Food and Beverage Service Management

FOOD AND BEVERAGE SERVICE MANAGEMENT

Ashim Gupta

CENTRUM PRESS
NEW DELHI-110002 (INDIA)

CENTRUM PRESS
H.O.: 4360/4, Ansari Road, Daryaganj,
New Delhi-110002 (India)
Tel: 23278000, 23261597, 23255577, 23286875
B.O.: No. 1015, Ist Main Road, BSK IIIrd Stage,
IIIrd Phase, IIIrd Block, Bengaluru-560085 (INDIA)
Tel: 080-41723429
Email: centrumpress@gmail.com
Visit us at: www.centrumpress.com

Food and Beverage Service Management

First Edition, 2012
ISBN 978-93-81293-85-0

PRINTED IN INDIA

Printed at Tarun Offset, Delhi

Contents

Preface

Food and beverage service management has been a skill and ability, but is fast stirring towards being a modern technology. One apparent way to get together the improved sensory safety, quality, health, nutrition, economy, and novelty demanded of food products by consumers is by improving the operations of food and beverage service management. Enhancement is connected to the improved prediction and control that follow quantitative description of the reactions, the chemistry changes that occur during the processing of food materials—the rates of changes and the factors influencing the changes. With today's importance on plummeting cost, improving class, and maximizing service, shared with the consumer's ever-increasing mission for value, the information in this book becomes more and more important. All chapters in this book gives exact information needed to keep away from downsides and focus on improving your bottom line.

It is my hope that by an understanding of the principles and practices of food and beverage cost control and profit improvement, Practical Food and beverage management can capture the discipline's rigour, intellectual richness, challenges and dynamism for all its readers.

Author

1

Introduction

FOOD AND BEVERAGE SERVICES MANAGEMENT

Food and beverage services are among the most visible locations at ski areas, and a ski area's environmental commitment is often judged by the environmental practices within these establishments. Food and beverage services at ski areas range from fine dining establishments to bars and cafeterias. Numerous programmes exist for the food and beverage service industry that help restaurants and their customers minimize environmental impacts. These programmes have established systematic approaches to help restaurants reduce their environmental impacts. Involvement in environmental programmes is a good way for a restaurant to learn more about environmental best practice opportunities.

Food and beverage serving and related workers are the front line of customer service in restaurants, coffee shops, and other food service establishments. These workers greet customers, escort them to seats and hand them menus, take food and drink orders, and serve food and beverages. They also answer questions, explain menu items and specials, and keep tables and dining areas clean and set for new diners. Most work as part of a team, helping coworkers to improve workflow and customer service.

Waiters and waitresses, the largest group of these workers, take customers' orders, serve food and beverages, prepare itemized checks, and sometimes accept payment. Their specific duties vary considerably, depending on the establishment. In coffee shops serving routine, straightforward fare, such as salads, soups, and sandwiches, servers are expected to provide fast, efficient, and courteous service. In fine dining restaurants, where more complicated meals are prepared and often served over several courses, waiters and waitresses provide more formal service emphasizing personal, attentive treatment and a more leisurely pace. They may recommend certain dishes and identify ingredients or explain how various items on the menu are prepared. Some prepare salads, desserts, or other menu items tableside. Additionally, they may check the identification of patrons to ensure they meet the minimum age requirement for the purchase of alcohol and tobacco products.

Waiters and waitresses sometimes perform the duties of other food and beverage service workers. These tasks may include escorting guests to tables, serving customers seated at counters, clearing and setting up tables, or operating a cash register. However, full-service restaurants frequently hire other staff, such as hosts and hostesses, cashiers, or dining room attendants, to perform these duties.

Bartenders fill drink orders either taken directly from patrons at the bar or through waiters and waitresses who place drink orders for dining room customers. Bartenders check identification of customers seated at the bar, to ensure they meet the minimum age requirement for the purchase of alcohol and tobacco products. They prepare mixed drinks, serve bottled or drought beer, and pour wine or other beverages. Bartenders must know a wide range of drink recipes and be able to mix drinks accurately, quickly, and without waste. Besides mixing and serving drinks, bartenders stock and prepare garnishes for drinks; maintain an adequate supply of ice, glasses, and other bar supplies; and keep the bar area clean for customers. They also may collect payment, operate the cash register, wash glassware and utensils, and serve food to customers seated at the bar. Bartenders usually are responsible for ordering and maintaining an inventory of liquor, mixes, and other bar supplies.

The majorities of bartenders directly serves and interact with patrons. Bartenders should be friendly and enjoy talking with customers. Bartenders at service bars, on the other hand, have less contact with customers. They work in small bars often located off the kitchen in restaurants, hotels, and clubs where only waiters and waitresses place drink orders. Some establishments, especially larger, higher volume ones, use equipment that automatically measures, pours and mixes drinks at the push of a button. Bartenders who use this equipment, however, still must work quickly to handle a large volume of drink orders and be familiar with the ingredients for special drink requests. Much of a bartender's work still must be done by hand to fill each individual order.

Hosts and hostesses welcome guests and maintain reservation or waiting lists. They may direct patrons to coatrooms, restrooms, or to a place to wait until their table is ready. Hosts and hostesses assign guests to tables suitable for the size of their group, escort patrons to their seats, and provide menus. They also schedule dining reservations, arrange parties, and organize any special services that are required. In some restaurants, they act as cashiers.

Dining room and cafeteria attendants and bartender helpers assist waiters, waitresses, and bartenders by cleaning tables, removing dirty dishes, and keeping serving areas stocked with supplies. Sometimes called backwaiters or runners, they bring meals out of the kitchen and assist waiters and waitresses by distributing dishes to individual diners. They also replenish the supply of clean linens, dishes, silverware, and glasses in the dining room and keep the bar stocked with glasses, liquor, ice, and drink garnishes.

Dining room attendants set tables with clean tablecloths, napkins, silverware, glasses, and dishes and serve ice water, rolls, and butter. At the conclusion of meals, they remove dirty dishes and soiled linens from tables. Cafeteria attendants stock serving tables with food, trays, dishes, and silverware and may carry trays to dining tables for patrons. Bartender helpers keep bar equipment clean and wash glasses. *Dishwashers* clean dishes, cutlery, and kitchen utensils and equipment.

Counter attendants take orders and serve food in cafeterias, coffee shops, and carryout eateries. In cafeterias, they serve food displayed on steam tables, carve meat, dish out vegetables, ladle sauces and soups, and fill beverage glasses. In lunchrooms and coffee shops, counter attendants take orders from customers seated at the counter, transmit orders to the kitchen, and pick up and serve food. They also fill cups with coffee, soda, and other beverages and prepare fountain specialties, such as milkshakes and ice cream sundaes. Counter attendants also take carryout orders from diners and wrap or place items in containers. They clean counters, write itemized checks, and sometimes accept payment. Some counter attendants may prepare short-order items, such as sandwiches and salads.

Some food and beverage serving workers take orders from customers at counters or drive-through windows at fast-food restaurants. They assemble orders, hand them to customers, and accept payment. Many of these are combined food preparation and serving workers who also cook and package food, make coffee, and fill beverage cups using drink-dispensing machines.

Other workers serve food to patrons outside of a restaurant environment, such as in hotels, hospital rooms, or cars. Food and beverage service workers are on their feet most of the time and often carry heavy trays of food, dishes, and glassware. During busy dining periods, they are under pressure to serve customers quickly and efficiently. The work is relatively safe, but care must be taken to avoid slips, falls, and burns.

Part-time work is more common among food and beverage serving and related workers than among workers in almost any other occupation. In 2004, those on part-time schedules included half of all waiters and waitresses, and 40 per cent of all bartenders.

Food service and drinking establishments typically maintain long dining hours and offer flexible and varied work opportunities. Many food and beverage serving and related workers work evenings, weekends, and holidays. Many students and teenagers seek part time or seasonal work as food and beverage serving and related workers as a first job to gain work experience or to earn spending money while in school.

Around one-fourth of food and beverage serving and related workers were 16 to 19 years old—about six times the proportion for all workers.

There are no specific educational requirements for food and beverage service jobs. Many employers prefer to hire high school graduates for waiter and waitress, bartender, and host and hostess positions, but completion of high school usually is not required for fast-food workers, counter attendants, dishwashers, and dining room attendants and bartender helpers. For many people a job as a food and beverage service worker serves as a source of immediate income, rather than a career. Many entrants to these jobs are in their late teens or early twenties and have a high school education or less. Usually, they have little or no work experience. Many are full-time students or homemakers. Food and beverage service jobs are a major source of part-time employment for high school and college students.

Restaurants rely on good food and quality customer service to retain loyal customers and succeed in a competitive industry. Food and beverage serving and related workers who exhibit excellent personal qualities—such as a neat clean appearance, a well-spoken manner, an ability to work as a member of team, and a pleasant way with patrons—will be highly sought after.

Waiters and waitresses need a good memory to avoid confusing customers' orders and to recall faces, names, and preferences of frequent patrons. These workers also should be comfortable using computers to place orders and generate customers' bills. Some may need to be quick at arithmetic so they can total bills manually. Knowledge of a foreign language is helpful to communicate with a diverse clientele and staff. Prior experience waiting on tables is preferred by restaurants and hotels that have rigid table service standards.

Jobs at these establishments often offer higher wages and have greater income potential from tips, but they may also have stiffer employment requirements than other establishments, such as prior table service experience or higher education. Usually, bartenders must be at least 21 years of age, but employers prefer to hire people who are 25 or older. Bartenders should be familiar with State and local laws concerning the sale of alcoholic beverages.

Most food and beverage serving and related workers pick up their skills on the job by observing and working with more experienced workers. Some full-service restaurants also provide new dining room employees with some form of classroom-type training that alternates with periods of actual on-the-job work experience. These training programmes communicate the operating philosophy of the restaurant, help establish a personal rapport with other staff and instill a desire to work as a team. They also provide an opportunity to discuss customer service situations and the proper ways of handling unpleasant circumstances or unruly patrons with new employees. Additionally, managers, chefs and servers may meet before each shift to discuss the menu and any new items or specials, review ingredients for any potential food allergies, or talk about any food safety concerns, coordination between the kitchen and the dining room, or any customer service issues from the previous day or shift.

Some employers, particularly those in fast-food restaurants, use self-instruction or on-line programmes with audiovisual presentations and instructional booklets to teach new employees food preparation and service skills. Some public and private vocational schools, restaurant associations, and large restaurant chains provide classroom training in a generalized food service curriculum. All employees receive training on safe food handling procedures and sanitation practices.

Some bartenders acquire their skills by attending a bartending or vocational and technical school. These programmes often include instruction on State and local laws and regulations, cocktail recipes, proper attire and conduct, and stocking a bar. Some of these schools help their graduates find jobs. Although few employers require any minimum level of educational attainment, some specialized training is usually needed in food handling and legal issues surrounding serving alcoholic beverages and tobacco. Employers are more likely to hire and promote based on people skills and personal qualities rather than education.

Due to the relatively small size of most food-serving establishments, opportunities for promotion are limited. After gaining experience, some dining room and cafeteria attendants and bartender helpers advance to waiter, waitress, or bartender jobs. For waiters, waitresses, and bartenders, advancement usually is limited to finding a job in a busier or more expensive restaurant or bar where prospects for tip earnings are better. Some bartenders, hosts and hostesses and waiters and waitresses advance to supervisory jobs, such as dining room supervisor, maitre d'hotel, assistant manager, or restaurant general manager. A few bartenders open their own businesses. In larger restaurant chains, food and beverage service workers who excel at their work often are invited to enter the company's formal management training programme.

EMPLOYMENT

Food and beverage serving and related workers held 6.8 million jobs in 2004. The overwhelming majority of jobs for food and beverage serving and related workers were found in food services and drinking places, such as restaurants, coffee shops, and bars. Other jobs were found primarily in traveller accommodation (hotels); amusement, gambling, and recreation industries; educational services; grocery stores; nursing care facilities; civic and social organizations; and hospitals.

Jobs are located throughout the country but are typically plentiful in large cities and tourist areas. Vacation resorts offer seasonal employment, and some workers alternate between summer and winter resorts, instead of remaining in one area the entire year.

Job Outlook

Job openings are expected to be abundant for food and beverage serving and related workers. Overall employment of these workers is expected to increase as fast as the average over the 2004-14 period as population, personal incomes, and employment expand. While employment growth will create many new jobs, the overwhelming majority of openings will arise from the need to replace the high proportion of workers who leave the occupations each year. There is substantial movement into and out of these occupations because education and training requirements are minimal and the predominance of part-time jobs are attractive to people seeking a short-term source of income rather than a career. However, keen competition is expected for bartender, waiter and waitress, and other food and beverage service jobs in popular restaurants and fine dining establishments, where potential earnings from tips are greatest.

Projected employment growth between 2004 and 2014 varies somewhat by type of job; however, average employment growth is expected for almost all food and beverage serving and related occupations. Employment of combined food preparation and serving workers, which includes fast-food workers, is expected to increase as fast as the average in response to the continuing fast-paced lifestyle of many Americans and the addition of healthier foods at many fast-food restaurants.

Average employment growth is expected for waiters and waitresses and hosts and hostesses because increases in the number of families and the more affluent, 55-and-older population will result in more restaurants that offer table service and more varied menus. Employment of bartenders, dining room attendants, and dishwashers will grow more slowly than other food and beverage serving and related workers because diners increasingly are eating at more casual dining spots, such as coffee bars and sandwich shops, rather than at the full-service restaurants and drinking places that employ more of these workers.

Earning

Food and beverage serving and related workers derive their earnings from a combination of hourly wages and customer tips. Earnings vary greatly, depending on the type of job and establishment. For example, fast-food workers and hosts and hostesses usually do not receive tips, so their wage rates may be higher than those of waiters and waitresses and bartenders in full-service restaurants, who typically earn more from tips than from wages. In some restaurants, workers contribute all or a portion of their tips to a tip pool, which is distributed among qualifying workers. Tip pools allow workers who don't usually receive tips directly from customers, such as dining room attendants, to feel a part of a team and to share in the rewards of good service.

In May 2004, median hourly earnings (including tips) of waiters and waitresses were $6.75. The middle 50 per cent earned between $6.04 and $8.34. The lowest 10 per cent earned less than $5.60, and the highest 10 per cent earned more than $11.27 an hour. For most waiters and waitresses, higher earnings are primarily the result of receiving more in tips rather than higher hourly wages. Tips usually average between 10 and 20 per cent of guests' checks; waiters and waitresses working in busy, expensive restaurants earn the most.

Bartenders had median hourly earnings (including tips) of $7.42 in May 2004. The middle 50 per cent earned between $6.34 and $9.26. The lowest 10 per cent earned less than $5.72, and the highest 10 per cent earned more than $12.47 an hour. Like waiters and waitresses, bartenders employed in public bars may receive more than half of their earnings as tips. Service bartenders often are paid higher hourly wages to offset their lower tip earnings.

Median hourly earnings (including tips) of dining room and cafeteria attendants and bartender helpers were $7.10 in May 2004. The middle 50 per cent earned between $6.24 and $8.25. The lowest 10 per cent earned less than $5.68, and the highest 10 per cent earned more than $9.88 an hour. Most received over half of their earnings as wages; the rest of their income was a share of the proceeds from tip pools.

Median hourly earnings of hosts and hostesses were $7.52 in May 2004. The middle 50 per cent earned between $6.48 and $8.63. The lowest 10 per cent earned less than $5.77, and the highest 10 per cent earned more than $10.49 an hour. Wages comprised the majority of their earnings. In some cases, wages were supplemented by proceeds from tip pools.

Median hourly earnings of combined food preparation and serving workers, including fast food, were $7.06 in May 2004. The middle 50 per cent earned between $6.18 and $8.25. The lowest 10 per cent earned less than $5.65, and the highest 10 per cent earned more than $9.85 an hour. Although some combined food preparation and serving workers receive a part of their earnings as tips, fast-food workers usually do not.

Median hourly earnings of counter attendants in cafeterias, food concessions, and coffee shops (including tips) were $7.53 in May 2004. The middle 50 per cent earned between $6.50 and $8.59 an hour. The lowest 10 per cent earned less than $5.80, and the highest 10 per cent earned more than $10.38 an hour.

Median hourly earnings of dishwashers were $7.35 in May 2004. The middle 50 per cent earned between $6.41 and $8.37. The lowest 10 per cent earned less than $5.76, and the highest 10 per cent earned more than $9.81 an hour.

Median hourly earnings of nonrestaurant food servers were $7.95 in May 2004. The middle 50 per cent earned between $6.64 and $9.98. The lowest 10 per cent earned less than $5.86, and the highest 10 per cent earned more than $12.53 an hour.

Many beginning or inexperienced workers start earning the Federal minimum wage of $5.15 an hour. However, a few States set minimum wages higher than the Federal minimum. Also, various minimum wage exceptions apply under specific circumstances to disabled workers, full-time students, youth under age 20 in their first 90 days of employment, tipped employees, and student-learners.

Tipped employees are those who customarily and regularly receive more than $30 a month in tips. The employer may consider tips as part of wages, but the employer must pay at least $2.13 an hour in direct wages. Employers also are permitted to deduct from wages the cost, or fair value, of any meals or lodging provided. Many employers, however, provide free meals and furnish uniforms. Food and beverage service workers who work full time often receive typical benefits, while part-time workers usually do not.

In some large restaurants and hotels, food and beverage serving and related workers belong to unions—principally the Hotel Employees and Restaurant Employees International Union and the Service Employees International Union.

FOOD AND BEVERAGE COST

This portion presents the professional techniques and methods used to effectively purchase, receive, and store food products. It teaches the formulas used to compute the true cost of the food you provide your guests, as well as a process for estimating the value of food you have used on a daily or weekly basis, by applying the food cost percentage method, which is the standard in the hospitality industry.

The U.S. Bureau of Labour Statistics consumer expenditure surveys reported that sales of food consumed away from home grew an average of 5% per year in the 1990s, with annual increases expected to be even higher in the 2000s. According to the National Restaurant Association's current forecasts, continued economic growth, gains in consumers' real disposable income, and changes in the lifestyles of today's busy American families are all spurring the sustained rise in the number of meals served away from home. This is good news for your career as a hospitality manager.

All this growth, activity, and consumer demand, however, will also create challenges for you. Consider the situation you would encounter if you used sales histories to project 300 guests for lunch today at the restaurant you manage. Your restaurant serves only three entrée items: roast chicken, roast pork, and roast beef. The question you would face is this, "How many servings of each item should we produce so that we do not run out of any one item?" If you were to run out of one of your three menu items, guests who wanted that item would undoubtedly become upset. Producing too much of any one item would, on the other hand, cause costs to rise to unacceptable levels unless these items could be sold for their full price at a later time.

Clearly, in this situation, it would be unwise to produce 300 portions of each item. While you would never run out of any one item, that is, each of your 300 estimated guests could order the same item and you would still have enough, you would also have 600 left overs at the end of your lunch period. What you would like to do, of course, is instruct your staff to make the "right" amount of each menu item. The right amount would be the number of servings that minimize your chances of running out of an item before lunch is over, while also minimizing your chance of having excessive leftovers. The answer to the question of how many servings of roast chicken, pork, and beef you should prepare lies in accurate menu forecasting. Let us return to the example cited previously. This time, however, assume that you were wise enough to have recorded last week's menu item sales on a form.

An estimate of 300 guests for next Monday makes sense because the weekly sales total last week of 1,500 guests served averages 300 guests per day (1,500/5 days 300/day). You also know that, on an average day, you sold 73 roast chicken (365 sold/5 days 73/day), 115 roast pork (573 sold/5 days 115/day), and 112 roast beef (562 sold/5 days 112/day).

Once you know the average number of people selecting a given menu item, and you know the total number of guests who made the selections, you can compute the popularity index, which is defined as the percentage of total guests choosing a given menu item from a list of alternatives. In this example, you can improve your "guess" about the quantity of each item to prepare if you use the sales history to help guide your decision. If you assume that future guests will select menu items much as past guests have done, given that the list of menu items remains the same, that information can be used to improve your predictions.

If we know, even in a general way, what we can expect our guests to select, we are better prepared to make good decisions about the quantity of each item that should be produced. In this example, your best guess of what your 300 guests are likely to order when they arrive. The basic formula for individual menu item forecasting, based on an item's individual sales history. The predicted number to be sold is simply the quantity of a specific menu item likely to be sold given an estimate of the total number of guests expected. Once you know what your guests are likely to select, you can determine how many of each menu item your production staff should be instructed to prepare. It is important to note that foodservice managers face a great deal of uncertainty when attempting to estimate the number of guests who will arrive on a given day because a variety of factors influence that number.

These, as well as other factors that affect sales volume, makes accurate guest count prediction very difficult. In addition, remember that sales histories track only the general trends of an operation. They are not able to estimate *precisely* the number of guests who may arrive on any given day. Sales histories, then, are a guide to what can be expected. In our example, last week's guest counts range from a low of 280 (Monday) to a high of 320 (Tuesday). In addition, the percentage of people selecting each menu item changes somewhat on a daily basis. As a professional foodservice manager, you must take into account possible increases or decreases in guest count and possible fluctuations in your predicted number to be sold computations when planning how many of each menu item you should prepare.

Forecasting can involve estimating the number of guests you expect, the dollar amount of sales you expect, or even what those guests may want to purchase. This forecasting is crucial if you are to effectively manage your food expenses. In addition, consistency in food production and guest service will greatly influence your overall success.

STANDARDIZED RECIPES

While it is the menu that determines what is to be sold and at what price, the standardized recipe controls both the quantity and the quality of what your kitchen will produce. A standardized recipe consists of the procedures to be used in preparing and serving each of your menu items. The standardized recipe ensures that each time a guest orders an item from your menu, he or she receives exactly what you intended the guest to receive.

Critical factors in a standardized recipe, such as cooking times and serving size, must remain constant so the menu items produced are always consistent. Guests expect to get what they pay for. The standardized recipe helps you make sure that they do. Inconsistency is the enemy of any quality foodservice operation.

It will make little difference to the unhappy guest, for instance, if you tell him or her that while the menu item he or she purchased today is not up to your normal standard, it will be tomorrow, or that it was the last time the guest visited your operation. Interestingly, despite their tremendous advantages, many managers refuse to take the time to develop standardized recipes. Of the preceding arguments, only the last one, staff's inability to read English, has any validity. The effective operator should have the standardized recipes printed in the language of his or her production employees. Standardized recipes have far more advantages than disadvantages.

Reasons for incorporating a system of standardized recipes include:

- Accurate purchasing is impossible without the existence and use of standardized recipes.
- Dietary concerns require some foodservice operators to know exactly the kinds of ingredients and the correct amount of nutrients in each serving of a menu item.
- Accuracy in menu laws require that foodservice operators be able to tell guests about the type and amount of ingredients in their recipes.
- Accurate recipe costing and menu pricing is impossible without standardized recipes.
- Matching food used to cash sales is impossible to do without standardized recipes.
- New employees can be better trained with standardized recipes.
- The computerization of a foodservice operation is impossible unless the elements of standardized recipes are in place; thus, the advantages of advanced

technological tools available to the operation are restricted or even eliminated.

In fact, standardized recipes are so important that they are the cornerstones of any serious effort to produce consistent, high-quality food products at an established cost. Without them, cost control efforts become nothing more than raising selling prices, reducing portion sizes, or lessening quality. This is not effective cost management. It is hardly management at all. Without established standardized recipes, however, this happens all too frequently.

Any recipe can be standardized. The process can sometimes be complicated, however, especially in the areas of baking and sauce production. It is always best to begin with a recipe of proven quality. Frequently, you may have a recipe designed to serve 10 guests, but you want to expand it to serve 100 people. In cases like this, it may not be possible to simply multiply each ingredient used by 10. A great deal has been written regarding various techniques used to expand recipes. Computer software designed for that purpose is now on the market. As a general rule, however, any item that can be produced in quantity can be standardized in recipe form and can be adjusted, up or down, in quantity.

When adjusting recipes, it is important that measurement standards be consistent. Weighing with a pound or an ounce scale is the most accurate method of measuring any ingredients. The food item to be measured must be recipe ready. That is, it must be cleaned, trimmed, cooked, and generally completed, save for its addition to the recipe. For liquid items, measurement of volume (i.e., cup, quart, or gallon, etc.) may be preferred. Some operators like to weigh all ingredients, even liquids, for improved accuracy.

PERCENTAGE METHOD

The percentage method deals with recipe weight, rather than with a conversion factor. It is sometimes more accurate than using a conversion factor alone. Essentially, the percentage method involves weighing all ingredients and then computing the percentage weight of each recipe ingredient in relation to the total weight of all ingredients. To facilitate the computation, many operators convert pounds to ounces prior to making their percentage calculations. These are converted back to standard pounds and ounces when the conversion is completed. To illustrate the use of the percentage method, let us assume that you have a recipe with a total weight of 10 pounds and 8 ounces, or 168 ounces. If the portion size is 4 ounces, the total recipe yield would be 168/4, or 42, servings. If you want your kitchen to prepare 75 servings, you would need to supply it with a standardized recipe consisting of the following total recipe weight: When adjusting recipes for quantity (total yield), two general methods may be employed.

They are:

- Factor method
- Percentage technique

FACTOR METHOD

When using the factor method, you must use the following formula to arrive at a recipe conversion factor: You now have all the information necessary to use the percentage method of recipe conversion. Note that% of total is computed as ingredient weight/total recipe weight. The proper conversion of weights and measures is important in recipe expansion or reduction. The judgment of the recipe writer is critical, however, since such factors as cooking time, temperature, and utensil selection may vary as recipe sizes are increased or decreased. In addition, some recipe ingredients, such as spices or flavorings, may not respond well to mathematical conversions. In the final analysis, it is your assessment of product taste that should ultimately determine ingredient ratios in standardized recipes. All recipes should be standardized and used as written. It is your responsibility to see that this is done.

INVENTORY CONTROL

With a knowledge of what is likely to be purchased by your guests (sales forecast) and a firm idea of the ingredients necessary to produce these items (standardized recipes), you must make decisions about desired inventory levels. A desired inventory level is simply the answer to the question, "How much of each needed ingredient should I have on hand at any one time?" It is clear that this question can only be properly answered if your sales forecast is of good quality and your standardized recipes are in place so you do not "forget" to stock a necessary recipe ingredient. Inventory management seeks to provide appropriate working stock, which is the amount of an ingredient you anticipate using before purchasing that item again, and a minimal safety stock, the extra amount of that ingredient you decide to keep on hand to meet higher than anticipated demand.

Demand for a given menu item can fluctuate greatly between deliveries periods, even when the delivery occurs daily. With too little inventory, you may run out of products and therefore reduce guest satisfaction. With too much inventory, waste, theft, and spoilage can become excessive. The ability to effectively manage the inventory process is one of the best skills a foodservice manager can acquire.

DETERMINING INVENTORY LEVELS

Inventory levels are determined by a variety of factors. Some of the most important ones are as follows:

- Storage capacity
- Item perishability
- Vendor delivery schedule
- Potential savings from increased purchase size
- Operating calendar
- Relative importance of stock outages
- Value of inventory dollars to the operator

Storage Capacity: Inventory items must be purchased in quantities that can be adequately stored and secured. Many times, kitchens lack adequate storage facilities. This may mean more frequent deliveries and holding less of each product on hand than would otherwise be desired. When storage space is too great, however, the tendency by some managers is to fill the space. It is important that this not be done, as increased inventory of items generally leads to greater spoilage and loss due to theft. Moreover, large quantities of goods on the shelf tend to send a message to employees that there is "plenty" of everything. This may result in the careless use of valuable and expensive products. It is also unwise to overload refrigerators or freezers. This not only can result in difficulty in finding items quickly, but also may cause carry overs (those items produced for a meal period but not sold) to be "lost" in the storage process.

Item Perishability: If all food products had the same shelf life, that is, the amount of time a food item retains its maximum freshness, flavour, and quality while in storage, you would have less difficulty in determining the quantity of each item you should keep on hand. Unfortunately, the shelf life of food products varies greatly. Because food items have varying shelf lives, you must balance the need for a particular product with the optimal shelf life of that product.

Serving items that are "too old" is a sure way to develop guest complaints. In fact, one of the quickest ways to determine the overall effectiveness of a foodservice manager is to "walk the boxes." This means to take a tour of a facility's storage area. If many products, particularly in the refrigerated area, are moldy, soft, overripe, or rotten, it is a good indication of a foodservice operation that does not have a feel for proper inventory levels based on the shelf lives of the items kept in inventory. It is also a sign that sales forecasting methods either are not in place or are not working well.

VENDOR DELIVERY SCHEDULE

It is the fortunate foodservice operator who lives in a large city with many vendors, some of whom may offer the same service and all of whom would like to have the operator's business. In many cases, however, you will not have the luxury of daily delivery. Your operation may be too small to warrant such frequent stops by a vendor, or the operation may be in such a remote location that daily delivery is simply not possible. Consider, for a moment, the difficulty you would face if you were the manager of a foodservice operation located on an offshore oil rig. Clearly, in a case like that, a vendor willing to provide daily dough nut delivery is going to be hard to find! In all cases, it is important to remember that the cost to the vendor for frequent deliveries will be reflected in the cost of the goods to you. Vendors will readily let you know what their delivery schedule to a certain area or location can be. It is up to you to use this information to make good decisions regarding the quantity of that vendor's product you must buy to have both working stock and safety stock.

POTENTIAL SAVINGS FROM INCREASED PURCHASE SIZE

Sometimes, you will find that you can realise substantial savings by purchasing needed items in large quantities. This certainly makes sense if the total savings actually outweigh the added costs of receiving and storing the larger quantity. For the large foodservice operator, who once a year buys canned green beans by the railroad car, the savings are real. For the smaller operator, who hopes to reduce costs by ordering two cases of green beans rather than one, the savings may be negligible. Generally, however, reduced packaging and shipping costs result in lower per unit costs when larger bags, boxes, or cartons of ingredients are purchased.

Remember, too, that there are costs associated with extraordinarily large purchases. These may include storage costs, spoilage, deterioration, insect or rodent infestation, or theft. As a general rule, you should determine your ideal product inventory levels and then maintain your stock within that need range. Only when the advantages of placing an extraordinarily large order are very clear should such a purchase be undertaken.

Operating Calendar

When an operation is involved in serving meals seven days a week to a relatively stable number of guests, the operating calendar makes little difference to inventory level decision making. If, however, the operation opens on Monday and closes on Friday for two days, as is the case in many school foodservice accounts, the operating calendar plays a large part in determining desired inventory levels. In general, it can be said that an operator who is closing down either for a weekend (as in school foodservice or a corporate dining situation) or for a season (as in the operation of a summer camp or seasonal hotel) should attempt to reduce overall inventory levels as the closing period approaches.

This is expecially true when it comes to perishable items. Many operators actually plan menus to steer clear of highly perishable items near their closing periods. They prefer to work highly perishable items, such as fresh seafood and some meat items, into the early or middle part of their operating calendar. This allows them to minimize the amount of perishable product that must be carried through the close-down period.

RELATIVE IMPORTANCE OF STOCK OUTAGES

In many foodservice operations, not having enough of a single food ingredient or menu item is simply not that important. In other operations, the shortage of even one menu item might spell disaster. While it may be all right for the local French restaurant to run out of one of the specials on Saturday night, it is not difficult to imagine the problem of the McDonald's restaurant manager who runs out of French fried potatoes on that same Saturday night! For the small operator, a mistake in the inventory level of a minor ingredient that results in an outage can often be corrected by a quick run to the grocery store.

For the larger facility, such an outage may well represent a substantial loss of sales or guest goodwill. Whether the operator is large or small, being out of a key ingredient or menu item is to be avoided, and planning inventory levels properly helps prevent it. In the restaurant industry, when an item is no longer available on the menu, you "86" the item, a reference to restaurant slang originating in the early 1920s (86 rhymed with "nix," a Cockney term meaning "to eliminate").

If you, as a manager, "86" too many items on any given night, the reputation of your restaurant as well as your ability to manage it will suffer. A strong awareness and knowledge of how critical this outage factor is help determine the appropriate inventory level. A word of caution is, however, necessary. The foodservice operator who is determined never to run out of anything must be careful not to set inventory levels so high as to actually end up costing the operation more than if realistic levels were maintained.

VALUE OF INVENTORY DOLLARS TO THE OPERATOR

In some cases, operators elect to remove dollars from their bank accounts and convert them to product inventory. When this is done, the operator is making the decision to value product more than dollars. When it is expected that the value of the inventory will rise faster than the value of the banked dollar, this is a good strategy. All too often, however, operators overbuy or "stockpile" inventory, causing too many dollars to be tied up in non-interest-bearing food products.

When this is done, managers incur opportunity costs. An opportunity cost is the cost of foregoing the next best alternative when making a decision. For example, suppose you have two choices, A and B, both having potential benefits or returns for you. If you choose A, then you lose the potential benefits from choosing B (opportunity cost).

In other words, you could choose to use your money to buy food inventory that will sit in your storeroom until it is sold, or you could choose not to stockpile food inventory and invest the money. If you stockpile the inventory, then the opportunity cost is the amount of money you would have made if you had invested rather than holding the excess inventory.

If the dollars used to purchase inventory must be borrowed from the bank, rather than being available from operating revenue, an even greater cost to carry the inventory is incurred since interest must be paid on the borrowed funds. In addition, a foodservice company of many units that invests too much of its money in inventory may find that funds for acquisition, renovation, or marketing are not readily available. In contrast, a state institution that is given its entire annual budget at the start of its fiscal year (a year that is 12 months long but may not follow the calendar year) may find it advantageous to use its purchasing power to acquire large amounts of inventory at the beginning of the year and at very low prices.

SETTING THE PURCHASE POINT

A purchase point, as it relates to inventory levels, is that point in time when an item should be reordered.

This point is typically designated by one of two methods:

1. As needed (just in time)
2. Par level

As Needed

When you elect to use the as-needed, or just-in-time, method of determining inventory level, you are basically purchasing food based on your prediction of unit sales and the sum of the ingredients (from standardized recipes) necessary to produce those sales. Then, no more than the absolute minimum of needed inventory level is secured from the vendor. When this system is used, the buyer compiles a list of needed ingredients and submits it to management for approval to purchase. For example, in a hotel foodservice operation, the demand for 500 servings of a raspberries and cream torte dessert, to be served to a group in the hotel next week, would cause the responsible person to check the standardized recipe for this item and, thus, determine the amount of raspberries that should be ordered. Then that amount, and no more, would be ordered from the vendor.

Par Level

Foodservice operators may set predetermined purchase points, called par levels, for some items. In the case of the raspberries and cream torte dessert referred to previously, it is likely that the torte will require vanilla extract. It does not make sense, however, to expect your food production manager to order vanilla extract by the tablespoon! In fact, you are likely to find that you are restricted in the quantity you could buy due to the vendor's delivery minimum, namely, bottle or case, or the manufacturer's packaging methods. In cases such as this, or when demand for a product is relatively constant, you may decide to set needed inventory levels for some items by determining purchase points based on appropriate par levels. When determining par levels, you must establish both minimum and maximum amounts required. Many foodservice managers establish a minimum par level by computing working stock, then adding 25 to 50% more for safety stock.

Then, an appropriate purchase point, or point at which additional stock is purchased, is determined. If, for example, you have decided that the inventory level for coffee should be based on a par system, the decision may be made that the minimum (given your usage) amount that should be on hand at all times is four cases. This would be the minimum par level. Assume that you set the maximum par level at ten cases. While the inventory level in this situation would vary from a low of four cases to a high of ten cases, you would be assured that you would never have too little or too much of this particular menu item.

If cases of coffee were to be ordered under this system, you would always attempt to keep the number of cases between the minimum par level (four cases) and the maximum par level (ten cases). The purchase point in this example might be six cases; that is, when your operation had six cases of coffee on hand, an order would be placed with the coffee vendor. The intention would be to get the total stock up to ten cases before your supply got below four cases. Since delivery might take one or two days, six cases might be an appropriate purchase point.

Whether we use the as-needed or the par level method, or, as in the case of most operators, a combination of the two, each ingredient or menu item should have a management-designated inventory level. As a rule, highly perishable items should be ordered on an as-needed basis, while items with a longer shelf life can often have their inventory levels set using a par level system. The answer to the question "How much of each ingredient should I have on hand at any point in time?" must come from you. Many factors will impact this decision. The decision, however, must be made and compliance monitored on a regular basis.

PURCHASING

Regardless of the method used to determine inventory levels, once the quantity needed on hand has been determined, you must then turn your attention to the extremely important area of purchasing.

Purchasing is essentially a matter of determining the following:

- What should be purchased?
- What is the best price to pay?
- How can a steady supply be assured?

What Should Be Purchased?

Just as it is not possible to determine inventory levels or items to be purchased without standardized recipes, it is not possible to manage costs where purchasing is concerned without the use of product specifications, or "specs." A product spec is simply a detailed description of an ingredient or menu item. A spec is a way for you to communicate in a very precise way with a vendor so that your operation receives the *exact* item requested every time.

A foodservice specification generally consists of the following information:

- Product name or specification number
- Pricing unit
- Standard or grade
- Weight range/size
- Processing and/or packaging
- Container size
- Intended use
- Other information such as product yield

It is very important to note that the product specification determines neither the "best" product nor the product that costs the least. It is the product that you have determined to be the *most appropriate* product for its intended use in terms of both quality and cost. A product specification that is written too loosely can be a problem because the needed level of item quality may not be delivered. On the other hand, if your product specifications are too tight, that is, if they are overly and unnecessarily specific, too few vendors may be able to supply the product, resulting in your paying excessively high costs for that item. The necessity of specifications will become clear if we listen in on a telephone call made by Louie, a manager who is about to place an order for bread with a new vendor, Sam's Uptown Bakery:

Louie:	*"Sam, I need bread for sandwiches."*
Sam:	*"Louie, you know I have the best bread in town!"*
Louie:	*"Well, send me 50 loaves as soon as possible."*
Sam:	*"No problem, Louie. We will deliver this afternoon!"*

Little does Louie know that Sam's definition of bread for sandwiches is *quite* different from his own. Louie is expecting 1pound, white, split, thin-sliced, 45-slices-to-the-bag bread. From Sam's exotic shop, however, he may well receive a 2-pound, thick-sliced, sesame seed–topped Italian loaf. Thus, even for a product as common as bread, a specification must be developed. Fortunately, the process is relatively simple because it depends mainly on your own view of appropriate product quality. Each menu item or ingredient should have its own spec. In fact, management should make it a habit to ensure that only telephone conversations such as the following take place:

Louie:	*"Sam, I need 50 loaves of my spec #617 as soon as possible."*
Sam:	*"Spec #617? Let's see, I've got it right here. That's your* white bread for sandwiches spec, right?"
Louie:	*"That's right, Sam."*
Sam:	*"No problem, Louie. We will deliver this afternoon!"*

Product Name

This may seem self-explanatory, but, in reality, it is not. Mangos are a fruit to those in the southwestern United States, but the word may mean a bell pepper to those in the Midwest. Bell peppers do not come only in green, their most common colour, but can also be purchased in yellow and red forms. Thus, the product name must be specific enough to clearly and precisely identify the item you wish to buy. Many canned hams are pear shaped, but a Pullman canned ham is square.

You may be requesting 100% maple syrup when you place a syrup order, but your vendor could assume maple-"flavored" syrup is the item you desire.

Purchasing food becomes even more difficult when you realise that, especially in the area of meats and seafood, different regions in the country may have different names for the same product. When developing the product specification, you may find it helpful to assign a number to the item as well as its name. This can be useful when, for example, many forms of the same ingredient or menu item may be purchased.

A deli-restaurant may use 10 to 20 different types of bread, depending on the intended use of the bread; thus, in our product specification example, bacon, which this operation uses in many forms, has both a name and a number assigned to the specification. The same may be true with a number of items such as cheese, which may come in a brick, sliced, shredded, or a variety of other forms, as well as several types.

PRICING UNIT

A pricing unit may be established in terms of pounds, quarts, gallons, cases, or any other commonly used unit. Parsley, for example, is typically sold in the United States by the bunch. Thus, it is also priced by the bunch. How much is a bunch? You must know. Grapes are sold by the "lug." Unless you are familiar with the term, you may not be able to buy that product in an effective way. Again, knowledge of the pricing unit, whether it is a gallon, pound, case, bunch, or lug, is critical when developing a product specification. You should insist that your vendor supply you with definitions of each pricing unit upon which that vendor bases his or her selling price.

Standard or Grade

Many food items are sold with varying degrees of quality or desirability. Because that is true, the U.S. Department of Agriculture, Bureau of Fisheries, and the Food and Drug Administration have developed standards for many food items. In addition, grading programmes are in place for many commonly used foodservice items. Trade groups such as the

National Association of Meat Purveyors publish item descriptions for many of these products. Consumers also are aware of many of these distinctions. Prime beef, in the consumer's mind, may be superior to choice beef. In a similar manner, you may wish to purchase and serve Coca-Cola rather than a lower cost generic fountain soda. When developing a specification, a specific brand name or product source (A-1 Steak Sauce, Maine lobster) may be included in this section. You should be cautious, however, about specifying a brand name unless it is actually critical to your operation. Unless several vendors are able to supply you with a product you need, the price you may pay to the vendor who does have the item may be too high.

Weight Range/Size

Weight range or size is important when referring to meats, fish, poultry, and some vegetables. In our standardized recipe example of roast chicken, the quarters were to have come from chickens in the 3- to 3_ pound range. This will make them very different than if they came from chickens in the 4- to 4_pound range. In the case of products requiring specific trim or maximum fat covering, that should be designated also, such as 10-ounce strip steak, maximum tail 1 inch, fat covering half inch. Four-ounce hamburger patties, 16-ounce T-bones, and one by fourth pound hot dogs are additional examples of items of the type that require, not a weight range, but an exact size. It is important to note that while the operator may specify such a specific weight, it is likely that he or she will pay a premium for such accuracy, especially in items such as steaks, where the supplier's ability to perfectly control product weight is somewhat limited.

Count, in the hospitality industry, is a term that is used to designate size. For example, 16- to 20-count shrimp refers to the fact that, for this size shrimp, 16 to 20 of the individual shrimp would be required to make 1 pound. In a like manner, 30- to 40-count shrimp means that it takes 30 to 40 of this size shrimp to make a pound. Many fruits and vegetables are also sold by count. For example, a 48-count avocado means that 48 individual avocados will fit in a standard case. In general, the larger the count, the smaller the size of the individual food items.

PROCESSING AND/OR PACKAGING

Processing and packaging refers to the product's state when you buy it. Apples, for example, may be purchased fresh, canned, or frozen. Each form will carry a price appropriate for its processed or packaged state. It is important to note that the term "fresh" is one with varying degrees of meaning. Fish that has been frozen and then thawed should be identified as such. Packaging is also extremely important when determining product yield. For example, 3 pounds of canned corn will not yield the same number of 3-ounce servings as 3 pounds of fresh ear corn. Fresh fruits and vegetables may be of excellent quality and low in cost per pound, but the effective food service operator must consider actual usable product when computing the price per pound. Also, the Labour cost of washing, trimming, and otherwise preparing fresh products must be considered when comparing their price to that of a canned or frozen product.

The U.S. food supply is one of great variety and quality. Food can come packed in a large number of forms and styles, including slab packed, layered cell packed, fiberboard divided, shrink packed, individually wrapped, and bulk packed. While it is beyond the scope of this text to detail all of the many varieties of food processing and packing styles, it is important for you to know about them. Your vendors will be pleased to help explain to you all the types of item processing and packaging they offer.

Container Size

This term refers to the can size, number of cans per case, or weight of the container in which the product is delivered. Most operators know that a 50-pound bag of flour should contain 50 pounds. Some may not be sure, however, what the appropriate weight for a "lug" of tomatoes would be.

Intended Use

Different types of the same item are often used in the same

foodservice operation, but in a variety of ways. Consider, for example, the operator who uses strawberries in a variety of ways. Obviously, perfect, large berries are best for chocolate-dipped strawberries served on a buffet table. Less-than-perfect berries, however, may cost less and be a perfectly acceptable form for sliced strawberries on strawberry shortcake. Frozen berries may make a good choice for a baked strawberry pie and would be much more cost effective. Breads, milk products, apples, and other fruits are additional examples of foods that come in a variety of forms; this requires you to know that the "best" form of a food product is not necessarily the most expensive.

Other Information Such as Product Yield

Additional information may be included in a specification if it helps the vendor understand exactly what you have in mind when your order is placed. An example is product yield. Product yield is simply the amount of product that you will have remaining after cooking, trimming, portioning, or cleaning. Product yield will help you and your vendor determine how much product you will have to purchase in order to have the desired product quantity after waste is removed.

WHAT IS THE BEST PRICE TO PAY?

Once purchase specifications have been developed and quantities to be purchased have been established, your next step is to determine how to buy these items at the best price. Some would say that determining the best price should be a simple matter of finding who has the lowest cost product and placing an order with that person. In fact, that is almost always a sure sign of a manager who lacks understanding of the way vendors operate. The best price, in fact, is more accurately stated as the lowest price that meets the long-term goals of both the foodservice operation and its vendor.

When you have a choice of vendors, each supplying the same product (your specification), it is possible to engage in comparison shopping. The vehicle used to do this is called the bid sheet. The bid sheet includes vendor information, buyer information, and item description, unit of bid, bid price, salesperson's signature, and date. It also includes the dates that the bid prices will be "fixed," which means the dates that the supplier agrees to keep the bid price in effect. The bid sheet would be sent to all meat vendors each week on Friday to be returned Monday for the weekly bid prices. Then you would compare the item prices to see which vendor you would buy.

After you have received bids from your suppliers, you can compare those bids on a price comparison sheet. A price comparison sheet typically has a place to list the category being bid on, namely, produce, dairy products, meats, and so on, the name of the vendors available to bid, bid date, item description, unit of purchase, best bid price, best company quote, and last price paid. This information may then be used to select a vendor, based on the best price. Once the best price is determined for each item, then a purchase order using the best prices can be developed for each vendor.

Bid sheets and price comparison sheets may be used to determine the specific vendor who can supply the *lowest* price, but they do not give enough information to determine the *best* price. This makes sense when you realise that your own guests do not necessarily go to the lowest-priced restaurants for all of their meals. If they did, there would be no hope of success for the operator who tried to provide a better food product, in a better environment, with better service. In fact, most foodservice operators would resent guests who came into their operation and claimed they could get the exact same item for a lower price down the street.

It is a truism that any product can be sold a little cheaper if quality is allowed to vary. Even with the use of product specifications, vendor dependability, quality of vendor service, and accuracy in delivery can be determining factors when attempting to determine the "best price." Bill's Produce may be the preferred vendor for these items if price alone is the issue. If, however, Bill's Produce is frequently late in delivery, has questionable sanitary habits, and frequently is short or unable to deliver the promised product, the lower price may be no bargain. Davis Foods, on the other hand, may have a reputation for quality products and service that make it the vendor of choice. Any foodservice operator who uses price as the only criterion when shopping will find it very difficult to develop any meaningful relationship with a supplier.

For the smaller operation, the manager may be interested in comparing the *total* price from each supplier, rather than the price of individual items. That is, each ordering day, the manager would multiply the quantity of an item needed by the best price. An approach such as this is used when buying strictly from the price comparison sheet may result in orders too small to meet a supplier's minimum order requirement, that is, the smallest order that can be placed with a vendor who delivers.

If the minimum order requirement cannot be met using the lowest prices, then the manager may have to choose the supplier with the next highest price to fill a complete order. In some cases, the vendor to be used by the foodservice operator has been determined in advance.

This is often true in a large corporate organization or in a franchise situation. Contracts to provide goods may be established by the central purchasing department of these organizations. When that happens, the designated vendor may have a national or a long-term contract to supply, at a predetermined price, items that meet the operation's specifications.

HOW CAN A STEADY SUPPLY BE ASSURED?

Unfortunately, very little has been written in the field of foodservice about managing costs through cooperation with vendors. Your food salesperson can be one of your most important allies in controlling costs. Operators who determine their supplier only on the basis of cost will find that they receive only the product they have purchased, whereas their competitors are buying more than just food! Or, as one food salesperson said when asked why he should be selected as the primary food vendor, "With my products, you also get me!"

And so it is; just as good foodservice operators know that guests respond to both products and personal service levels, so, too, do effective food suppliers.

Assuring a steady supply of quality products at a fair price is extremely important to the long-term success of a foodservice operator, yet many operators treat their suppliers as if they were the enemy. In fact, suppliers can be of immense value in assuring a steady supply of quality products at a fair price if you remember the following points.

Suppliers have Many Prices, not Just One

Unlike the restaurant business, which tends to hold its prices steady between menu reprints and generally charges the same price to all who come in the door, suppliers have a variety of prices based on the customer to whom they are quoting them. Therefore, when an operator gets a quote on a case of lettuce, the telephone conversation may sound like this:

Foodservice manager:	*"Hello, is this Ready Boy Produce?"*
Ready boy:	*"Yes, how can I help you?"*
Foodservice operator:	*"What is your price on lettuce today?"*
Ready boy:	*"$28.50 per case."*
This conversation should really be interpreted, as follows:	
Foodservice operator:	*"Hello, is this Ready Boy Produce?"*
Ready boy:	*"Yes, how can I help you?"*
Foodservice operator:	*"What is my price on lettuce today?"*
Ready boy:	*"Based on our relationship, it is $28.50 per case."*

Suppliers Reward Volume Customers

It is simply in the best interest of a supplier to give a better price to a high-volume customer. The cost of delivering a $1,000 order is not that much different from the cost of delivering a $100 order. It still takes one truck and one driver. Those operators who decide to concentrate their business in the hands of fewer suppliers will, as a general rule, pay a lower price.Of course, the volume of products you must buy from a vendor to meet his or her minimum delivery requirement will vary. In addition, larger foodservice units certainly have a greater degree of flexibility in selecting multiple vendors because managers of these large units can more easily meet supplier requirements while still minimizing overall costs.

Cherry Pickers are Serviced Last

Cherry pickers is the term used by suppliers to describe the customer who gets bids from multiple vendors, then buys only those items each vendor has "on sale" or for the lowest price. If an operator buys only a vendor's low-end item, the vendor will usually respond by providing limited service. It is a natural reaction to the foodservice operator's failure to take into account varying service levels, long-term relationships, dependability, or any other vendor characteristic, except cheapest price.

It is important to remember, however, that a foodservice manager who meets minimum delivery requirements and buys regularly from the same vendor is not seen as a cherry picker just because he or she buys each item from the vendor with the lowest price. The key concept here is to develop a history of regular buying and cooperation with your vendor.

Slow Pay Means High Pay

Those operators who do not pay their bills in a timely manner would be surprised to know what their competitors are paying for similar products. In most cases, operators who are slow to pay will find that the vendor has decided to add the extra cost of carrying their account to the price the operator pays for his or her products.

Vendors can Help Reduce Costs

Vendors have a knowledge of the products they sell that exceeds that of the average foodservice operator. This skill can be used to help the competition, or it can be harnessed for your own good use. Vendors can be a great source of information related to new products, cooking techniques, trends, and alternative product usage.

ONE VENDOR VERSUS MANY VENDORS

Every operator is faced with the decision of whether to

buy from one vendor or many vendors. In general, the more vendors there are, the more time must be spent in ordering, receiving, and paying invoices. Many operators, however, fear that if they give all their business to one supplier, their costs may rise because of a lack of competition. In reality, the likelihood of this occurring is extremely small. Just as foodservice operators are unlikely to take advantage of their best guests (and, in fact, would tend to offer additional services not available to the occasional guest), so, too, does the vendor tend to behave in a manner that is preferential to the operator who does most of his or her buying from that vendor.

In fact, it makes good business sense for the vendor to do so. It is never advisable, however, to be at the mercy of a particular vendor. A good business relationship can only occur among equals; thus, many operators strive to maintain both a primary and a secondary supplier of most products. Using one or two vendors tends to bring the average delivery size up and should result in a lower per item price. On the other hand, giving one vendor all of the operation's business can be dangerous and costly if the items to be purchased vary widely in quality and price. Staples and nonperishables are best purchased in bulk from one vendor. Orders for meats, produce, and some bakery products are best split among several vendors, perhaps with a primary and a secondary vendor in each category so that you have a second alternative should the need arise. If you are using bid buying as a purchasing method, having three vendors is advisable so that you have an adequate choice of prices and services.

Purchasing Ethics

Purchasing food products is an area that can test the ethics of even the most conscientious manager. Ethics have been defined as the choices of proper conduct made by an individual in his or her relationships with others. Ethics come into play in purchasing products because of the tendency for some suppliers to seek an unfair advantage over the competition by providing "personal" Favours to the buyer. These Favours can range from small holiday gifts given in appreciation for another year's partnership to outright offers of cash "bribes"/kickbacks to the buyer in exchange for volume purchases. Some suppliers have been known to offer buyers computers, monthly cash payments, trips to Hawaii, and other such "big ticket" items to guarantee business.

Although you, as a buyer, might personally benefit from these items, the foodservice operation, your employer, will ultimately "pay" for these kickbacks through higher product prices. Should you get caught accepting these items, it is possible that you will be fired. It is the wise manager who knows the boundaries of appropriate behaviour with suppliers. Some large foodservice organizations have formal codes of conduct for their buyers. When these are in place, they should, of course, be carefully reviewed and followed. If your organization does not have a formal set of ethical guidelines for buying, the following self-tests can be helpful in determining whether a considered course of action with your supplier is indeed ethical.

Ethical Guidelines

- Is it legal?
  - Any course of action that violates written law or company policy and procedure is wrong.
- Does it hurt anyone?
  - Are benefits accruing to the buyer that rightfully belong to the owner of the business? Discounts, rebates, and free products are the property of the business, not the buyer.
- Am I being honest?
  - Is the activity one that you can comfortably say reflects well on your integrity as a professional, or will the activity actually diminish your reputation with other suppliers?
- Would I care if it happened to me?
  - If you owned the business, would you be in Favour of your buyer behaving in the manner you are considering? If you owned multiple units, would it be good for the business if all

of your buyers followed the considered course of action?

- Would I publicize my action?
  - A quick way to review the ethical merit of a situation is to consider whom you would tell about it. If you are comfortable telling your boss and your other suppliers about the considered course of action, it is likely ethical. If you would prefer that your actions go undetected, you are probably on shaky ethical ground.

DAILY INVENTORY SHEET

Before you can place an order, you will need to find out what you need! The process is much like going through your house and making a shopping list of all items before you go to the store. Some managers say that they intuitively "know" what they need without looking at their storage areas. If you have ever gone grocery shopping without a list, however, you know that you will inevitably miss a few items. We have all been in a situation in which we went to the store, purchased what we thought we needed, only to find that we forgot an important item!

You, as a foodservice manager, will want to have a detailed look at your inventory before you place an order. A good way to make sure that you have checked all your items in your storage areas is to use a daily inventory sheet. A daily inventory sheet will have the items listed in your storage areas, the unit of purchase, and the par value preprinted on the sheet. In addition, the form will have the following columns: on hand, special order, and order amount.

A preprinted list of all your items in storage and unit of purchase is important so that you will not have to write down the items every time you check the inventory. The list should be in the same order that you store the items so that you can quickly and easily locate your products. The par value is listed so that you know how much inventory you should have in storage at any given time. You may also want to list the purchase point, if appropriate. To use the daily inventory sheet, you would physically walk through your storage areas to determine what items (and amounts) you should order for the following day. Under the "On Hand" column, you would list how many of each item you have on hand, that is, sitting on the shelf. You also need to list any "Special Order" amounts needed above the par level. An example of this would be extra cases of perishables, such as strawberries, ordered for a banquet.

PREPARING THE PURCHASE ORDER

Some items will be purchased daily, others weekly, and some, perhaps, monthly. In addition, you may be able to choose from a variety of ways to communicate with your supplier. Of course, much purchasing is done face-to-face, but the technology available for placing orders today is significant and includes the fax machine, telephone keypad, e-mail, and direct access to the vendor's order system via modem on software supplied to you by that vendor. Some vendors will also come to your business and place orders for you on their laptop computers and then transfer your order electronically. In addition, more and more vendors are posting current prices on their Web pages, thus ensuring a rapid transfer of information to their customers.

Regardless of your communication method, however, it is critical that you prepare a written purchase order, or record of what you have decided to buy. The purchase order (PO) should be made out in triplicate (three copies). One copy goes to the receiving area for use by the receiving clerk. One copy is retained by management for the bookkeeping area. The original is, of course, sent to the vendor. If the purchase order is developed by telephone, management retains the original copy, with a notation in the Comments section, stating that the vendor has not seen the PO. In all cases, however, it is important to place all orders using a purchase order form. If this is not done, the receiving clerk will have no record of what is coming in on the delivery. Purchase order preparation can be simple or complex, but, in all cases, the written purchase order form should contain space for the following information:

Purchase Order Information

- Item name
- Spec number, if appropriate
- Quantity ordered
- Quoted price
- Extension price
- Total price of order
- Vendor information
- Purchase order number
- Date ordered
- Delivery date
- Ordered by
- Received by
- Delivery instructions
- Comments

Each order you place should result in the preparation of a PO. This is true even if the vendor is delivering a standing order on a daily basis.

The advantages of a written purchase order are many and include the following:

- Written verification of quoted price
- Written verification of quantity ordered
- Written verification of the receipt of all goods ordered
- Written and special instructions to the receiving clerk, as needed
- Written verification of conformance to product specification
- Written authorization to prepare vendor invoice for payment

The chef has used a sales forecast to determine the quantity of products needed for next Thursday's delivery. A check of the produce walk-in lets the chef know what is on hand and the quantity of each product required. This information allows for the accurate preparation of the PO. In this case, the order is then faxed to Scooter's Produce. The receiving clerk at the Ardmoor is now prepared with the information necessary to effectively receive the product from Scooter's.

RECEIVING

Once the PO has been prepared by the purchasing agent, it is time to prepare for the acceptance or receiving of the goods. This function is performed by the receiving clerk in a large operation or may be performed in a smaller operation by you, as the manager, or by a staff member you designate. In all cases, however, it is wise for you to establish the purchasing and receiving functions so that one individual places the order, while another individual is responsible for verifying delivery and acceptance of the product.

When this is not done, the potential for fraud or theft is substantial. Auditors, those individuals responsible for reviewing and evaluating proper operational procedures, have frequently found that the purchasing agent in an operation ordered a product, signed for its acceptance, and thus authorized invoice payment when, in fact, no product was ever delivered! In this case, the purchasing agent could be getting cash payment from the purveyor or supplier without the manager's knowledge. This could happen unless there are additional individuals in the purchasing chain. If it is not possible to have more than one person involved in the buying process, the work of the purchasing agent/receiving clerk must be carefully monitored by management to prevent fraud. There is probably no area of the foodservice establishment more ignored than the area in which receiving takes place. This is truly unfortunate, since this is the area where we are ensuring we receive the quality of products we ordered.

Proper receiving includes all of the following features:

- Proper location
- Proper tools and equipment
- Proper delivery schedules
- Proper training

PROPER LOCATION

The "back door," which is usually reserved for receiving, is often no more than that—just an entrance to the kitchen. In fact, the receiving area must be adequate to handle the job of receiving, or product loss and inconsistency will result. First, the receiving area must be large enough to allow for checking products delivered against both the invoice, which is the supplier's record of products delivered and price charged, and the PO, which is the operation's record of the same thing. In addition to space required to allow for counting and weighing, accessibility to equipment required to move products to their proper storage area and to dispose of excess packaging is important.

A location near refrigerated areas is helpful in maintaining refrigerated and frozen products at their desired temperatures. You should make sure the area stays free of trash and clutter, as these make it too easy to hide delivered food items that may be taken home at the end of the dishonest employee's shift. It is important to remember that the delivery person is also a potential thief.

While most suppliers are extremely careful to screen their delivery personnel for honesty, it is a fact that a delivery person has access to products and has a truck available to *remove* as well as deliver goods. For this reason, it is important that the receiving clerk work in an area that has a clear view of both delivery personnel and their vehicles.

The receiving area should be kept extremely clean, since you do not want to contaminate incoming food, or provide a carrying vehicle for pests. Often, suppliers themselves are responsible for delivering goods that can harbor roach eggs or other insects. A clean receiving area makes it easier to both prevent and detect this type of problem.

The area should be well lit and properly ventilated. Excessive heat in the receiving area can quickly damage delivered goods, especially if they are either refrigerated or frozen products. Too little light may cause product defects to go unnoticed; therefore, the receiving area should be well lit. Flooring should be light in colour and of a type that is easily cleaned. In colder climates, it is important that the receiving area be warm enough to allow the receiving clerk to carefully inspect products. The outside dock area in February, if the temperature is below freezing, is no place for an employee to conduct a thorough inspection of incoming products!

PROPER TOOLS AND EQUIPMENT

While the tools and equipment needed for effective receiving vary by type and size of operation, some items are standard in any receiving operation. These include the following:

Scales

Scales should be of two types: those accurate to the fraction of a pound (for large items) and those accurate to the fraction of an ounce (for smaller items and pre-portioned meats). Scales should be calibrated regularly to ensure accuracy.

Wheeled Equipment

These items, whether hand trucks or carts, should be available so that goods can be moved quickly and efficiently to their proper storage areas.

Box Cutter

This item, properly maintained and used, allows the receiving clerk to quickly remove excess packaging and thus accurately verify the quality of delivered products. Of course, care must be taken when using this tool, so proper training is essential.

Thermometer

Foods must be delivered at their proper storage temperatures. You must establish the range of temperatures you deem acceptable for product delivery. For many operators, those temperatures would be the following:

Item Acceptable Temperature Range

- °F °C
- Frozen Foods 10°F or less _12°C or less
- Refrigerated Foods 30–45°F _1–7°C

Calculator

Vendor calculations should always be checked, especially when the invoice has been prepared by hand. It is especially useful if the calculator has a physical tape that can be used by the receiving clerk when needed. The calculator should also be available in case the original invoice is either increased or decreased in amount due to incorrect vendor pricing or because of items that were listed on the invoice but not delivered. In addition, invoice totals will change when all or a portion of the delivery was rejected because the items were of substandard quality.

Records Area

This area should, in the best of cases, include a desk, telephone, computer/fax, copy machine, file cabinet, and ample office supplies such as pens, pencils, and a stapler. Obviously, larger operations are more likely to have such an area. In a smaller operation, however, the need for basic equipment still exists. In all cases, the records area should include a copy of all product specifications so there is no confusion about whether a delivered food or supply item meets the spec and, thus, should be accepted or rejected.

PROPER DELIVERY SCHEDULES

In an ideal world, you would accept delivery of products only during designated hours. These times would be scheduled during your slow periods, when there would be plenty of time for a thorough checking of the products delivered. In fact, some operators are able to demand that deliveries be made only at certain times, say between 9:00 A.M. and 10:30 A.M. These are called acceptance hours. In a case such as this, the operation may refuse to accept delivery at any other time.

Some large operations prefer to establish times in which they will *not* accept deliveries, say between 11:00 A.M. and 1:00 P.M. These are called refusal hours. Since a busy lunchtime may make it inconvenient to accept deliveries at this time, some operators will simply not take deliveries then. In both cases, however, the assumption is that the operator is either a large enough or a good enough customer to make demands such as these. You may find yourself in a situation, however, where the supplier will determine when goods are delivered. While this may seem inconvenient (and often is), remember that all foodservice units would like to have their deliveries made during the slow periods, between peak meal times. In many cases, it is simply not possible for the supplier to stop his or her trucks for several hours to wait for a good delivery time. In fact, in a remote location, some foodservice operators will be told only the day a delivery will be made, not a specific time! The key to establishing a successful delivery schedule with suppliers is, quite simply, to work with them.

If an operator is seen as especially difficult or costly to do business with, the supplier will pass those costs on, in the form of higher prices. On the other hand, the foodservice operator must make the supplier understand that there are certain times of the day when it is just not possible to accept delivery. While every relationship between operator and supplier is somewhat different, both sides, working together, can generally come to an acceptable solution on delivery hours. If you do decide to post either acceptance hours or refusal hours, these should be equally enforced with all vendors.

PROPER TRAINING

Receiving clerks should be properly trained to verify the following product characteristics:

- Weight
- Quantity
- Quality
- Price

Weight

One of the most important items to verify when receiving food products is, of course, their weight. It is simply true that 14 pounds of ground beef in a box looks exactly like 15 pounds. There is no way to tell the difference without putting the product on the scale. Receiving clerks should be required to weigh all meat, fish, and poultry delivered.

The only exception to this rule would be unopened Cryovac (sealed) packages containing items such as hot dogs, bacon, and the like. In this situation, the entire case should be weighed to detect shortages in content. Often, meat deliveries consist of several items, all of which are packaged together.

When the receiving clerk or supplier is very busy, the temptation exists to weigh all of the products together. The following example shows why it is important to weigh each item rather than the entire group of items as a whole.

Assume that you ordered 40 pounds of product from Bruno's Meats. When the Bruno's delivery person arrived, all three items were in one box and the deliverer was in a hurry. He, therefore, suggested that your receiving clerk simply weigh the entire box. Your receiving clerk did just that and found that the contents weighed 40 1 2 pounds. Since the box itself weighed about 1 2 pound, she signed for delivery.

If you called the supplier to complain about the overcharge ($248.50 total price $232.75 actual value $15.75 overcharge), you would likely be told that the misdelivery was simply a mistake caused by human error. It may well have been, but the lesson here is to always instruct your receiving personnel to weigh delivered items individually, even if they are in a hurry. When an item is ordered by weight, its delivery should be verified by weight. It is up to the operator to train the receiving clerk to *always* verify that the operation is charged only for the product weight delivered. Excess packaging, ice, or water in the case of produce can all serve to increase the delivered weight. The effective receiving clerk must be aware of and be on guard against deceptive delivery practices as far as the delivery of the agreed-upon product is concerned.

Quantity

The counting of products is as important as weighing them. It is a fact that suppliers make more mistakes in not delivering products than they do in excessive delivery. Products delivered but not charged for cost the supplier money. Products *not* delivered but charged for cost you money. If you order five cases of green beans, then, of course, you want to receive and pay for five cases. This is important for two reasons. First, you only want to pay for products that have been delivered. Second and just as important, if you have prepared your purchase order correctly, you truly need five cases of green beans.

If only three are delivered, you may not be able to prepare the menu items that are necessary to service your guests. If this means you will run out of an item or have to make a substitute, you may be forced to deal with unhappy diners. Shorting is the term used in the industry to indicate that an ordered item has not been delivered as promised. When a vendor shorts the delivery of an item you ordered, that item may or may not appear on the invoice. If it does not appear, note must be taken so that management knows that the item is missing and appropriate action can be taken.

If the item is listed on the invoice, the delivery driver should sign a credit memo. The credit memo should be filled out in triplicate (three copies). One copy goes to the receiving area to be filed. One copy is retained by management for the bookkeeping area. The original is, of course, sent to the vendor. Note that the credit memo has a place for the signature of a representative from your operation, as well as that of the vendor. It must be signed by both. The credit memo is simply a formal way of notifying the vendor that an item listed on the original invoice is missing, and, thus, the value of that item should be deducted from the invoice total. If a supplier consistently shorts your operation, that supplier is suspect in terms of both honesty and lack of concern for your operation's long-term success.

The counting of boxes, cases, sacks, barrels, and the like must be routine behaviour for the receiving clerk. Counting items, such as the number of lemons or oranges in a box, should be done on a periodic basis, but the value of counting items such as these on a regular basis is questionable. While an unscrupulous supplier might be able to remove one or two lemons from each box delivered, the time it would take for an employee to detect such behaviour is hardly worth the effort expended. It is preferable to do a periodic check and to work with reputable vendors. The direct delivery of products to a foodservice operator's storeroom or holding area is another cause for concern. The delivery person may deliver some items, such as bread, milk, and soda, directly to the storage area, thus bypassing the receiving clerk. This should not be allowed. After such an activity, it simply may be impossible to verify the accurate quantity of items delivered. If this process must be used, product dates on each item can help assure that all products listed on the invoice were indeed delivered.

Quality

No area of your operation should be of greater concern to you than that of the appropriate quality of product delivered. If you go to the trouble of developing product specifications, but then accept delivery of products that do not match these specifications, you are simply wasting time and effort. Without product specifications, verification of quality is difficult because management itself is unsure of the quality level that is desired. Some foodservice operators think that all food items are basically alike.

Nothing could be further from the truth. Suppliers know their products. They also know their customers. Some customers will accept only those items they have specified. Others will accept anything that comes in the back door because they do not take the time to verify a product's quality when it is delivered. If you were a supplier and you had a sack of onions that was getting a bit old, which customer would you deliver it to?

Unscrupulous suppliers can cost your operation guests because of both overcharging and shortchanging. Imagine, for example, a restaurant manager who requests a ¼-inch fat cover on all New York strip steaks ordered. Instead, the meat company delivers steaks with a ½-inch fat cover. The operation will, of course, pay too much for the product, since steaks with a ¼-inch fat covering sell at a higher price per pound than those with a ½-inch covering. Guests, however, will hold the operator responsible for steaks that suddenly seem to be a little "fatter" than they used to be. Coincidentally, the guests who eat the fatter steaks may tend to be a bit fatter themselves in the future! Checking for quality means checking the entire shipment for conformance to specifications. If only the top row of tomatoes in the box conforms to spec, it is up to the receiving clerk or manager to point that out to the vendor. If the balance of the box does not meet the specification, it should be refused. The credit memo can then be used to reduce the total on the invoice to the proper amount.

Sometimes, quality deficiencies are not discovered until after a delivery driver has left your establishment. When that is the case, you should notify the vendor that a thorough inspection has uncovered substandard product. The vendor is then instructed to pick up the nonconforming items. Many managers use the same "Additional Information" section of the credit memo to record this requested pickup. When the product is picked up, the pickup information is recorded. Alternatively, a separate memo to the vendor requesting a product pickup could be produced. It is best, however, to keep the number of cost control forms to a minimum whenever possible, especially when minor modifications of one form will allow that form to serve two purposes.

Vendors are sometimes out of a product, just as you may sometimes run out of a menu item. In cases such as these, the receiving clerk must know whether it is management's preference to accept a product of higher quality, lower quality, or no product at all, as a substitute. If this information is not known, one can expect that suppliers will be able to downgrade quality simply by saying that they were "out" of the requested product and did not want the operator to be "shorted" on the delivery. Training your receiving clerk to assess and evaluate quality products is a continuous process. The effective receiving clerk should develop a keen eye for quality. This is done not merely to protect the operation and ensure that it gets what it pays for, but also to ensure that guests get what they pay for. The receiving clerk might accept a lower quality. Your guests, however, may not. In fact, accepting a lower-quality substitute merely because it costs less is almost always a sure sign that management is unclear about the concept of establishing quality standards and sticking to them.

Price

In the area of training for price, two major concerns are to be addressed.

They are:

1. Matching PO unit price to invoice unit price
2. Verifying price extensions and total

Matching Purchase Order Unit Price to Invoice Unit Price

When the person responsible for purchasing food for the operation places an order, the confirmed quoted price should be written on the purchase order because it is never safe to assume that the delivered price will match the price on the purchase order. While most suppliers are honest, it is amazing how often the price quoted on the telephone or in person ends up being lower than the price the operation is charged at delivery time. Often, this variation is said to be "computer error" or a "clerical mistake."

It is interesting to note, however, that the errors most often result in the foodservice operator being overcharged and rarely result in an undercharge. As an ethical manager, you should not be happy with either an overcharge or an undercharge for a purchased product. Just as you would hope that a guest would inform you if a waiter forgot to add the price of a bottle of wine to the dinner check, a good receiving clerk works with the supplier to ensure that the operation is fairly charged for all items delivered.

The proper acceptance of products puts the integrity of both supplier and operator on the line. Honesty and fair play must govern the actions of both parties. If the receiving clerk has a copy of the purchase order, it is a simple matter to verify the quoted price and the delivered price. If these two do not match, management should be notified immediately. If management notification is not possible, both the driver and the receiving clerk should initial the "Comments" section of the purchase order, showing the difference in the two prices, and a credit memo should be prepared. Obviously, if the receiving clerk has no record of the quoted price, from either a purchase order or an equivalent document, price verification of this type is not possible. An inability to verify the quoted price and the delivered price *at the time of delivery* is a sure indication that all is not well in the food cost control system.

Some operators deal with suppliers in such a way that a contract price is established. A contract price is simply an agreement between buyer and seller to hold the price of a product constant over a defined period of time. For example, Bernardo uses Dairy O Milk. Dairy O agrees to supply Bernardo with milk at the price of $2.55 per gallon for three months from January 1 through March 31. Bernardo is free to buy as much or as little as he needs.

The milk will always be billed at $2.55 per gallon; $2.55, then, is the contract price. The advantage to Bernardo is that he knows exactly what his per-gallon milk cost will be for the three-month period. The advantage to Dairy O is that it can offer a lower price in the hope of securing all of Bernardo's milk business. Even in the case of a contract price, however, the receiving clerk must verify the invoice delivery price against the established contract price.

Verifying Price Extensions and Total

Price extension is just as important for you to monitor as is the ordered/delivered price. Price extension is the process by which you compute extended price. Extended price is simply the unit price multiplied by the number of units delivered. Extended price verification is extremely important. It is critical that the receiving clerk verify: Unit prices Number of units delivered Extended price computations (unit price _ number of units delivered) Invoice totals There seem to be two major reasons why operators do not always insist that the receiving clerk verify the extended prices and invoice totals. The most common reason is the belief that there is not enough time to do so. The driver may be in a hurry and the operation may be very busy. If that is the case, the process of verifying the extended price can be moved to a slower time. Why? Because there is a written record provided by the vendor of both the unit price and the number of units delivered. Remember that verification of price extensions is a part of the receiving verification process that need not be done at the time of delivery. Extension errors are vendor errors, in the vendor's own handwriting! Or, more accurately, today they are in the vendor's own computer. The second reason operators sometimes ignore price extensions is related to these same computers. Some operators believe that if an invoice is computer generated, the mathematics of price extension must be correct. Nothing could be further from the truth.

Anyone familiar with the process of using computers knows that there are many possible entry errors that can result in extension errors. Once all extensions have been verified, it is always a good idea to check the invoice total against the sum of the individual, correct price extensions. Managers must ensure that delivery clerks verify both extension prices and invoice totals. If this cannot be done at the time of delivery, it must be done as soon thereafter as possible. Errors are made, and they can cost your operation greatly if they go undetected.

RECEIVING RECORD OR DAILY RECEIVING SHEET

Some large operations use a receiving record when receiving food. This method, while taking administrative time both to prepare and to monitor, does have some advantages.

A receiving record generally contains the following information:

- Name of supplier
- Invoice number
- Item description
- Unit price
- Number of units delivered
- Total cost
- Storage area (unit distribution)
- Date of activity

Note that some items are placed directly into production areas (direct use), while others may be used in specific units or sent to the storeroom. Sundry items, such as paper products, ashtrays, matches, and cleaning supplies, may be stored in specific nonfood areas. Note also that subtotals for storage areas can be determined in terms of both units or dollars, as the operator prefers.

In all cases, the sums for each distribution area should equal the total for all items received during the day. Receiving reports can be useful to management if it is important to record where items are to be delivered or where they have been delivered. While some foodservice operators will find the receiving report useful, many will not, since most of the information it contains is also included in the receiving clerk's copy of the purchase order.

STORAGE

The ideal situation for you and your operation would be for you to store only the food you will use between the time of a vendor's delivery and the time of that vendor's next delivery. This is true because storage costs money, both in terms of providing the storage space for inventory items and in terms of money that is tied up in inventory items and, thus, unavailable for use elsewhere. It is always best, whenever possible, to order only the products that are absolutely needed by the operation. In that way, the vendor's storeroom actually becomes your storeroom. The vendor then absorbs the costs of storing your needed products. In all cases, however, you must have an adequate supply of products on hand to service your guests. They are your main concern. If you are doing your job well, you will have many guests and will need many items in storage! Once the receiving clerk has properly accepted the food products you have purchased, the next step in the control of food costs is that of storing those items.

The storage process, in most foodservice establishments, consists of essentially four main parts:

- Placing products in storage
- Maintaining product quality and safety
- Maintaining product security
- Determining inventory value

PLACING PRODUCTS IN STORAGE

Food products are highly perishable items. As such, they must be moved quickly from your receiving area to the area selected for storage. This is especially true for refrigerated and frozen items. An item such as ice cream, for example, can deteriorate substantially if it is at room temperature for only a few minutes. Most often, in foodservice, this high perishability dictates that the same individual responsible for receiving the items is the individual responsible for their storage. Consider the situation of Kathryn, the receiving clerk at the Fairview Estates, an extended care facility with 400 residents. She has just taken delivery of seven loaves of bread. They were delivered in accordance with the purchase order and now must be put away. While Kathryn stores these items, she must know whether management requires her to use the LIFO (last in, first out) or FIFO (first in, first out) method of product rotation.

LIFO System

When using the LIFO storage system, the storeroom operator intends to use the most recently delivered product (last in) before he or she uses any part of that same product previously on hand. If Kathryn decides, for example, to use the new bread first, she would be using the LIFO system. In all cases, you must strive to maintain a consistent product standard. In the case of *some* bread, pastry, dairy, fruit, and vegetable items, the storeroom clerk could practice the LIFO system, if these items have been designed as LIFO items by management. With LIFO, you will need to take great care to order only the quantity of product needed between deliveries. If too much product is ordered, loss rates will be very high. Costs can rise dramatically when LIFO items must eventually be discarded or used in a way that reduces their revenue-producing ability. For most items you will buy, the best storage system to use is the FIFO system.

FIFO System

First in, first out (FIFO) means that you intend to rotate your stock in such a way that product already on hand is sold prior to the sale of more recently delivered product. If this is the case, the storeroom clerk must take great care to place new stock behind or at the bottom of old stock. It is the tendency of employees not to do this. Consider, for example, the storeroom clerk who must put away six cases of tomato sauce. The cases weigh about 40 pounds. The FIFO method dictates that these six cases be placed *under* the five cases already in the storeroom. Will the clerk place the six newly delivered cases underneath the five older cases? In many instances, the answer is no. Unless management strictly enforces the FIFO rule, employees may be tempted to take the easy way out.

FIFO is the preferred storage technique for most perishable and nonperishable items. This is because it is generally a good idea to sell the oldest stock first. Failure to implement a FIFO system of storage management can result in excessive product loss due to spoilage, shrinkage, and deterioration of quality. All of these must be avoided if you are to effectively manage food expenses. Decisions about storing food items according to the LIFO or FIFO method are your decisions. Once these decisions have been made, they should be communicated to the storeroom clerk and monitored on a regular basis to ensure compliance. To ensure that this is so, some foodservice managers require the storeroom clerk to mark or tag each delivered item with the date of delivery.

These markings provide a visual aid in determining which product should be used first. This is especially critical in the area of highly perishable and greater-cost items such as fresh meats and seafood. Special meat and seafood date tags will be available from your vendor. These tags contain a space for writing in the item name, quantity, and delivery date. The use of these tags or an alternative date tracking system is strongly recommended. If the supplier has computerized his or her delivery, the box or case may already bear a strip identifying both the product and the delivery date. When this is not the case, however, the storeroom clerk should assume this function.

Storage Areas

The food and related products you buy will generally be placed in one of the following three major storage areas within your facility:

1. Dry storage

2. Refrigerated storage
3. Frozen storage

Dry Storage

Dry-storage areas should generally be maintained at a temperature ranging between 65°F (18°C) and 75°F (24°C). Temperatures lower than those recommended can be harmful to food products. More often, however, dry-storage temperatures can get very high, exceeding by far the upper limit of temperature acceptability. This is because storage areas are frequently in poorly ventilated closed-in areas of the building. Excessive temperatures damage dry-storage products. Many dry-storage areas are not air conditioned, so it may be necessary to monitor the temperature of these areas with a thermometer. Shelving in dry-storage areas must be easily cleaned and sturdy enough to hold the weight of dry products. Local health codes can vary, but shelving should generally be placed at least 6 inches above the ground to allow for proper cleaning beneath the shelving and to ensure proper ventilation.

Dry-goods products should never be stored directly on the ground, and it is a violation of all local health codes to do so. Slotted shelving is generally preferred over solid shelving when storing food, because slotted shelving allows better air circulation around the product. Can labels should face out for easy identification. For those bulk items stored in bins or large containers, wheels on these containers should be used whenever possible so that heavy lifting and resulting employee injuries can be avoided. Most important, dry-storage space must be sufficient in size to handle your operation's needs. Cramped and cluttered dry-storage areas tend to increase costs because inventory cannot be easily rotated, maintained, and counted. Theft can go undetected, and you may find yourself accidentally using the FIST (first in, still there!) method of inventory storage because products get "lost" in the storeroom.

Refrigerated Storage

Refrigerator temperatures should generally be maintained

between 32°F (0°C) and 36°F (2°C). In fact, the refrigerator itself will vary as much as four degrees (F) between its coldest spot (near the bottom) and its warmest spot. The bottom tends to be coldest in a refrigerator because warm air rises and cold air falls. Refrigerators actually work by removing heat from the contents, rather than "making" food cold. This is an important point to remember when refrigerating food. Foods that are boiling hot should be precooled to 160°F (71°C) before placing them in the refrigerator. This results in lower operating costs for the refrigerator, but is still well above the potentially hazardous food danger zone, which most food experts place at 40°F to 140°F (4°C to 60°C).

Refrigerators should have easily cleaned shelving units that are at least 6 inches off the floor and are slotted to allow for good air circulation. They should be properly cleaned on a regular basis and should be opened and closed quickly, both to lower operational costs and to ensure that the items in the refrigerator stay at their peak of freshness. Carryover items should be properly labeled, wrapped, and rotated so that items can be found easily, resulting in both greater employee efficiency and reduced energy costs because refrigerator doors will be opened for shorter periods of time. Many managers find that requiring foods to be stored in clear plastic containers also helps in this regard.

Freezer Storage

Freezer temperatures should be maintained between 0°F and 10°F (18°C and 23°C). What is usually called a freezer, however, is more properly a "frozen-food storage unit." The distinction is an important one. To be frozen at its peak of freshness, a food item must be frozen very quickly. This involves temperatures of 20°F (29°C) or lower. Freezer units in a foodservice operation do not generally operate at these temperatures; thus, they really are best at "holding" foods that are already frozen, rather than freezing food. Frozen foods comprise an increasingly large portion of the foods you are likely to buy. Therefore, the conversion of dry or refrigerated space to frozen-food storage is highly recommended. Most foodservice operators also find that their carryover items will, in many cases, have a longer shelf life when held frozen rather than in refrigeration. Frozen foods should be wrapped securely to reduce moisture loss, and newly delivered products should be carefully checked with a thermometer when received to ensure that they are at the proper temperature. In addition, these items should be carefully inspected to ensure that they have not been thawed and refrozen.

Frozen-food holding units must be regularly maintained, a process that includes cleaning inside and out and constant temperature monitoring to detect possible improper operation. A thermometer permanently placed in the unit or read from outside the unit, as is the case with digital displays, is required in most areas. It is also a good idea to periodically check that gaskets on freezers, as well as refrigerators, tightly seal the food cabinet. This will not only reduce operating costs, but will also maintain food quality for a longer period of time.

STORAGE BASICS

Regardless of the storage type, food and related products should be stored neatly in some logical order. This makes them easier to find and to count when the need arises. You may decide, for example, to arrange your stored products on the basis of how often your staff uses them. That is, frequently used items are placed near the front of the storage area. When a few items constitute a majority of the sales volume in your unit, this can be an effective storage technique. No matter what type of storage system you choose, make sure your inventory sheet matches the physical order of items in storage. This saves time in taking inventory, and it results in fewer errors. It is also important to note that the objective of a neat storage area is both to maximize storage space and to minimize the time it takes to locate the item in storage. When possible, the storage area should be in close proximity to the area in which the product will be used. This reduces unnecessary time lost in traveling to remote storage areas to secure needed products.

In this regard, proper storage techniques, while assisting in lowering the cost of food products, also help in reducing costs associated with Labour. It is sometimes amazing how long it can take an employee to go to the storeroom for a can of beans! In an improperly maintained storage area, employees can claim that it took a long time to "find" the desired product. When a storage area is well located, properly labeled, kept clean, and monitored regularly, problems such as this will not occur.

MAINTAINING PRODUCT QUALITY AND SAFETY

It is a fact that food product quality rarely improves with increased storage time. In most cases, the quality of ingredients you buy is at its peak when the product you ordered is delivered to you. From then on, the products can only decline in freshness, quality, and nutrition. The only exception to this might be the gourmet restaurant that elects to age some of its own products. The general case, however, is that your storeroom clerk must make every effort to maintain food quality in all of your storage areas, since food quality tends to diminish during the storage process. The primary method for ensuring product quality while in storage is through proper product rotation and high standards of storeroom sanitation. Storage areas are excellent breeding grounds for insects, some bacteria, and also rodents.

To protect against these potentially damaging hazards, you should insist on a regular cleaning of all storage areas. Compressor units on refrigerators and frozen-food holding units should be checked regularly for the buildup of dust and dirt. Interior storage racks should be kept free of spills and soil. Refrigerators and frozen-food holding units remove significant amounts of stored product moisture, causing shrinkage in meats and produce and freezer burn in poorly wrapped or stored items kept at freezing temperatures.

Unless they are built in, refrigerators and frozen-food holding units should be high enough off the ground to allow for easy cleaning around and under them to prevent cockroaches and other insects from living beneath them. Both refrigerators and frozen-food holding units should be kept 6 to 10 inches from walls to allow for the free circulation of air around, and efficient operation of, the units. Drainage systems in refrigerators should be checked at least weekly. Ideally, frozen-food holding units and refrigerators should have *externally visible* internal thermometers, whether they are read as a digital display or in the more traditional temperature scale. In larger storage areas, hallways should be kept clear and empty of storage materials or boxes. This helps both in finding items in the storage area and in reducing the number of hiding places for insects and rodents.

Maintaining Product Security

Food products are the same as money to you. In fact, you should think of food inventory items in exactly that way. The apple in a produce walk-in is not just an apple. It represents, at a selling price of $2.00, that amount in revenue to the airport foodservice director, who hopes to sell a crisp, fresh apple to a weary traveller. If the apple disappears, revenue of $2.00 will disappear also. When you think of inventory items in terms of their sales value, it becomes clear why product security is of the utmost importance. As such, systems must be in place to reduce employee, vendor, and guest theft to the lowest possible level.

All foodservice establishments will experience some amount of theft, in its strictest sense. The reason is very simple. Some employee theft is impossible to detect. Even the most sophisticated, computerized control system is not able to determine if an employee or vendor's employee walked into the produce walk-in and ate one green grape. Similarly, an employee who takes home two sugar packets per night will likely go undetected for a great length of time. In neither of these cases, however, is the amount of loss significant, and certainly not enough to install security cameras in the walk-in or to frisk your employees as they leave for home at the end of their shifts.

What you do want to do, however, is to make it difficult to remove significant amounts of food from storage without authorization, so that you can know when that food has been removed. Good cost control systems must be in place if you are to achieve this goal. It is amazing how large the impact of theft can be on profitability. Consider the following example. Jesse is the receiving clerk at the Irish Voice sports bar. On a daily basis, Jesse takes home $2.00 worth of food products. How much, then, does Jesse cost the bar in one year? The answer is a surprising $14,600 in sales revenue! If Jesse steals $2.00 per day for 365 days, the total theft amount is $730 (365 days $2.00 per day $730). If the bar makes an after-tax profit of 5% on each dollar of food products sold, the operation must sell $730 $14,600 to recover the lost $730.

In order to recover the dollar amount of Jesse's theft, the sports bar must sell $14,600 of food per year and make 5 cents per dollar sold on these sales. In the case of a smaller bar, $14,600 may well represent several days' sales revenue. Clearly, small thefts can add up to large dollar losses! Most foodservice operators attempt to control access to the location of stored products. This may be done, in some areas, by a process as simple as keeping the dry-storage area locked and requiring employees to "get the keys" from the manager or supervisor. In other situations, cameras may be mounted in both storage areas and employee exit areas.

While the physical layout of the foodservice operation may prevent management from being able to effectively lock and secure all storage areas, too much traffic is sure to cause theft problems. This is not because employees are basically dishonest. Most are not. Theft problems develop because of the few employees who either feel that management will not miss a few of whatever is being stolen or feel that they "deserve" to take a few things because they work so hard and are paid so little! It is your responsibility to see to it that the storeroom clerk maintains good habits in securing product inventory. As a general rule, if storerooms are to be locked, only one individual should have the key during any shift. The temptation sometimes exists for management to hang the key by the door, that is, to have the storeroom locked, but give the key to any employee who says that he or she needs it. This obviously defeats the purpose of the locked system. In reality, it is simply not possible to keep all inventory items under lock and key. Some items must be received and immediately sent to the kitchen for processing or use. Also, what would happen if you or another designated "key holder" were gone from the operation for a few minutes? Most operators find that it is impossible to operate under a system where all food products are locked away from the employees.

Storage areas should, however, not be accessible to guests or vendor employees. Unlocked storage areas near exits are extremely tempting to the dishonest individual. If proper control procedures are in place, employees will know that you can determine if theft has occurred. Without such control, employees are aware that theft can go undetected. This must, and can, be avoided.

Determining Inventory Value

The inventory you have on hand should be maintained in a way that makes it easy to issue (place into production), as well as to count and to determine its monetary value. This is because you must be able to answer this fundamental question: "What is the value of the products I currently have on hand?" The answer to this question is critical because it is simply not possible to know your actual food expense without an accurate inventory. In fact, the mathematical formula used to determine the cost of food sold (food expense) is driven primarily by knowing the dollar value of all food products in inventory. The process of determining inventory value is quite simple, even if the actual task can be very time consuming. Valuing, or establishing a dollar value for your entire inventory, is done by using the following inventory valuation formula:

Item Amount Item Value Item Inventory Value

Item Amount

Item amount may be determined by counting the item, as in the case of cans, or by weighing items, as in the case of meats. Volume, that is, gallons, quarts, and the like, is another method of establishing product amounts. If an item is purchased by the pound, it is generally weighed to determine item amount. If it is purchased by the piece or case, the appropriate unit to determine the item amount may be either pieces or cases. If, for example, canned pears are purchased by the case, with six cans per case, management might decide to consider the item either as case or as can.

That is, three cases of the canned pears might be considered as three items (by the case) or as 18 items (by the can). Any method you use to accurately establish the amount of product you have on hand is acceptable. If product is undercounted, your expenses will appear higher than they actually are. If, on the other hand, you erroneously (or on purpose) compute overstated, or padded inventory, costs will appear artificially low until the proper inventory values are determined.

Item Value

An item's actual value can be more complicated to determine than its amount. This is because the price you pay for an item may vary slightly each time you buy it. Assume, for example, that you bought curly endive for $2.20 per pound on Monday, but the same item was $2.50 per pound on Wednesday. On Friday, you see that you have one pound of the curly endive in your refrigerated walk-in. Is the value of the item $2.20 or $2.50? Item value is, generally speaking, determined by using either the LIFO or the FIFO method. When the LIFO method is in use, the item's value is said to be the price paid for the least recent (oldest) addition to item amount. If the FIFO method is in use, the item value is said to be the price paid for the most recent (newest) product on hand. In the hospitality industry, most operators value inventory at its most recently known value; thus, FIFO is the more common method. A simple illustration may help. Peggy purchased grapes on Monday and paid $30.00 per lug. On Friday, she again purchased grapes, but paid $40.00 per lug. On Saturday morning, she took inventory and found that she had 1_12_ lugs of grapes.

What is their inventory value? The LIFO system says that Peggy's grapes have an inventory value of $45.00 ($30.00 LIFO price 1.5 lugs $45.00). The FIFO method places a value of

$60.00 on the grapes ($40.00 FIFO price _ 1.5 lugs _ $60.00). Because it is closest to the actual replacement cost of the inventory item, choosing to value inventory at the most recently paid price (FIFO) is the best method for establishing item value for the majority of hospitality operators. This inventory valuation sheet has a place for all inventory items, the quantity on hand, and the unit value of each item.

There is also a place for the date the inventory was taken, a spot for the name of the person who counted the product, and another space for the person who extended or established the value of the inventory. It is recommended that these two be different individuals to reduce the risk of inventory valuation fraud. The inventory valuation sheet should be completed each time the inventory is counted. It can be preprinted from a computerized list of items, a process that saves much in the way of staff time and effort. Regardless of the form used, the item's inventory value is determined as described earlier.

Thus, if we have five cases of fresh beets in our inventory, and each case has a value of $20.00, the inventory value of our beets is value of the item by the number of units on hand. The process becomes more difficult when one realises that the average foodservice operation has hundreds of items in inventory. Thus, "taking the inventory" can be a very time-consuming task. A physical inventory, one in which the food products are actually counted, must, however, be taken to determine your actual food usage. Some operators take this inventory monthly, others weekly or even daily! Some, unfortunately, feel that there is no need to ever take inventory. These operators cannot effectively control their costs because they do not know what their costs are.

DETERMINING ACTUAL FOOD EXPENSE

Assume that you own and manage a small ice cream store that makes its own products. You have reviewed your records for the past month and found the following: You have determined your revenue figure from the sales history you maintained. You have determined your food expense by adding the dollar value of all the properly corrected delivery invoices that you accumulated for the month. That is, you totaled the value of all food purchased and delivered between the first day of the month and the last.

Would it be correct to say that your food expense for the month of January is $39,000? The answer is No. Why not? Because you may have more, or less, of the food products required to make your ice cream in inventory on the last day of January than you had on the first day. If you have more food products in inventory on January 31 than you had on January 1, your food expense is less than $39,000. If you have fewer products in inventory on January 31 than you had on January 1, your food expense is higher than $39,000. To understand why this is so, you must understand the formula for computing your actual food expense.

BEGINNING INVENTORY

Beginning inventory is the dollar value of all food on hand at the beginning of the accounting period. It is determined by completing an actual count and valuation of the products on hand.

Purchases

Purchases are the sum cost of all food purchased during the accounting period. It is determined by adding all properly tabulated invoices for the accounting period.

Goods Available for Sale

Goods available for sale is the sum of the beginning inventory and purchases. It represents the value of all food that was available for sale during the accounting period.

Ending Inventory

Ending inventory refers to the dollar value of all food on hand at the end of the accounting period. It also is determined by completing a physical inventory.

Cost of Food Consumed

The cost of food consumed is the actual dollar value of

all food used, or consumed, by the operation. Again, it is important to note that this is not merely the value of all food sold, but rather the value of all food no longer in the establishment and includes the value of any meals eaten by employees.

Employee Meals

Employee meal cost is a Labour-related, not food-related cost. Free or reduced-cost employee meals are a benefit much in the same manner as medical insurance or paid vacation. Therefore, the value of this benefit, if provided, should be transferred and charged not as a cost of food but as a cost of employee benefits. The dollar value of food eaten by employees is subtracted from the cost of food consumed to yield the cost of food sold.

Cost of Food Sold

As stated earlier, the cost of food sold is the actual dollar value of all food expense incurred by the operation except for those related to employee meals. It is not possible to determine this number unless a beginning inventory has been taken at the start of the month, followed by another inventory taken at the end of the month. Without these two numbers, it is impossible to accurately determine the cost of food sold. In the ice cream store example, had you completed such a form, you would have known your actual cost of food sold. Every manager should, on a regular basis, compute the actual cost of food sold because it is not possible to improve your cost picture unless you first know what your costs are.

VARIATIONS ON THE BASIC COST OF FOOD SOLD FORMULA

Unit to Another

This is the case when, for example, an operator seeks to compute one cost of food sold figure for a bar and another for the bar's companion restaurant. In this situation, it is likely that fruits, juices, vegetables, and similar items are taken from the kitchen for use in the bar, while wine, sherry, and similar items may be taken from the bar for use in the kitchen. The formula for cost of food sold in this situation would be as follows:

Cost of Food Sold		
Accounting Period: to ______		
Unit Name: ______		
Beginning Inventory	$ ______	
Plus		
Purchases	$ ______	
Goods Available for Sale		$ ______
Less		
Ending Inventory		$ ______
Cost of Food Consumed		$ ______
Less		
Employee Meals		$ ______
Cost of Food Sold		$ ______

It is important for you to know exactly which formula or variation is in use when analyzing cost of food sold. The variations, while slight, can make big differences in the interpretation of your cost information. In all cases, it is critical that accurate beginning and ending inventory figures be maintained if accurate cost data are to be computed. In the following example, both beginning inventory and ending inventory figures are known, thus enabling you to determine your actual cost of food sold.

It is important to note that ending inventory for one accounting period becomes the beginning inventory figure for the next period. For example, in the case of your ice cream store, the January 31 ending inventory figure of $27,500 will become the February 1 beginning inventory figure. In this manner, it is clear that physical inventory need only be taken one time per accounting period, not twice. Again, while the physical inventory process can be time consuming, it must be performed in order to determine actual food expense. While there is no reliable method for replacing the actual counting of inventory items on hand, there are many computer programmes on the market programmed to allow an individual to scan the bar codes on products using a handheld scanning device and, thus, perform both the counting and the price extension process necessary to develop actual inventory valuations. Using technology in this manner can make a time-consuming task much less tedious and more efficient.

FOOD COST PERCENTAGE

Food expense is often expressed as a percentage of total revenue or sales. Since you can now determine your actual cost of food sold, you can also learn to compute and evaluate your operation's food cost percentage. Again, this is both the traditional way of looking at food expense and generally the method used by most operators when preparing the profit and loss statement. Food cost% represents that portion of food sales that was spent on food expenses. In the case of the ice cream store discussed previously, you know that the cost of food sold equals $33,275.

Estimating Daily Cost of Food Sold

Many operators would like to know their food usage on a much more regular basis than once per month. When this is the case, the physical inventory may be taken as often as desired. Again, however, physical inventories are time consuming. It would be convenient if you could have a close estimate of your food usage on a weekly or daily basis without the effort of a daily inventory count. Fortunately, such an approximation exists. One of them is to estimate food cost% on a daily or weekly basis. As an example, assume that you own an Italian restaurant that serves no liquor and caters to a family-oriented clientele. You would like to monitor your food cost percentage on a more regular basis than once a month, which is your regular accounting period. You have decided to use a sixcolumn form to estimate your food cost percentage. Since you keep track of both daily sales and purchases, you can easily do so. In the space above the first two columns, write the word Sales. Above the middle two columns, write Purchases, and above the last two columns, enter the term Cost%. You then proceed each day to enter your daily sales revenue in the column labeled Sales Today. Your invoices for food deliveries are totaled daily and entered in the column titled Purchases Today. Dividing the Purchases Today column by the Sales Today column yields the figure that is placed in the Cost% Today column. Purchases to Date (the cumulative purchases amount) is divided by Sales to Date (the cumulative sales amount) to yield the Cost% to Date figure. You buy most of your food at the beginning of the week, while sales are strongest in the later part of the week. This is a common occurrence at many foodservice establishments. As can also be seen, your daily cost percentage ranges from a high of 130% (Monday) to a low of 0% (Sunday), when no deliveries are made. In the Cost% to Date column, however, the range is only from a high of 130% (Monday) to a low of 39.20% (Sunday). What is your best estimate about what your food cost% actually is as of Sunday? The answer is that it will be slightly less than 39.20%. Why? Let us go back to the formula for cost of food sold.

Before we do, we must make one important assumption: "For any time period we are evaluating, the beginning inventory and ending inventory amounts are the same." In other words, over any given time period, you will have approximately the same amount of food on hand at all times. If this assumption is correct, the six-column food cost estimate is, in fact, a good indicator of your food usage. The reason is very simple. The formula for cost of food sold asks you to add beginning inventory and then later subtract ending inventory. If these two numbers are assumed to be the same, they can be ignored, since adding and subtracting the same number to any other number will result in no effect at all. For example, if we start with $10, add $50, and subtract $10, we are left with $50. In terms of the cost of food sold formula, when beginning inventory and ending inventory are assumed to be the same figure, it is the mathematical equivalent of adding a zero and subtracting a zero. To continue our example, if we start with $0, add $50, and subtract $0, we are left, again, with $50.

Therefore, as stated earlier, if you assume that your inventory is constant, your cost of food sold for the one-week period is a little less than $4,034.21, or 39.20% of sales. Why a little less? Because we must still subtract the value of employee meals, if any are provided, since they are an employee benefit and not a food expense. How accurate is the six-column form?

For most operators, it is quite accurate and has the following advantages:

- It is very simple to compute, requiring 10 minutes or less per day for most operations.
- It records both sales history and purchasing patterns.
- It identifies problems before the end of the monthly accounting period.
- By the ninth or tenth day, the degree of accuracy in the To Date column is very high.
- It is a daily reminder to both management and employees that there is a very definite relationship between sales and expenses. The use of a six-column food cost estimator is highly recommended for the operator who elects to conduct a physical inventory less often than every two weeks.

The control of food expense is critical to all foodservice operations. From the purchase of the raw ingredient to its receiving and storage, the effective foodservice operator strives to have the proper quality and quantity of product on hand at all times. Food represents a large part of your overall expense budget. Protecting this product and accounting for its usage are extremely important in helping to manage overall costs.

2

Effects and Impacts of Control Process

INTRODUCTION

In general, control means exercising governing power over events and situations such that an outcome can be achieved or prevented. In our personal lives we can normally exercise governing power over our actions, and thus control, to achieve or prevent various outcomes. For example, we leave our homes for work or school each day early enough so that we arrive at a specific time. We drink alcoholic beverages to achieve a desired glow, but we must limit the amount we drink if we do not want to get drunk or sick.

Many people give up smoking cigarettes to prevent the possibility of getting lung cancer. Governments, employers, and parents frequently exercise governing power. In the process, our freedom to act becomes more limited. For example, legislatures enact laws that limit our freedom when driving on the roads—a speed limit of 65 miles per hour on the interstate highway, stopping at a red light, and so on.

These laws have the intention of making driving safer so that accidents can be prevented and others are not harmed. Parents make rules for their children in an attempt to control their behaviour. Managers of businesses make work rules and establish procedures of various kinds for their employees. In each of these situations, there are consequences if we choose not to follow the laws, regulations, procedures, and rules that are established. If we do not arrive at school on time, there is the possibility of a penalty for being late for class. If we drive faster than the established speed limit, there is the possibility of a speeding ticket and eventual loss of driving privileges.

Exercising control generally means that there is some human involvement. Humans either take some form of action or prevent others from taking an action in order to achieve an outcome. It is important to point out that in the food and beverage industry, *control* really means controlling people rather than things. Consider the following: Food does not disappear by itself, without help. Excess quantities of liquor do not get into drinks unless put there by bartenders. Employees' wage calculations are not based on the wrong numbers of hours unless someone gives the wrong information to the paymaster. Food is not consumed by rodents unless human beings make that food accessible. Customers seldom leave without paying unless staff members make that possible.

In every one of these instances, the problem is the result of human action or lack of it. If a business is to operate profitably and reach its financial goals, people's actions must be managed, or, in some cases, limited. "People" may include more than simply the personnel of the food and beverage operation; they may include customers of the establishment and, in some cases, intruders who seek to steal the resources of the establishment—obviously, without the knowledge and consent of management. Thus, installing locks on both the front and back doors is one of the most basic control measures one can use to prevent intruders from entering and stealing food, beverages, equipment, and cash when the operation is closed. Locating the cashier near the front door helps prevent customers from leaving without paying their food and beverage charges.

Instituting various sanitation procedures may serve effectively to control infestation by various insects and rodents. Obviously, loss of food due to nonhuman invaders surely constitutes unwarranted additional cost to any restaurant. The time clock for employees is an example of a simple control device. This serves many purposes, one of which is to prepare accurate payroll records so that Labour costs will be correct.

Another good example is the bartender's use of a measuring device to ensure that each drink will contain the correct amount of a particular alcoholic ingredient.

In the food and beverage business, control is a process used by managers to direct, regulate, and restrain the actions of people so that the established goals of an enterprise may be achieved. Probably the most common goal for all private enterprises is financial success—a particular profit or return on investment Other goals may include operating the best restaurant in the city, having a low Labour turnover (dedicated employees who stay with the restaurant for many years), or promoting better health by providing nutritional information on the menu. To achieve these goals, management must set up any number of subgoals compatible with its primary goals. These tend to be more specific and usually more immediate in nature. For example, to achieve the goal of operating the best restaurant in the city, it might be necessary to have a subgoal of hiring an excellent chef and to purchase the finest ingredients. To have a low Labour turnover, it generally is necessary to have a subgoal of establishing a pleasant working environment, good pay, and suitable fringe benefits.

A discussion of general business goals is beyond the scope of a text on cost control. On the assumption that appropriate goals have been established, the discussion in this chapter is restricted to the control procedures employed by foodservice managers to achieve one basic goal of business: operating profitably. Therefore, the focus is on establishing control over costs and sales in food and beverage operations. Attention is centered on the particular methods and procedures used by foodservice managers to direct, regulate, and restrain the actions of people, both directly and indirectly, to keep costs within acceptable bounds, to account for revenues, and to earn a profit in the process.

COST CONTROL

Cost control is defined as the process used by managers to regulate costs and guard against excessive costs. It is an ongoing process and involves every step in the chain of purchasing, receiving, storing, issuing, and preparing food and beverages for sale, as well as training and scheduling the personnel involved. The particular methods used to control costs vary from one establishment to another, depending, in part, on the nature and scope of operations, but the principles behind these methods are constant. The obvious objective is to eliminate excessive costs for food, beverages, and Labour—to exert some governing power over costs in all areas to ensure that the enterprise will operate at a profit.

Two of the principal causes of excessive costs are inefficiency and waste. For example, storing food in refrigerators that are not cold enough or bottled beer in a warm, sunny room will cause spoilage and excessive cost. So will the preparation of an inedible beef stew or an unpalatable drink. When the stew is thrown into the garbage can or the drink is poured down the drain, the costs of operation are increased, but sales are not. Because profit is essentially the difference between sales and costs, it is apparent that any increases in cost that do not lead to corresponding increases in sales can have only one effect—a reduction in profits. Clearly, management must take steps to guard against such excessive costs.

SALES CONTROL

Although cost control is critically important to the profitable operation of any business, cost control alone will not ensure profitability. Additional steps must be taken to ensure that all sales result in appropriate income to the business (sales control). For example, profits will be adversely affected if a steak listed in the menu for $18.95 is sold to a customer for $15.95 or if the drink priced to sell for $4.50 is sold for $2.50, or if food and drink are given away. Therefore, it is important to require that each employee records each sale accurately. In addition, it is useful to compare sales records to production records to ensure that all quantities produced are accounted for. Although it is unfortunate that some employees are not completely honest, it is a fact of life that must be taken into account in food and beverage operations. Therefore, guest checks are usually numbered to ensure accountability. Sometimes duplicate copies of the checks, clearly identified as duplicates so they are not confused with the originals, are used to reconcile kitchen production with recorded sales.

When the checks and duplicates are numbered sequentially, missing numbers can be noted and investigated at once. Establishments that use industry-specific computer programmes find that control is much easier to institute than at establishments without such programmes. For example, this chapter illustrates one such programme that makes it very difficult for menu items to be priced incorrectly, makes it very easy to reconcile kitchen production with recorded sales, and allows management to determine that all sales have been accounted for, either in cash or by credit.

RESPONSIBILITY FOR CONTROL

Responsibility for every aspect of any food and beverage enterprise rests with management. Control, therefore, is clearly a responsibility of management. In some food and beverage enterprises—probably the majority— managers take personal charge of directing and supervising the control procedures in every phase of operations. In others, managers delegate some or all of the work to subordinates. The nature, size, and scope of operations help determine the extent to which managers can exercise direct control rather than delegate that control to someone else. In general, the larger and more complex the operation, the more likely it is that control procedures will be supervised by subordinates. Job titles for these subordinates include food controller, beverage controller, assistant manager, supervisor, and a number of others.

Throughout this text, several job titles are used for those having responsibility for supervising food, beverage, or Labour control procedures. In the majority of food and beverage enterprises, one is likely to find control procedures supervised directly by managers, so that title is used most often. In larger operations, one may find food controllers and beverage controllers. Today, there are comparatively few of these, but the job titles are still useful in discussions of control principles and will appear in various chapters. The use of one job title rather than another in this text is not intended to suggest that any particular task should be assigned to any particular job title. In that sense, the specific job titles used are of little importance. The significant point is that management is ultimately responsible for seeing that appropriate control procedures are established, either by attending to the work personally or by assigning it to others.

Instituting Control

The food and beverage business can be characterized as one that involves raw materials purchased, received, stored, and issued for the purpose of manufacturing products for sale. In respect to these functions, there are many similarities between the food and beverage business and other manufacturing businesses. For example, consider the steps involved in the production of wood furniture. The furniture manufacturer must determine the kinds of wood that are best suited to the types of furniture to be manufactured and must purchase appropriate quantities of lumber at Favourable prices.

When the wood is delivered, the shipment must be checked to ensure that the material delivered is exactly as ordered. Then it must be moved into appropriate storage facilities, partly to prevent theft and partly to ensure that the characteristics of the wood will not be adversely affected by climate. The wood must then be issued in appropriate amounts for the production of various kinds of tables and chairs. During the manufacturing process, some effort must be made to maintain balanced quantities of parts so that, for example, one tabletop is made for each four legs.

After the tables have been manufactured and sold to customers, care must be taken to ensure that each sale is properly recorded, that the correct price is charged for each table sold, and that the total dollar value of each sale is collected. The motel coffee shop, the school cafeteria, the hotel dining room, the resort cocktail lounge—all share the same need for purchasing, receiving, storing, and issuing raw materials for the production of finished products for sale. In food and beverage operations, we deal with fruits, vegetables, meat, poultry, and a large number of other foods— fresh, frozen, and canned—as well as alcoholic beverages in many establishments; but these really serve the same purposes in our business that wood serves in the furniture manufacturing business. Thus, in a very real sense, the food and beverage industry is a manufacturing business.

All restaurants take raw material and "manufacture" them into a final product. Some restaurants use raw materials to a greater extent than others. A fine dining establishment, for example, will use relatively few convenience foods. By contrast, fast-food restaurants and institutional operations will generally purchase foods that require less preparation to serve.

In both restaurants and manufacturing operations, raw materials must be carefully selected, always with the desired final products in mind, and appropriate quantities of each must be ordered to meet expected production needs.

Orders for materials are typically placed with a vendor at the most Favourable prices. As materials are received, they are checked to see that the business is getting what it pays for. Then the materials are stored appropriately until needed. When the person in charge of production requests materials from storage, they are made available for the production of finished items for sale.

At each stage of operation, it is necessary to institute control in order to prevent the kinds of problems mentioned earlier. Control may be accomplished in a variety of ways, and anyone who attempts to manage a food and beverage operation should be aware of the range of techniques available. The particular techniques selected for use in a given situation depend on the nature of the material or service requiring control and on the degree of difficulty inherent in instituting such control. Deciding on the appropriate control technique to adopt in a given situation is not always simple. Some of the more common techniques are discussed in the following paragraphs.

CONTROL TECHNIQUES

The control techniques available to a manager include the following:

- Establishing standards
- Establishing procedures
- Training
- Setting examples
- Observing and correcting employee actions
- Requiring records and reports
- Disciplining employees
- Preparing and following budgets

Establishing Standards

Standards are defined as rules or measures established for making comparisons and judgments. In business these standards are set by management and are used for judging the extent to which results meet expectations. Several types of standards are useful in establishing control over food and beverage operations. It is important to develop a working understanding of these several types of standards before proceeding.

Quality standards are used to define the degree of excellence of raw materials, finished products, and, by extension, work. In one sense, establishing quality standards is a grading process. Most food items are graded according to degree of excellence (many of them by government: the Department of Agriculture in the United States and similar agencies in other nations), and management should establish a quality standard for each food item that is to be purchased. Beef, for example, is generally available in a number of different grades for restaurant and institutional use, and it is important to determine which grade will be used for the preparation of a particular menu item.

Beverage items also require quality standards. For example, some spirits improve with age, and a 12-year-old scotch whiskey is generally considered to be of a higher quality than one that is only 8 years old. Management in beverage operations must determine which beverage items are of appropriate quality to ensure customer satisfaction. Quality standards must also be determined for the workforce. In some hotels and fine restaurants, higher degrees of skill are required for the production and service of elaborate menu items. Lower levels of skill would probably be acceptable in the average roadside diner.

Quantity standards, defined as measures of weight, count, or volume, are used to make comparisons and judgments. Management must establish a number of quantity standards. Standard portion sizes for food and beverage products and standards for work output are simple examples. The portion size for every food item served must be clearly established. Each shrimp cocktail should contain a predetermined number of shrimp of specified size, a certain measure of sauce, and clearly identified quantities of garnishes. A portion of soup should be identified as to size of bowl or cup to be used, or the size of the ladle used to portion it, and the quantity of any garnish to be added. Similarly, entrée items must be identified as to the number of ounces or pieces. Surrounding items, such as vegetables, should be portioned with a spoon of a particular size, as with peas, or identified by count, as with asparagus spears.

In bar operations, management must establish a standard quantity for each measure of liquor used. In many instances, bars operate with standard drink recipes indicating the specific quantities of ingredients to be used in preparing particular drinks. Quantity standards are often important in the control of Labour costs as well. When planning staff schedules, it is useful to know, for example, the number of tables or seats a server can cover during a given period or the number of sandwiches a pantry worker can make per hour. In addition to quality and quantity standards, it is ultimately necessary to determine and set cost standards for operation. Cost standards are more commonly referred to as standard costs.

The term standard cost is defined as the cost of goods or services identified, approved, and accepted by management. Standard costs are used for various purposes. They may be compared with actual costs in order to make judgments about the actual costs, and they may be used as a basis for establishing sales prices. Paradoxically, a standard cost is simultaneously both realistic and an ideal. For example, if one bottle of liquor containing 33.8 ounces costs $16.90 to purchase, each ounce has a value of $0.50. That is, the standard cost of 1 ounce is $0.50. If the entire bottle is used to prepare drinks, each of which contains 1 ounce of the liquor, the standard cost of the liquor in each drink is $0.50. Based on the actual purchase price of the bottle, that is the real cost of 1 ounce. However, this is an ideal: It does not take into account the possibility of spillage or evaporation, both of which are likely to occur in bar operations.

Standard costs are useful in measuring the effectiveness of operations in food and beverage establishments. As discussed later, comparing standard costs with actual costs can help determine how effectively food and beverage materials and Labour resources are being used in day-to-day operations. Standard costs are particularly useful in cost control because they provide a means for management to compare what is actually happening in an enterprise with what *should* be happening, given the standards established for operations. Standard costs must be calculated. There are various methods for doing this, each of which is discussed in detail in later chapters. In the case of foods and beverages, various kinds of calculations are necessary, the simplest form of which has been previously illustrated in the discussion of the standard cost of 1 ounce of liquor. In the case of Labour, determination of standard costs is rather more complex.

Establishing Procedures

In addition to establishing standards for quality, quantity, and cost, food and beverage managers must establish standard procedures. Procedures are the methods employed to prepare products or perform jobs. Standard procedures are those that have been established as the correct methods, routines, and techniques for day-to-day operations. As discussed in later chapters, maintaining effective control over food, beverage, and Labour costs requires establishing standard procedures for every phase of operations. Ordering and purchasing procedures must be standardized to ensure that ingredients used to make food and beverage products are purchased at appropriate times in needed quantities, at the most Favourable prices, and are of appropriate quality for their intended use. Receiving procedures must be standardized so that all goods received conform in quality, quantity, and cost to those ordered.

Standard storing procedures must be put into effect to guard against both spoilage and theft, either of which will lead to excessive costs. Issuing must be standardized so that food and beverage items will be used in the order in which they are received, thus preventing spoilage and the resulting excessive costs. To further guard against spoilage and theft, the quantities of foods and beverages issued must be linked to carefully determined production needs. Moreover, records of issues can be used to calculate cost per item produced; such costs can then be compared with standard costs to determine the efficiency of production and the effectiveness of operations.

Production procedures must be standardized for a number of reasons. One of the most important of these is customer satisfaction. Any given item should be produced by the same method and with the same ingredients every time it is served. It should also be served in the same quantity each time, partly so that regular customers will be given the same quantity each time they order the item, and partly to maintain cost standards.

Training

Although establishing standards and standard procedures is necessary for control, doing so is really just the first step in a process. None of the standards are of any significance unless employees are aware of them, and employees will not become aware of the standards unless management is willing to undertake staff training. Training is a process by which managers teach employees how work is to be done, given the standards and standard procedures established. For example, if management has established a standard 4-ounce portion size for hamburgers, then all employees responsible for producing portions of hamburgers must be made aware that 4 ounces is the correct portion size. Moreover, each of these employees must be trained to produce portions of the standard size at his or her workstation, using the correct equipment and supplies provided for doing so.

If all employees are not aware of the relevant standards and standard procedures established for their work and are not trained to follow these standards, the standards are completely useless. Any foodservice manager who trains employees would doubtlessly agree that training is difficult, frustrating, time-consuming, and, in the short run, costly. Perhaps that is why a substantial number of poor managers ignore it and simply put new employees to work without devoting any time to demonstrating and explaining what they are to do. Sometimes a new employee is merely introduced to a co-worker, who is then expected to train the new person.

Occasionally this works reasonably well; more often it does not, frequently because the co-worker is either unwilling or unable to train the new employee. After all, the typical foodservice employee is not hired for his or her ability to train others. If employees are not suitably trained to follow established standards and standard procedures, the control aspects of the manager's job become difficult, at best; sometimes control becomes impossible. This topic is discussed further in relevant sections of the text and in the chapters on Labour control.

Setting Examples

Sometimes the process of establishing standards and standard procedures is not quite as formal as the foregoing discussion may suggest. In many instances, standards are established in a very informal way: Employees in an operation follow the examples set by the manager— the manager's behaviour, manner, responses to questions, and even a failure to speak or take action in some situations.

In general, the behaviour of individuals in a group tends to be influenced by the actions, statements, and attitudes of their leaders. The attitudes and work habits of a manager are evident as he or she performs various tasks in the course of a workday. The behaviour of the manager will influence the manner in which employees perform their work. If the manager who has occasion to help employees plate food for the dining room serves incorrect portion sizes, employees will be more likely to do the same when the manager is not there. Similarly, if a manager is inclined to wrap parcels of food to take home for personal use, employees will be more likely to do so.

And if the manager observes them doing so and fails to end the practice, the amount of food leaving the premises will usually increase. It must be noted that any manager must be consistent in setting examples, as well as in directing, regulating, and restraining employees and their actions. In far too many cases, managers appear not to have long-range and short-range goals clearly in mind as they go about the business of managing. Consequently, their examples, actions, directions, and responses to employees' questions do not present a clear and consistent view to subordinates. Such inconsistency confuses employees and has the effect of working against the control processes and procedures in effect.

Observing and Correcting Employee Actions

If a manager were to see a bartender mixing drinks without measuring the ingredients and did not take the time to remind the individual to measure quantities carefully, then the bartender may reasonably assume that his or her work met the manager's standards. The manager would have missed an excellent opportunity to improve the bartender's work habits and to maintain control. Similarly, if a manager were to observe a receiving clerk failing to verify that quantities of meat delivered conformed to the quantity on the invoice and did not correct the individual, the employee might never know that his or her performance was unacceptable.

One of a manager's important tasks is to observe the actions of all employees continually as they go about their daily jobs, judging those actions in the light of the standards and standard procedures established for their work. If any are failing to follow the standards, it is a manager's responsibility to correct their performance to the extent necessary at the appropriate time.

Requiring Records and Reports

Obviously, no manager can be in all places at all times to observe employees' actions. The owner/manager of a small operation can observe employee actions to a far greater extent than can the manager of a larger operation—one consisting, for example, of several bars and dining rooms, seating hundreds of guests and employing hundreds of personnel. The larger the establishment, the more likely it is that managers' observations must be indirect rather than direct.

Their "observations" must be abstracted and inferred from a variety of records and reports. The statement of income summarizes cost and sales information for a particular period. The figures in the statement of income can be used to calculate cost-to-sales ratios of various kinds. These are normally compared with ratios for previous periods, and judgments are made about operations on the basis of these comparisons.

If the comparisons are considered satisfactory to management, this implies, in general, that the performance of employees has been acceptable during the period covered by the statement. If the comparisons are unsatisfactory, the implication is that some or all of the standards and standard procedures have not been followed.

A manager cannot normally pinpoint specific problems from such a general report as the statement of income; other more specific and more timely reports and records are usually required. Some of these may be developed daily, others weekly or monthly, as discussed in later chapters. At this point, it is important to recognize that managers need timely information to determine whether primary goals and subgoals are being met. If timely records and reports are not available, opportunities for taking corrective action may be lost. The variety and extent of the records and reports developed and used for control purposes are discussed in greater detail in later chapters.

Disciplining Employees

Discipline is defined as action taken to admonish, chastise, or reprimand an employee for work performance or personal behaviour incompatible with established standards. It is a term with negative connotations, suggesting the threats and punishments used on children by some parents. Discipline, therefore, is a difficult topic to address.

Foodservice managers generally prefer to avoid the need for discipline by improving the hiring practices in their organizations. By selecting the right people for the various jobs—those with the experience, skill, and personal characteristics that match the job requirements—the number of individuals requiring some level of discipline can be reduced to a bare minimum. However, every manager must face the fact that at times, an individual staff member must be disciplined. Discipline is used as a control technique in many food and beverage operations and may take any of a number of forms, as discussed in the following paragraphs. It is a valuable technique if used properly and judiciously.

Discipline is not the same as observing and correcting employee actions; it is the next step beyond. Before resorting to discipline, managers are likely to have made reasonable, though unsuccessful, efforts to correct the actions of an employee. Discipline is called for only if corrective action has failed. At this point, managers commonly resort to some words or actions that employees normally regard as punishing, in the broadest sense of that term. One assumes that the standards for work performance and personal behaviour are known and understood by all employees, either because they have been given appropriate training and instruction by management or because they should be aware of the norms for acceptable behaviour in the workplace.

For example, suppose an employee has been trained to follow specific performance standards for serving food in the dining room and does not do so. A supervisor, given his responsibility to observe and correct employees' actions, notices the employee's failure to follow the performance standards and calls his attention to the need to adhere to the standards in which he was trained. If repeated efforts aimed at obtaining improved performance from the employee are entirely unsuccessful, some discipline is required. The employee's poor performance is called to his attention again by his supervisor, probably more directly and forcefully.

On this second occasion, the supervisor's approach is likely to be more severe. Most responsible managers hope that the second such occasion will be the last and that the admonition will bring about the necessary improvement. However, if it does not, then it will be necessary to take progressively more stern, forceful, and, finally, punishing actions, the last of which would be firing. If an employee was worth hiring, he or she should be worth keeping, and all suitable efforts should be made to bring that employee's job performance into line. Therefore, this final step—firing—is normally reserved for use only if it is simply impossible to modify the employee's job performance or personal behaviour. On some rare occasions—in the case of theft, for example—it is used immediately.

On another level, a manager responsible for poor financial performance in one unit of a chain organization may have this fact pointed out to him or her by top management in any number of ways. The possibilities range from quiet discussion to heated admonition, or from demotion or transfer to firing. Finally, no employee at any level of an organization is completely immune from the possibility of disciplinary action. It is important to recognize the desirability of keeping the number of individuals terminated to a minimum. A high rate of employee turnover because of excessive firings can be very costly, leading to such additional expenses as newspaper advertising for new help, higher rates for unemployment insurance contributions (in some states), lower rates of productivity, higher training costs, and a number of other costs.

On one hand, it must be understood that the object of discipline is to change or modify employees' job performance or personal behaviour— to improve performance so that the work is done in conformance with the standards and procedures that management has identified as those most likely to achieve the organization's goals and objectives. On the other hand, it should be apparent that disciplinary action generally has negative connotations in the minds of employees, most of whom would normally prefer to avoid any such unpleasantness.

If certain behaviour patterns (those that follow the standards and procedures established by management) lead to positive and pleasant rewards, and others (those that ignore management's standards and procedures) bring the negative and unpleasant consequences associated with disciplinary action, then most employees will generally work towards the former and avoid the latter. The very fact that employees know that continual failure to follow established standards can lead to unpleasantness tends to have the desired effect of making job performance and personal behaviour conform to appropriate standards.

PREPARING AND FOLLOWING BUDGETS

Preparing and following budgets may be the most common technique for controlling business operations. A budget is defined as a financial plan and may be described as a realistic expression of management's goals and objectives expressed in financial terms. Many businesses establish budgets for specific aspects of operation. Thus, there are sales budgets, cash flow budgets, capital equipment budgets, and advertising budgets, among others.

Food and beverage operations also use budgets—many of the same types of budgets that are used in other businesses. Many restaurants prepare capital equipment budgets, for example, because of the ongoing need to replace equipment that wears out and to purchase new types of equipment that becomes available in the market. Capital equipment is typically very costly, and a financial plan must be established before making such purchases. Advertising budgets are established so that appropriate levels of funds can be made available to generate a particular level of sales. The most important type of budget a food and beverage manager can prepare is an operating budget. Stated in dollar terms, this is a forecast of sales activity and an estimate of costs that will be incurred in the process of generating sales. By extension, the budget indicates the profit that should result after the costs of producing those sales have been met. An operating budget is clearly a financial plan for the period it covers. In this text, the discussion of budgets is restricted to operating budgets, because the operating budget is most closely aligned with food, beverage, and Labour cost control.

For established restaurants, preparation of an operating budget normally begins with historical information—the financial records of the business. In addition, one needs estimates of anticipated changes in costs and sales and in the business environment. Thus, if federal or state laws will affect wage rates paid to employees in the period covered by the budget being prepared, this information must be factored into the planning. Similarly, if the establishment's real estate tax rates have been increased or decreased, that information should be reflected in the budget. More difficult to deal with, but equally important, are the effects of poor weather conditions on future crops, anticipated shortages of beef due to ranchers' reductions in herds, and other such general conditions, including trends in the local and national economy that may affect future costs and sales.

In new establishments that lack financial statements for previous years, information derived from a market analysis and from a manager's previous experience in the industry provide the best alternative sources of data for budget preparation. When no market analysis is available, or when the manager is not widely experienced in the food and beverage business, or when both of these are true, it may be that no effort is made to prepare a budget. When this is the case, management has missed an opportunity to use one of the most useful of all control techniques.

PREPARING AN OPERATING BUDGET

As previously stated, an operating budget is normally prepared using historical information from previous budgets and other financial records. This information, together with anticipated changes in sales and costs, provides the basic data needed to prepare an operating budget for an upcoming period. Operating budgets can be prepared for any period of time—a day, a week, a month, a quarter, six months, or a full year. Typically, an operating budget for one full year is prepared first and then broken down into smaller units for shorter time periods.

Budgets for these shorter periods may not reflect equal sales and costs in every instance. This is the case in seasonal restaurants. Thus, for example, if the budget for a restaurant forecasts $1,600,000 in sales for the year, each quarter would not necessarily forecast sales of $400,000.

The first and fourth quarters might be busy periods for the restaurant, whereas the second and third quarters might be slow. The manager might forecast $500,000 in sales for the first and fourth quarters and only $300,000 in sales for each of the second and third quarters. In addition, the manager might forecast substantial profits for the busy quarters and very little for the slow quarters.

A static budget is one that is prepared for only one level of business activity for the period (i.e., $1,600,000 in sales for the year). To prepare an operating budget, it is necessary to determine which costs are fixed and which are variable. That can be more complex than it sounds, and the determinations made by management in one restaurant may be incorrect or inappropriate for another.

Using those assumptions, we begin the process of preparing an operating budget for the Grandview Bistro for the coming fiscal year. The initial step in this process is to examine sales figures from the recent past to note evident trends, if any. In some establishments, the examination of sales records may reveal regular increases in sales from year to year; in others, decreases may be seen; in still others, changes from year to year may show no discernible pattern. In any case, it is the responsibility of the owner or manager to analyse past sales for this purpose. Information from such an analysis can be of great value in projecting sales levels for the period to be covered by the budget. The next step in the budgeting process is to examine the external environment and assess any conditions or factors that could affect sales volume in the coming year. These include general economic conditions in the nation and in the immediate geographical area; population changes; changes that may affect transportation to the establishment, including new highways and bus routes; and any number of other external variables, including new competition from planned restaurants.

Another important step is to review any planned changes in the operation that will affect sales volume. For example, any plans to increase or decrease menu prices will clearly affect sales volume, and the impact of such changes must be clearly assessed. The impact of such varied possibilities as anticipated changes in the number of seats in the restaurant, in the number of items listed in the menu, in the particular menu items offered, and in levels of advertising must also be considered.

After conducting the aforementioned assessments, the next logical procedure is to determine the nature and extent of changes in cost levels, some of which will be dictated by anticipated changes in sales volume and others of which will occur independent of volume changes. Some variable costs are certain to be affected by changes in volume, but may also be affected by other factors. Increased sales volume may necessitate hiring additional servers, and a union Labour contract may include a new hourly wage for all employees.

There are many other possibilities for cost increases—a clause in a lease dictating a rent increase effective on a particular date, higher utility rates, anticipated increases in the costs of particular foods, and any number of others. Any anticipated changes in cost and sales levels must be considered and factored into the new operating budget. Assume that the management of the Grandview Bistro has carefully examined past cost and sales figures and has assessed the impact of various anticipated changes in both internal and external conditions on costs and sales.

The following changes are anticipated:

- Both food and beverage sales are expected to increase by 5 per cent.

- Fixed salaries and wages will increase by 4 per cent.
- Variable salaries and wages will continue to be the same percentage of sales.
- The cost of employee benefits will increase, but will continue to be the same percentage of salaries and wages.
- Other controllable costs will increase by $6,500.
- Occupancy costs will increase by $2,000.
- Food and beverage cost percentages will remain the same.
- Interest and depreciation will remain the same.

Assuming that the projections in the operating budget for sales, costs, and profits are acceptable to management, the budget will be adopted as the plan of action for the covered period. If the projections are unacceptable, management will reexamine both the assumptions on which the budget was based and the budget figures themselves.

A reexamination of this nature may suggest the desirability of additional changes affecting sales or costs that may lead to more acceptable results. Before the adoption of the budget, the effects of such potential changes can be tested by means of the techniques of cost/volume/profit analysis, the principal subject of the following chapter. Once an operating budget is accepted and adopted for an upcoming period, it becomes a standard against which operating performance is measured as the fiscal year progresses.

To use it effectively for this purpose, the operating budget may be broken down into smaller units for shorter time periods, as discussed earlier. This may result in monthly or quarterly budgets, with sales and cost projections with which actual figures can be compared. The budget projections become the standards or targets for the covered periods.

If cost and sales figures for a given period do not meet expectations as identified in the budget, there will be an effort to identify the causes. Once the causes have been identified, it is possible and desirable to take remedial actions to ensure better performance in the next operating period. If, for example, sales do not meet budget projections and costs are too high for the level of sales recorded, some remedial action will clearly be required. If payroll or any other controllable cost is greater than the amount budgeted, then management should attempt to determine the causes of the excessive costs and take appropriate measures to keep future costs at more suitable levels.

One must recognize that budget projections are merely targets and are often incorrect. Sales levels are often higher or lower than projections, because the people who prepare budgets—owners, managers, and accountants—are seldom able to predict and thus project the future accurately. Sometimes this is caused by their failure to take all of the information at hand into account when preparing the operating budget.

A new office building down the street, for example, may generate additional luncheon business that was not accurately anticipated, or planned advertising may bring in more customers than the manager had expected. Conversely, unexpected road construction outside a restaurant may cause a significant decrease in sales volume for some period of time, or the unexpected closing of a nearby manufacturing facility may bring about a loss of business.

To counteract the inherent shortcomings of fixed operating budgets, a manager can prepare a budget designed to project sales and costs for several levels of business activity. This is called a flexible budget.

Flexible budgets are normally prepared for levels of business volume above and below the expected level. The idea is that if the level of sales is higher or lower than expected, management already has a new operating budget available with appropriate projections of costs for the particular sales level.

THE CONTROL PROCESS

As indicated earlier in this chapter, control in the food and beverage business was defined as a process by which managers attempt to direct, regulate, and restrain the actions of people in order to achieve desired goals.

The control process consists of four steps:

1. Establish standards and standard procedures for operation.
2. Train all individuals to follow established standards and standard procedures.
3. Monitor performance and compare actual performances with established standards.
4. Take appropriate action to correct deviations from standards.

Sometimes investigation reveals that an established standard is actually unrealistic or inappropriate. If that is the case, then management should consider changing the standard. To illustrate the relevance of the control process to food and beverage management, consider the following example. Imagine a restaurant owner who has taken great care to establish goals for his business.

One of those goals is to serve the finest food in the area. To reach this goal, the owner has established standards and standard procedures that help define his meaning of "the finest." For one menu item—prime sirloin steak—the standard is made clear by the use of the term *prime*, which specifies certain specific characteristics in beef. The standards and standard procedures for the chef and the steward reflect the owner's wish that only prime beef is to be purchased for the production of this menu item.

Employees receiving deliveries of meat from purveyors have been trained to follow standard procedures, which include checking the quality of the beef delivered by examining it and verifying that the USDA grade stamp is present. The restaurant manager must monitor operations regularly, checking to see personally that the beef purchased meets the standards set. This may be done in any number of ways, one of which is by examining the raw beef in the refrigerator. The manager knows that if operations are not monitored and this results in orders placed for a lower grade of beef, regular customers will notice the difference.

Some will complain; most will not—they will simply find a restaurant that really has the prime beef promised by its menu. Therefore, whenever the manager finds that the quality of beef purchased deviates from the standards, appropriate remedial action must be taken if the owner's goal of offering the finest food is to be met. There is a clear need for control in every phase of food and beverage operations. Control is one key to successful food and beverage management and must be established if success is to be achieved. Experience throughout the industry has long proven that establishing control means instituting the four-step process identified in the preceding list.

CONTROL SYSTEMS

Control system is the term used to describe that collection of interrelated and interdependent control techniques and procedures in use. Historically, control systems in foodservice and related enterprises were heavily dependent on paper-and-pencil methods. Many systems required difficult and time-consuming calculations. In recent years, however, various time- and Labour-saving devices have been introduced to decrease our industry's historical reliance on paper-and-pencil calculations and extensive paper records. Fortunately, paper-and-pencil methods are disappearing from today's food and beverage operations.

Some operations rely on electronic cash registers, for example, programmed to keep records of numbers of portions sold and to print out simple reports to management at the end of a day. Many restaurants depend on computers, with software designed to accumulate and summarize information that was simply not available in the past. Still others have invested in amazingly complex computer systems to assist in maintaining control over operations in ways that previously were not possible.

One of the primary reasons that the Grandview Bistro has been able to control its costs so well is that it has a computer system with software designed specifically for restaurant operations. A file server located in the manager's office functions as the hub of the computer network. Terminals with touch-screen monitors and printers, as well as credit-card imprinters, have been installed at two servers' stations. One workstation is on the manager's desk. Remote printers have been installed at the bar and at the cook's station.

The control features for purchasing, receiving, issuing, producing, and selling described in the following chapters have been programmed into the software. In addition, the system provides managers with full access to sales and cost information at any time. Operations proceed along the following lines: Servers arriving for work change into uniforms on a lower level (not shown on the diagram), and then proceed to the manager's office to sign in. They record their arrival for work much as they would with a traditional time clock except they log in at the terminal in the manager's office.

Guests enter the dining room, leaving coats in the coatroom. They are seated by the supervisor, who leaves menus at the table. A server greets the guests and takes their orders for drinks; the orders are written on a captain's pad or an ordinary white pad rather than on a guest check. Having taken the orders, the server proceeds to a terminal and opens an account in computer memory. This account is equivalent to a guest check. The process requires the server to enter a personal identification code, the table number, and the number of guests as shown on the monitor. With the account opened, the server manipulates a touch-screen POS system to enter the customers' orders for drinks.

This information, along with the time of the order, is now in computer memory, which has been programmed with correct prices for all drinks. The system is programmed to send the recorded drink orders to the bartender at the bar, where they are printed on a remote printer. The hard copy, provided by the remote printer, is an order for the bartender to prepare the drinks. This hard copy includes the server number, table number, and order time. The bartender removes the order from the printer, makes the drinks, and places the printed order on the tray with the drinks, thus eliminating questions about which drinks are for which server and what time the orders were entered. At the appropriate time, the server follows similar procedures for placing food orders. The computer is programmed to send food orders only to the remote printers at the cook's station. All ordered items are stored in memory, but the only items appearing on the remote printer at any preparation station are those appropriate to that station. Thus, food orders are not sent to the bar, and orders for coffee, handled by the servers themselves, do not appear on any remote printers. After a diner has finished the meal, the server obtains the guest check by requesting it via the terminal and printer at the sidestand. With this system, the guest check is merely a hard copy of the data stored in the computer, accessed by table and server number. This hard copy is torn from the printer and given to the diner.

IN THE GRANDVIEW

Bistro each server acts as a cashier for his or her own checks, and settlement is recorded for each check as the server receives cash or a credit card. At the end of a shift the server reports to the manager's office to turn in the cash, checks, and credit-card vouchers for his or her sales. Bill Young, the owner, sits at his terminal to obtain summary data showing charge and cash sales for that particular server. He collects cash and charge vouchers accordingly. Before changing out of uniform and leaving the premises, each server logs out, using the manager's terminal. At any time of day, Bill Young can monitor operations at will. Data include gross sales volume, numbers of customers served, numbers of checks outstanding, sales mix, numbers of portions of particular items sold, and any number of other kinds of information that may be of special interest at given times throughout the day.

At the conclusion of business, Bill prints a detailed breakdown of the day's business. The software has been programmed to provide total dollar sales categorized into cash sales and charge sales, with the charge sales divided by type of credit card; total dollar sales separated into food sales and beverage sales, with the food sales broken down into dollar sales by menu category or by individual menu items; average dollar sale per customer, per server, per seat, per table, or per hour, or any combination of these; seat turnover; number of customers per server, per hour, per meal, and per day; number of orders of each food and beverage item sold (a reflection of the sales mix); total dollar sales per hour; sales in any category for the period to date; total payroll cost for the day, for any part of the day, or for the period to date; and a vast amount of food and beverage cost data, including standard costs.

Today most food and beverage operators are using some type of computer control system as an aid to managing. For some, the computer system is simply a modern electronic cash register with features that earlier cash registers were not able to provide. In growing numbers of operations, however, the computer systems are increasingly complex and designed to provide both quick access to needed information and sophisticated managerial control over most or all operations in the restaurant.

COST/BENEFIT RATIO

An important concept in the control process is cost/benefit ratio: the relationship between the costs incurred in instituting and maintaining a single control or control system, and the benefits or savings derived by doing so. It should be obvious that no control measure can be instituted without some cost. Sometimes that cost is relatively insignificant. Yet sometimes it is so great that careful consideration must be given to the extent of the expected benefit before one feels justified in incurring the cost. Occasionally the cost may prove to be completely prohibitive. A relatively insignificant cost is required to institute one basic control measure: locking the front and back doors at night to prevent burglary, for example.

In contrast, relocating a restaurant cashier's desk to a position judged to be more suitable for preventing customers from leaving without paying the checks may be somewhat more costly. Installing a sophisticated new computer system and hiring a new employee trained to operate it would require even greater, ongoing costs. Establishing a new control department, hiring a food and beverage controller and appropriate support staff, and supplying the staff with equipment and supplies would obviously require large—and possibly prohibitive—amounts of money. In judging whether the cost of any control procedure is justified, one must take into consideration how long a period of time will be required for the savings to pay for the cost of the new procedure—the payback period. For example, purchasing and installing locks for food storage facilities to prevent employee theft costs a relatively small amount of money and could result in immediate savings.

The payback period might be only one month or less and would clearly be justified. Relocating the cashier's station to a more suitable position may result in only minimal savings, and might have a payback period of a year or longer. Purchasing a new computer system might have a payback period of more than one year, but be judged necessary nevertheless. Establishing a new control department, hiring a food and beverage controller and appropriate support staff, may have annual costs that would exceed the financial savings and thus never justify the costs incurred.

One must keep clearly in mind the primary purposes of cost and sales control measures: to guard against excessive costs and to ensure that all sales result in appropriate income. In other words, some identifiable financial benefit must be obtainable from the introduction of any control device or control procedure or from the hiring of any staff member responsible for instituting controls. Benefits must always exceed costs. Before instituting any new procedures for control, management should first determine that the anticipated savings will be greater than the cost of the new procedures.

If controls cost more than the benefits they deliver, their value is doubtful at best. In normal circumstances, it is not sensible to institute any controls that cost more than they save. Stated in other terms, one might say that one should not normally spend a dollar to save dollar. In numeric terms, one might say that the ratio of cost to benefit should always be less than 1/1. Before instituting any control procedure and incurring the consequent dollar costs, one should also look at the nonquantifiable effects. Some of these may be beneficial; others may not. Control systems and procedures generally affect many aspects of an operation, sometimes in negative ways not anticipated by management. For example, a system designed to verify that all food transported by servers from kitchen to dining room is appropriately recorded on guest checks may slow down service, reduce seat turnover, and even result in cold food being served to guests. Similarly, the installation of a time clock to obtain accurate data for payroll purposes may cause resentment among longtime, loyal, and valued employees, some of whom might seek other employment rather than punch a time clock. Thus, management should carefully estimate the nonmonetary outcomes of any control system or procedure before putting it into effect.

3

Menus

To plan a profitable menu in the foodservice industry, the menu planner must be knowledgeable about foods, management, and financing. This chapter discusses facts and practical work experience that are essential in planning a profitable menu in the institutional, industrial, and commercial segments of the foodservice industry.

OBJECTIVES

- To give the student an understanding of the knowledge that a menu planner must have in order to prepare menus in each of the three foodservice segments
- To help the student effectively apply the knowledge of planning menus to writing menus
- To identify special characteristics in each of the foodservice segments

BACKGROUND OF A MENU PLANNER

Who can plan a menu? Anyone can plan a menu in its simplest form. The definition of a menu is simply "a listing of foods." If people are hungry, they can mentally plan a menu by choosing the foods they would like to eat. To plan a simple menu does not take years of experience and education. On the other hand, planning a successful and profitable menu for a commercial foodservice operation does take foodservice experience and a culinary education. Menus planned for a commercial foodservice operation are different from those planned for an institutional or industrial foodservice operation.

The person planning menus for an institutional, industrial, or commercial foodservice operation must be knowledgeable about a number of aspects of the foodservice industry. A professional menu planner must be knowledgeable about food, finances, and management. The menu planner must have a good understanding of all three of these areas in order to be able to plan a profitable menu. For a person to acquire enough knowledge in these three areas requires a combination of educational theory (know-how) and practical working experience (howto) in each area.

When planning a menu, it is helpful and important for the menu planner to categorize the information into two categories:

1. Necessary information
2. Helpful information.

Information that is not necessary in menu planning for a commercial foodservice operation might be very necessary in menu planning for an institutional foodservice operation. For example, it is not essential to know the sodium dietary needs of customers when planning a menu for a commercial foodservice operation. Yet, this information would be necessary when planning a menu for a patient in an institutional foodservice operation. In addition to knowing the type of market (customer) that will be patronizing the foodservice operation, the menu planner needs to have a knowledge of food, finances, and management when planning a menu.

FOOD

In the area of food, the menu planner must know the following:

- The customer's likes and dislikes regarding food. Knowing which foods are preferred definitely helps the saleability of a product.
- How to identify the various food products that are available in the markets.
- How to explain the different criteria that establish the quality grades of food products.
- The availability of the food products. Knowing when a food product is available helps keep food costs down and profits up.

- How the food items are prepared, produced, plated, served, and consumed by the guest. This information allows the menu planner to specify the type of equipment necessary to produce the food product. This knowledge also will indicate the level of skill necessary for the cooks.
- How the food product is packaged, shipped, received, and stored, as well as the shelf life of the product. This information helps the menu planner to establish a quality menu for the foodservice operation.
- Which foods are complementary to one another for the proper garnishing of dishes and for achieving an aesthetic and nutritionally balanced menu.
- The yields of food products, which will help in setting up recipes.
- How to do recipe conversions, how to merchandise, and how to market the food product.
- How to cross-utilize products. Cross-utilization refers to using a menu product in more than one menu or in more than one product.

For example, if a chef placed baked scallops with buttered bread crumbs on the menu, scallops should also appear in at least one or two more entrées, such as fried scallops or scallops in a casserole with cheese sauce. Just having scallops listed once on the menu would present product and cost problems, unless scallops were extremely popular and the amount purchased was used for only one entrée selection. Cross-utilization should be followed throughout the menu, not just in entrées. Most institutional menus use cross-utilization of food products exceptionally well.

FINANCES

The menu planner must understand the relationship between food costs and other expenses, such as Labour and overhead. The menu planner must be able to produce a menu that is profitable. Thus, the menu planner must understand how the portion cost affects the selling price. The prices on the menu must be appealing to the consumer, yet still allow the foodservice operation to make a profit. The menu planner must know how to cost a recipe. Portion cost and markup must be related to volume in order to make a profit. Recipe costing is essentially finding a portion cost and marking it up to a selling price that the market will accept. A menu planner must have an awareness of how a sales history is developed and an understanding of how to prepare a sales mix or a scatter sheet, which is used in forecasting. Knowing how to establish a check average and how to project annual sales are also essential. The menu planner must understand financing as it applies to the foodservice industry as a whole and to the menu in particular.

MANAGEMENT

To successfully design a profitable menu, it is important that the menu planner be aware of the foodservice owner's wants and needs. Profit, check average, type of operation, style of the menu, theme of the operation, style of service to be used, atmosphere, the mood that is to be achieved, the skill level of personnel, and the market all must be considered. The menu planner must know as much as possible about customers' food preferences and the price that customers are willing to pay in order to design the type of menu appropriate for a particular foodservice operation.

INSTITUTIONAL FOODSERVICE

The institutional foodservice category is composed of:

- Grade schools
- High schools
- Colleges and universities
- Private and federally funded hospitals
- Nursing homes and assisted-living facilities
- Correctional facilities
- Armed services

Each of these operations has its own dietary requirements that must be followed on the menu. The most important factor in planning an institutional menu is that the offerings must be nutritious. All institutional menus should include the five basic food groups: bread, cereal, rice and pasta; vegetables; fruit; milk, yogurt, and cheese; meat, poultry, fish, dry beans, eggs, and nuts.

When planning a menu for any institution, the following factors should be considered:

- The type of operation and the diet required by its patrons
- Budget restrictions
- Ages of the patrons
- Food preferences of the patrons
- Type of service needed
- Hours of feeding
- Storage area
- Equipment needed to produce the menu
- Government regulations
- Religious and ethnic backgrounds of the patrons

TYPES OF OPERATIONS AND REQUIRED DIETS

The menu offered will depend on the type of institutional operation. In a hospital setting the menu planner must follow strict dietary regulations that have been set by the registered dietician.

The five main diets used in hospitals include:

1. The Regular or house diet
2. The liquid diet
3. The mechanical soft diet
4. The diabetic diet
5. The cardiac diet

It is vital that a patient's meal be planned very carefully to assist the patient in making a faster recovery. If these diets are not followed as prescribed, illness or accidental death could result.

BUDGET RESTRICTIONS

Most institutional foodservices today are operated by large foodservice companies, such as ARAMARK, ARA, Service Master, and Sodexho. The hospital, nursing home, or school will establish a *per diem* (dollar per day sum) under which the facility must operate. The menu need not stay within this sum each day; rather, it must remain within this budget over an accounting period, thus allowing the menu planner some flexibility in meal planning. In most cases institutional cafeterias are set up on a break-even basis or on a 1 to 2 per cent profit. The institution itself is not in business for the purpose of making a large profit in the foodservice operation. Thus, many institutional facilities charge very little for their food items.

AGES OF PATRONS

When a menu planner decides to plan a particular menu, the ages of the patrons who will consume the food must be considered. As we grow older our bodies require and are able to handle different foods. At infancy our digestive systems are very delicate and are able to digest only delicate foods. As our digestive systems mature, we are able to digest a much larger variety of foods. When we age, our digestive systems grow frail and we can digest a lesser variety of foods.

Age has a direct effect on the items selected for a particular menu. Since hospital patients vary in age, the menu planner must have food items on the menu that appeal to all age groups, as well as making sure that these items together comprise a nutritionally balanced menu. In an elementary or secondary school setting, the menu planner does not have to consider as many age groups as in a hospital. Planning menus for elementary and secondary school students is a much simpler task than planning menus for hospitals.

The college or university population presents more of a challenge to the menu planner. The ages of this group may vary from young adults to much older adults. College students also tend to be more demanding than young school children. Many students today are paying high tuition and room and board costs, and they expect to get adequate menu selections and quality food.

FOOD PREFERENCES

Although, in many cases, institutions such as hospitals and

schools are under strict dietary regulations or government regulations, the menu planner must take a careful look at what the patient or patron wants to eat within the institution. This process can be accomplished by a number of different methods. A survey might be taken to determine which foods are popular or to determine which foods patrons hope to see on the menu in the future.

The menu planner can review the surveys and make important evaluations that can help improve future menus. If possible, the menu planner should eliminate those foods that prove to be unpopular. Another method of determining food preferences is to put suggestion boxes in the cafeteria. This idea does not work as well as the food survey. People will usually take a survey more seriously than placing suggestions in a box. At times an employer will make it mandatory for employees to fill out the survey, whereas suggestions in a suggestion box are entirely optional.

TYPE OF SERVICE NEEDED

In most institutional settings, the service is cafeteria style, which utilizes a tray line. Another popular service system is the scatter system. This system allows a large volume of people to move quickly, bypassing food stations from which they do not wish to select food. This system allows for much more customer involvement.

It is important to serve food that has good holding qualities, both hot and cold. In many institutions, hot food is served in steam tables and is allowed to continue to cook or to evaporate excess moisture. Stews, casseroles, and quiches are good examples of foods that have good holding qualities and that do not become overcooked or dried out if the temperature is properly set at a steam table. Items such as fried fish or roast beef can be served on a steam table, but only a few orders can be cooked or sliced at a time.

Fried fish becomes soggy on the line if a cover is put over it. Roast beef tends to dry out and shrink when a cover is left on for a long period of time. Cold items placed on a cafeteria service line should be placed on a bed of ice. Salads and dairy desserts require refrigeration units. It would be unwise to serve oysters or clams on the half shell because of their poor holding qualities; they lose their freshness when they are served at room temperature.

In a hospital, food is cooked and plated in the kitchen, placed in a refrigerated or heated cart, and transported to the patients' rooms. Another method of serving hot foods is to precook the food in the kitchen and to finish cooking it in a prep kitchen on the individual floor. In a hospital, it is very important to be accurate about serving foods at their proper temperatures in order to avoid the development of foodborne diseases, such as salmonella.

Note: Overall, when planning menus for institutional foodservice operations, the menu planner must look at the type of service to be used in order to maintain a quality food product.

HOURS OF FEEDING

Within the institutional framework, hours of feeding will help determine the types of items that will be offered on the menu. If the hours of feeding are from 8 A.M. to 4 P.M., the menu planner must plan menus for breakfast and lunch. If an institution is operating a 24-hour feeding system, then breakfast, lunch, and dinner menus have to be planned.

STORAGE AREA

In an institutional setting, the storage area that is available helps to determine the type of food that will be offered on the menu. In many cases, institutions have limited walk-in freezer space. Limited freezer space indicates that many items on the menu must either be fresh foods that require refrigerated space or canned foods that require storeroom facilities. The menu planner must take into consideration the amount and type of storage area available and balance the variety of food products on the menu accordingly.

EQUIPMENT NEEDS

Many institutions purchase their equipment first and then

set up the menu. It is only afterward that management may realise that some of the equipment that it has procured is not necessary for the production of the menu. Always plan the menu first; then analyse it to decide the type of equipment needed to produce the menu. This part of the planning process is called a foodservice equipment analysis. Most institutions have limited equipment because of budget restrictions. This fact makes menu planning even more important in the institutional setting.

GOVERNMENT STIPULATIONS

In most institutional facilities, the government plays an important role in menu planning. In elementary and secondary schools, the foodservice systems must follow the school lunch requirements set up by the U.S. Department of Agriculture (USDA). All branches of the armed services and veterans hospitals fall under strict government stipulations as well. It is important to keep abreast of the laws enacted by our governments (state and federal) that set dietary guidelines. Government financial aid may be suspended if laws or regulations are not followed when planning menus for government-funded institutions.

RELIGIOUS AND ETHNIC BACKGROUNDS

In institutional foodservice operations, religious and ethnic backgrounds of the people being served play an important role in the planning of menus. For example, in a Jewish hospital, strict cultural dietary requirements must be followed: dairy and meat products cannot be mixed and have to be kept in separate reach-ins; yet, eggs, fish, and vegetables, which are considered pareve, can be used with dairy or meat meals; lard or any other animal fat cannot be used, but soybean, palm, or vegetable oils are acceptable. All nationalities have their own Favourite foods. The Italian culture offers a variety of sausages, pasta products, and pastry products. The Irish culture offers a variety of stews, sauces and dessert coffees. It is important to offer employees or patients their preferred food items on the menu.

INDUSTRIAL FOODSERVICE

The industrial segment of the foodservice industry is composed of:

- Corporations
- Companies
- Factories

and any other type of business that employs enough people to warrant the need for an in-plant foodservice operation. For the menu planner to plan a successful menu within the industrial segment of the foodservice industry, the following factors must be taken into consideration:

- Management's reasons for having a foodservice operation inhouse
- The food preferences of the employees to be fed
- The type of work the employees are doing
- The time allotted for meals
- The amount of money the employees have to spend on meals

PROFIT

Management will spend money to make money. How does an industrial foodservice operation make a profit for management? It does so by keeping employees at or near their working stations during their meal period. Most employees are given a half-hour or an hour for their meal period. Employees will slow down or quit production five to ten minutes before eating, and many workers are five to ten minutes late in returning from eating when a business does not have a cafeteria or a foodservice operation in-house. Keeping the employees on the grounds of the business for meals helps to reduce the number of workers who return late from lunch, which increases production and, in turn, increases profits.

OPERATING METHODS

The two methods of operating an industrial foodservice operation are for management to contract with a professional foodservice company to manage the operation or to take full responsibility of controlling the feeding system as a part of the business. Contracting an outside professional foodservice company to handle the responsibility of feeding employees is popular and, in most cases, a profitable choice.

There are several methods of feeding employees for which management may contract:

- Computerized vending units
- Full table service
- Cafeteria service
- Coffee-deli shops
- Fast-food service

The two most important factors in choosing industrial foodservice establishments are offering fast service and providing menus that fit the needs of the employees.

PRICING

When pricing an industrial foodservice menu, management has a choice of setting the price in one of three ways:

1. Setting a large profit percentage (10 to 15 per cent)
2. Setting a small profit percentage (1 to 2 per cent)
3. Setting a break-even price (food is sold at a price that covers only the cost of the food, Labour, and overhead, and the company does not make a profit)

FOOD PREFERENCES

The menu planner must be familiar with employee food preferences in order to be able to plan a successful menu. A food survey should be conducted to determine employees' preferences in foods. Some employees may prefer a nutritional menu that includes poultry, fish, salads, fruits, and vegetables rather than a menu that includes hamburgers, hot dogs, sandwiches, and French fries. The survey should be conducted every three months in order to accommodate employee turnover and also because attitudes and tastes can change over time.

TYPE OF WORK

The menu planner needs to know the type of work that employees do. Are employees involved in physical activity, or are they sitting at their desks all day? This information helps to determine food portions, the amount and variety of foods to offer, and whether the items should be hearty and of a heavy calorie count. With jobs that require physical Labour, employees are burning large amounts of calories, so the menu should offer a selection of foods that will replace lost calories. When employees do limited physical work, the menu selections should be light in calories and smaller in portion size.

TIME

Knowing the amount of time allotted for the meal period is an important consideration. Food items that take a long time to prepare should not be included on the menu. Most employees are given only a half hour or an hour to eat. If an item takes too long to produce, employees will not have enough time to finish their meals and will feel rushed. Thus, employees will be dissatisfied with the foodservice operation.

PRICE

The amount of disposable income that an employee has or is willing to spend for a meal on a daily basis may be limited. Disposable income is income that is available for the employee's use after federal, state, and city taxes, and personal bills have been paid. The menu planner should not select foods that have a high food cost and offer them at an even higher cost, because the average employee cannot afford to buy that product on a daily basis. The average employee does not want to spend more than $5 on each meal. The menu planner needs to offer food items that are of good quality and that are reasonably priced.

COMMERCIAL FOOD SERVICE

The commercial segment of the foodservice industry includes:

- Hotels
- Restaurants
- Clubs
- Diners
- Fast-food operations
- Specialty shops

- Cafeterias
- Catering businesses
- Vending businesses
- Dinner theaters
- Delicatessens

In each of these foodservice operations, the menu planner must know management's point of view on the following:

- How the operation is run
- The type of clientele that management would like to attract (also known as the market)
- Check average
- Decor
- Profit margin
- Competition
- Market trends

HOW THE OPERATION IS TO RUN

Although there are many philosophies on how to operate a foodservice operation, there are three basic approaches: fast food, family, and fine dining. Management must recognize and have a full understanding of an operation's philosophy in order to achieve a maximum profit. Management must be completely dedicated to the philosophy selected and should avoid mixing different philosophies that would only serve to confuse the market.

FAST-FOOD OPERATION

Characteristics of the fast-food philosophy and operation are as follows:

- *Low check average*: $4 to $8
- *High turnover of capacity and high volume of sales*: the National Restaurant Association indicates a $1,000 to $5,000 sales amount per hour as high volume
- *Limited square footage per person for dining*: 7 to 9 square feet
- *Bright lights*: almost a shadowless lighting scheme
- *The use of bold, bright, and loud primary colours*: red, blue, and yellow

- Rapid employee movement, which tends to affect the customer's pace
- *Limited seat comfort*: the use of plastic nonmoveable seats provides less comfort than a cushioned, unfixed seat
- *High noise (decibel) level*: the use of nonacoustic materials (made from a hard substance, such as stone, brick, ceramic tile, or stainless steel)
- The use of styrofoam cups and plates, and paper napkins
- *Limited menu*: the selection of food items on the menu is limited to no more than 30 items, to reduce the time it takes for customers to read the menu and to decide on their orders

With this philosophy, the goal is to create an atmosphere that will allow the customer to eat and leave the foodservice operation as quickly as possible, usually within a 30-minute time period. Management must design the entire building (interior and exterior), in order to allow for rapid movement (flow) of customers. Every detail is geared towards getting the customer in and out of the foodservice operation as quickly as possible, without making the dining experience an uncomfortable, rushed, or negative one for the customer.

FAMILY OPERATION

The objective of the family philosophy is designed to appeal to the market that falls between the fast-food and the finedining market. The term "family" indicates that management must take into consideration the desires of a wide range of customers—from grandchildren to grandparents.

Characteristics of the family philosophy are as follows:

- *Moderate check average*: $8 to $15 per person
- *Moderate turnover rate*: one-and-a-half to two-and-a-half times per hour with a 100-seat capacity
- *Square footage per person*: 12 to 14 square feet
- *Illumination (lighting) level*: balanced, not dim or bright, but adequate
- Colour scheme that incorporates a blend of pastel and bright colours

- *Employee movement*: prompt, not slow or too rapid
- Seating that is moderately comfortable; good quality chairs used
- *Noise (decibel) level*: ranges from 60 decibels (calm conversation) to 90 decibels (a loud argument), with a balanced use of acoustic and nonacoustic material
- *Menu selections include 45 to 150 items*: of all the types of menus, this type of menu takes the longest time to read, because graphics (such as photographs) accompany the description of the food products

This philosophy incorporates objectives from both the fast-food and fine-dining philosophies. The objective of not rushing customers is borrowed from the fine-dining philosophy, while the goal of not allowing the customer to take two hours to dine stems from the fast-food philosophy.

FINE DINING

The fine-dining philosophy is, in many ways, the opposite of the fast-food philosophy. The objective of the fine-dining philosophy is to provide the customer with a relaxing and pleasant dining experience.

Characteristics of this philosophy include:

- *High check average*: $45 to $100 per person
- *A low turnover rate*: a 100-seat capacity foodservice operation will have a three-quarter to one-and-a-half turnover capacity
- *Square footage per person*: 24 to 30 square feet to provide greater room and privacy, which allows the customer to be more relaxed
- *Illumination level (lighting)*: low
- *Colours selected are relaxing*: pastel and earth-tone colours, such as tan and beige
- Employee movement in the dining room is not so rapid as to give a rushed impression and not so slow as to suggest indifference
- *Seating is very comfortable*: the use of fabric-padded seats provides more comfort
- *Noise (decibel) level*: a quiet, relaxing level of 30 to 70

decibels, facilitated by the use of soft acoustic material (wood, plants, carpets, fabric wallpaper, or other materials that absorb sound waves)

- Menu selections that are extensive (60 to 125 items) or limited (20 to 45 items), with more of a description accompanying the food items so as to enhance a person's appetite (when done correctly)
- *High-quality interior decor*: an atmosphere that encourages customers to relax, enjoy themselves, and spend money It is important that a foodservice operation select only one philosophy.

A combination of two or three philosophies during various hours of operation will only serve to confuse the customers and to deter them from identifying who you are and what you are all about. Very few foodservice operations can successfully combine philosophies and achieve a profitable margin.

CLIENTELE

It is critical that the menu planner know the type of clientele for whom the menu is being planned. In the commercial segment, the primary motive for going into business is profit. To generate a maximum profit, the menu must satisfy the clientele. The menu is one of management's ways of meeting the demands of the clientele. The menu needs to reflect these demands through food selections, price, and creativity.

CHECK AVERAGE

The *check average* is used to indicate the amount of money that people are spending. Foodservice managers use this information to evaluate and to set financial goals. If a foodservice operation sets a $12.50 check average per person as a goal prior to opening and is achieving only a $9.50 check average per person after it has opened, this information allows management to analyse why the check average is $3 short and to make the necessary changes. If management does not use this information, it will fall short of its financial goals, which could lead to indebtedness or failure.

DÉCOR

The decor, or decoration, of a foodservice establishment should project an image with which the market can identify. All of the exterior and interior design (such as landscaping, painting of the building, colour of the menu, the type of artwork, the wallpaper, the style of windows, the size and shape of the parking lot) must be done to accommodate the taste and style of the market.

The first impression of the interior is derived from the appearance of the exterior of a property. A littered parking lot reflects a negative image—one of messiness and filth that is certainly not appealing or attractive to the customer who has never been to the establishment. To know what the market is looking for, you must do a market survey.

PROFIT MARGIN

Profit margin is the amount of money made on a food or beverage product. All food and beverage products generally have different profit margins, even if they have the same food cost percentage. The profit margin is calculated when the food and beverage product is marked up from a preliminary selling price to a final selling price. For example, a slice of apple pie may cost $.35 to make. To make a profit, the slice of pie is sold for $1.75.

The difference between $.35 and $1.75 is $1.40, which will pay for the ingredients, the cost of Labour, the cost of the equipment, and the energy to make the pie, and will also contain a percentage for profit. When the price of the pie is increased to $2.25, the true margin of profit increases. If the price is lowered to $1.50, the margin of profit is lowered. Management will always make a profit on the piece of apple pie if it is priced correctly. The question is, how much profit? The answer is determined by how much the market is willing to pay for the slice of pie. If the market will pay $3.50 for the slice of apple pie, then management can price it at $3.50 on the menu.

COMPETITION

Competition in the foodservice industry, as in all business

endeavors, keeps operations at a competitive edge. Management must keep its standards high or the customer will go elsewhere.

Competition does the following:

- It keeps the prices of menu items under control and competitive. A food operation will not overprice a product such as coffee, which is common among all operations.
- It decreases advertising costs. If an independent foodservice operation locates next to a national foodservice chain organization, the independent operation can reduce spending on advertising, since the chain operation brings customers into and next to the independent foodservice operation.

MARKET TRENDS

The market is always changing. To be successful, the menu in a commercial foodservice operation needs to keep pace with the changes in the market. The menu planner and management must accurately forecast the demands of the market.

This task is not simple. The following items must be considered:

- New developments in food products, menu styles, decor concepts, as well as a variety of other trends occurring in the foodservice industry;
- The economy and how it is affecting the market; and
- The social needs of the market.

4

Skills in Restaurant Industry

Ask any restaurant operator about the alphabet soup known as ASPs, WAN, LAN, SAN, VPN, SQL, and POS, and you may get a puzzled look or a response that adds to your restaurant technology vocabulary. We have come a long way from the momand- pop operators and their proverbial cigar box. Independent operators may not require— or be able to afford—the sophistication of technology that chain operators are using.

However, it is hard to overlook the progress in making technology available and affordable for independent restaurants. This chapter will examine some of the better-known systems used and identify their applications in the restaurant industry. Most restaurants divide their technology into two parts: back and front of the house. Many systems integrate these so that operators can input and draw on the information from both programmes.

RESTURANT

Eating is one of life's pleasure and pride—so is cooking and serving good food to others. A restaurant is a commercial outfit which specializes in the preparation of quality food and to serve them to satisy the customer's demands. Their motto is "Customers are our assets and satisfied customers are our source of wealth".

Restaurants do have state of the art kitchens in their premises, where food items are prepared, following a fixed menu to serve the customers. Most restaurants are also equipped with infrastructure facilities, table settings, dining halls of various sizes to cater to needs of small gatherings to grandiose banquets to suit customer demands and above all, trained personnel to provide a satisfactory service. The term restaurant first appeared in the 16th century, meaning "a food which restores", and referred specifically to a rich, highly flavoured soup.

The modern sense of the word was born around 1765 when a Parisian soup-seller named Boulanger opened his establishment. Whilst inns and taverns were known from antiquity, these were establishments aimed at travellers, and in general locals would rarely eat there. The modern formal style of dining, where customers are given a plate with the food already arranged on it, is known as service à la russe, as it is said to have been introduced to France by the Russian Prince Kurakin in the 1810s, from where it spread rapidly to England and beyond.

A restaurant is a retail establishment that serves prepared food to customers. Service is generally for eating on premises, though the term has been used to include take-out establishments and food delivery services. The term covers many types of venues and a diversity of styles of cuisine and service. Restaurants are sometimes a feature of a larger complex, typically a hotel, where the dining amenities are provided for the convenience of the residents and of course, for the hotel with a singular objective to maximise their potential revenue. Such restaurants are often also open to non-residents.

Restaurants range from unpretentious lunching or dining places catering to people working nearby, with simple food and fixed menu served in simple settings at low prices, to expensive establishments serving expensive speciality food and wines in a formal setting. In the former case, customers usually wear casual clothing.

In the latter case, depending on culture and local traditions, customers might wear semi-casual, semi-formal, or even in rare cases formal wear. Typically, customers sit at tables, their orders are taken by a waiter, who brings the food when it is ready, and the customers pay the bill before leaving.

In class or porche restaurants there will be a host or hostess or even a maître d'hôtel to welcome customers and to seat them. Other staff's waiting on customers include busboys and sommeliers.

CLASSIFICATION OF RESTAURANTS

Restaurants can be classified by whether they provide places to sit, whether they are served by wait-staff and the quality of the service, the formal atmosphere, and the price range.

Restaurants are generally classified into three groups:

1. *Quick Service*: Also known as fast-food restaurants. They offer limited menus that are prepared quickly. They usually have drive-thru windows and take-out. They may also be selfservice outfits.
2. *Mid scale*: They offer full meals at a medium price that customers perceive as "good value." They can be o f full service, buffets or limited service with customers ordering at the counter and having their food brought to them or self service.
3. *Upscale*: Offer high quality cuisine at a high end price. They offer full service and have a high quality of ambience.

TYPES OF RESTAURANTS

Restaurants often specialize in certain types of food or present a certain unifying, and often entertaining, theme. For example, there are seafood restaurants, vegetarian restaurants or ethnic restaurants. Generally speaking, restaurants selling "local" food are simply called restaurants, while restaurants selling food of foreign origin are called accordingly, for example, a Chinese restaurant and a French restaurant. Depending on local customs and the policy of the establishment, restaurants may or may not serve alcoholic beverages. Restaurants are often prohibited from selling alcohol without a meal by alcohol sale laws; such sale is considered to be activity for bars, which are meant to have more severe restrictions. Some restaurants are licensed to serve alcohol and / or permit customers to 'bring your own' alcohol.

CAFETERIAS

A cafeteria is a restaurant serving mostly cooked ready to food arranged behind a food-serving counter. There is little or no table service. Typically, a patron takes a tray and pushes it along a track in front of the counter. Depending on the establishment, servings may be ordered from attendants, selected as ready-made portions already on plates, or self-serve of food of their own choice.

In some establishments, a few items such as steaks may be ordered specially prepared rare, medium and well done from the attendants. The patron waits for those items to be prepared or is given a number and they are brought to the table. Beverages may be filled from selfservice dispensers or ordered from the attendants. At the end of the line a cashier rings up the purchases. At some self-service cafeterias, purchases are priced by weight, rather than by individual item.

The trays filled with selected items of food are taken to a table to eat. Institutional cafeterias may have common tables, but upscale cafeterias provide individual tables as in sit-down restaurants. Upscale cafeterias have traditional cutlery and crockery, and some have servers to carry the trays from the line to the patrons' tables, and/ or bus the empty trays and used dishes. Cafeterias have a wider variety of prepared foods. For example, it may have a variety of roasts ready for carving by a server, as well as other cooked entrées, rather than simply an offering of hamburgers or fried chicken.

FAST-FOOD RESTAURANTS

Fast-food restaurants emphasize speed of service and low cost over all other considerations. A common feature of newer fastfood restaurants that distinguishes them from traditional cafeteria is a lack of cutlery or crockery; the customer is expected to eat the food directly from the disposable container it was served in using their fingers.

There are various types of fast-food restaurant:

- One collects food from a counter and pays, then sits down and starts eating; sub-varieties:
- One collects ready portions

- One serves oneself from containers
- One is served at the counter
- A special procedure is that one first pays at the cash desk, collects a coupon and then goes to the food counter, where one gets the food in exchange for the coupon.
- One orders at the counter; after preparation the food is brought to one's table; paying may be on ordering or after eating.
- A drive-through is a type of fast-food restaurant without seating; diners receive their food in their cars and drive away to eat

Most fast-food restaurants offer take-out: ready-to-eat hot food in disposable packaging for the customer to eat off-site.

CASUAL RESTAURANTS

A casual dining restaurant is a restaurant that serves moderately-priced food in a casual atmosphere. Except for buffetstyle restaurants, casual dining restaurants typically provide table service. Casual dining comprises of a market segment between fast food establishments and fine dining restaurants.

FAST CASUAL-DINING RESTAURANTS

A fast casual restaurant is similar to a fast-food restaurant in that it does not offer full table service, but promises a somewhat higher quality of food and atmosphere. Average prices charged are higher than fast-food prices and non-disposable plates and cutlery are usually offered.

This category is a growing concept that fills the space between fast food and casual dining. Counter service accompanied by handmade food is typical. Alcohol may be served. Dishes like steak, which require experience on the part of the cook to get it right, may be offered. The menu is usually limited to an extended over-counter display, and options in the way the food is prepared are emphasized. Many fast casual-dining restaurants are marketed as healthconscious: healthful items may have a larger number of items than normal portion of the menu and high-quality ingredients such as freerange chicken and freshly made salsas may be advertised. Overall, the quality of the food is presented as a much higher class than conventional factory-made fast food. An obvious ethnic theme may or may not be present in the menu.

OTHER RESTAURANTS

Most of these establishments can be considered subtypes of fast casual-dining restaurants or casual-dining restaurants.

Cafe

Cafés and coffee shops are informal restaurants offering a range of hot meals and made-to-order sandwiches. Cafés offer table service. Many cafés are open for breakfast and serve full hot breakfasts. In some areas, cafés offer outdoor seating.

Coffee House

Coffee houses are casual restaurants without table service that emphasize coffee and other beverages; typically a limited selection of cold foods such as pastries and perhaps sandwiches are offered as well. Their distinguishing feature is that they allow patrons to relax and socialize on their premises for long periods of time without pressure to leave promptly after eating.

Pub

A pub is a bar that serves simple food fare. Traditionally, pubs were primarily drinking establishments with food in a decidedly secondary position, whereas the modern pub business relies on food as well, to the point where gastropubs are known for their high-quality pub food. A typical pub has a large selection of beers and ales on tap.

Bistros and Brasserie

A brasserie is a café doubling as a restaurant and serving single dishes and other meals in a relaxed setting. A bistro is a familiar name for a café serving moderately priced simple meals in an unpretentious setting. Especially in Paris, bistros have become increasingly popular with tourists. When used in English, the term bistro usually indicates either a fast casual-dining restaurant with a European-influenced menu or a café with a larger menu of food.

Family Style

"Family style restaurants" are restaurants that have a fixed menu and fixed price, usually with diners seated at a communal table such as on bench seats. More common in the 19th and early 20th century, they can still be found in rural communities, or as theme restaurants, or in vacation lodges. There is no menu to choose from; rather food is brought out in courses, usually with communal serving dishes, like at a family meal. Typical examples can include crabhouses, German-style beer halls, BBQ restaurants, hunting lodges, etc. Some normal restaurants will mix elements of family style, such as a table salad or bread bowl that is included as part of the meal.

BYO Restaurant

BYO Restaurant are restaurants and bistros which do not have a liquor license.

Delicatessens Restaurant

Restaurants offering foods intended for immediate consumption. The main product line is normally luncheon meats and cheeses. They may offer sandwiches, soups, and salads as well. Most foods are precooked prior to delivery. Preparation of food products is generally simple and only involves one or two steps.

Ethnic Restaurants

They range from quick-service to upscale. Their menus usually include ethnic dishes and / or authentic ethnic foods. Specialize in a particular multicultural cuisine not specifically accommodated by any other listed categories. Example: Asian Cuisine, Chinese cuisine, Indian Cuisine, American Cuisine etc.

Destination Restaurants

A destination restaurant is one that has a strong enough appeal to draw customers from beyond its community.

Example: Michelin Guide 3-star restaurant in Europe, which according to the restaurant guides is "worthy of a journey".

STAFF ORGANISATION

Staff organization is basically concerned with matters such as the decision of tasks within the restaurant, position of responsibility and authority and the relationship between them. It helps in introducing the conceps of span of control, level of management and delegation of power and responsibilities. However smaller organizations may combine a number of responsibilities according to the needs of the particular facility.

THE DUTIES AND RESPONSIBILITIES OF RESTAURANT STAFF

All types of catering establishments require a variety of staff positions in order to operate effectively and efficiently. The food and beverage service department usually has the largest staff. Able leadership and supervision is required to effectively direct the department and guide the staff.

The personnel in the food and beverage service industry require practical knowledge of operations as even a small error can cause displeasure to the guest. Coordination of activities of all outlets is essential to provide the guest with quality service at all times. Teamwork is the watchword in any food and beverage service department.

A dedicated and committed team, with able leadership, under ideal working conditions, helps in fulfilling the establishment's ultimate goal of guest satisfaction The important duties and responsibilities of the restaurant staffs are discussed in this section.

FOOD AND BEVERAGE MANAGER

The food and beverage manager is the head of the food and beverage service department, and is responsible for its administrative and operational work. Food and Beverage Managers direct, plan and control all aspects of food and beverage services. Food and Beverage Managers require excellent sales and customer service skills, proven human resource management skills, and good communication and leadership skills. Desired knowledge for this position includes knowledge of the products, services, sector, industry and local area, and knowledge of relevant legislation and regulations, as well. Hence it is said that food and beverage manager is a Jack-of-all-trades, as the job covers a wide variety of duties.

In general, food and beverage manager is responsible for:

- *Budgeting*: The food and beverage manager is responsible for preparing the budget for the department. He should ensure that each outlet in the department achieves the estimated profit margins.
- *Compiling New Menus and Wine Lists*: In consultation with the chef, and based on the availability of ingredients and prevailing trends, the food and beverage manager should update and if necessary, compile new menus. New and updated wine lists should also be introduced regularly.
- *Quality Control*: The food and beverage manager should ensure quality control in terms of efficiency in all service areas, by ascertaining that the staffs are adequately trained in keeping with the standards of the unit.
- *Manpower Development*: The food and beverage manager is responsible for recruitment, promotions, transfers and dismissals in the department. He should hold regular meetings with section heads, to ensure that both routine as well as projected activities of the department go on as planned. He must also give training, motivate and effectively control staff.

ASSISTANT FOOD AND BEVERAGE MANAGER

The assistant food and beverage manager assists the food and beverage manager in running the department by being more involved in the actual day-to-day operations. This position exists only in large organisations.

An assistant food and beverage manager's job includes:

- Assisting section heads during busy periods.

- Taking charge of an outlet, when an outlet manager is on leave.
- Setting duty schedules for all the outlet managers and monitoring their performance.
- Running the department independently in the absence of the food and beverage manager.

RESTAURANT MANAGER

Restaurant Manager is responsible for directing and supervising all activities pertaining to employee relation, food production, sanitation, guest service and operating profits. The restaurant manager is either the coffee shop manager, bar manager or the specialist restaurant manager. The restaurant manager reports directly to the food and beverage manager and has overall responsibility for the organisation and administration of a particular outlet or a section of the food and beverage service department.

The restaurant manager's job includes:

- Setting and monitoring the standards of service in the outlets.
- Administrative duties such as setting duty charts, granting leave, monitoring staff positions, recommending staff promotions and handling issues relating to discipline.
- Training the staff by conducting a daily briefing in the outlet.
- Playing a vital role in public relations, meeting guests in the outlets and attending to guest complaints, if any.
- Formulating the sales and expenditure budget for the outlet.
- Planning food festivals to increase the revenue and organising advertisement campaign of the outlet along with the chef and the food and beverage manager.

ROOM SERVICE MANAGER

The room service manager reports directly to the food and

beverage manager and is responsible for the room service outlet. The room service manager checks that the service rendered to the guests conforms to the standards set by the hotel. He also monitors all operational aspects of the outlet such as service, billing, duty charts, leave and absenteeism, in addition to attending to guest complaints regarding food and service. The room service manager is also in charge of the sales and expenditure budget.

The room service is most liable to have problems. The room service manager should ensure coordination among the room service order taker, the captain and the waiter. It is necessary for the room service manager to be present in the outlet during peak hours to interact with other departments of the hotel and to take regular momentums of all the equipment used In the event of the hotel offering valet service and the room service manager takes charge of that service as well.

BAR MANAGER

Bar Manager organises and controls a bar's operations. A bar manager arranges the purchase and pricing of beverages according to budget; selects, trains and supervises bar staff; maintains records of stock levels and financial transactions; makes sure bar staff follow liquor laws and regulations; and checks on customer satisfaction and preferences. The bar manager should have good interpersonal skills and good memory. He must be efficient and speedy, must enjoy working with people. He should have good cash-handling skills.

BANQUET MANAGER

The banquet manager supervises the banquet operations, sets up break-down service according to the standards established by the hotel. He co-ordinates the banquet service in conjunction with other departments involved and prepares weekly schedules for the banquet personnel. From the time the bookings are done till the guest settles the bill, the banquet manager is in charge of all aspects of banquet and conference operations. He supervises the work of the banquet sales assistants, who do the banquet bookings and the captains and waiters who perform the food and beverage service activities under his guidance. He is responsible for organising everything right down to the finest detail. The banquet manager projects the budget of the banquets, and works in close coordination with the chef in preparing menus. He is responsible for making an inventory of all the banquet equipment and maintaining a balance between revenue and expenditure. Banquet managers may also be designated as assistant managers in the food and beverage service department.

OTHER STAFF DESIGNATIONS AT VARIOUS LEVELS

The following are the various designations with their job specifications in the food and beverage department.

Senior Captain or Maitre d' Hotel

The senior captain has overall responsibility for operations. He prepares the duty charts in consultation with the outlet manager. He oversees the Mise-en-place, cleaning, setting up of the outlet and staffing to ensure that the outlet is always ready for service. The senior captain receives the guests and hands them over to the captain or station holder. He takes orders from guests if the captain is unable to do so. The senior captain should be an able organiser and also be prepared to take over the duties of any member of the staff as and when required.

Reception Head Waiter

This staff member is responsible for accepting any booking and for keeping the booking diary up-to-date. He / she will reserve tables and allocate these reservations to particular stations. The reception head waiter greets guests on arrival and takes them to the table and seats them.

Captain / Chef De Rang

This position exists in large restaurants, as well as in the food and beverage service department of all major hotels. The captain is basically a supervisor and is in charge of a particular section. A restaurant may be divided into sections called Sations, each consisting of 4 to 5 tables or 20 to 24 covers. A captain is responsible for the efficient performance of the staff in his station.A captain should possess a sound knowledge of food and beverage, and be able to discuss the menu with the guests. He should be able to take a guest's order and be an efficient salesperson. Specialised service such as gueridon work involves a certain degree of skill, and it is the captain who usually takes the responsibility to do this work.

Waiters/Commis De Rang/Server

The waiters serve the food and beverage ordered by a guest and is part of a team under a station captain. They should be able to perform the duties of a captain to a certain extent and be a substitute for the captain if he is busy or not on duty. They should; also be knowledgeable about all types of food and beverages, so that they can effectively take an order from a guest, execute the order and serve the correct dish with its appropriate garnish and accompaniment. They should be able to efficiently coordinate with the other staff in the outlet.

Trainee/Commis De Barraseur

The trainees work closely with the waiters, fetching orders from the kitchen and the bar, and clearing the side station in a restaurant. They serve water and assist the waiter. They are mainly responsible for the mise-en-place, and stacking the side board with the necessary equipment for service. The debarrasseur is the 'learner', having just joined the food service staff, and possibly wishing to take up food service as a carreer.

Wine Waiter/Sommelier

Wine waiters have an important role to play in reputed establishments. Their job is to take orders for the service of wine and alcoholic beverages and serve them during the meal. Hence they should be knowledgeable about wines that accompany a particular dish and the manner in which they should be served. They should also be aware of the licensing laws prevalent in the city and should be efficient sales persons.

Room Service Waiters/Chef D'etage

Room service waiters work in the room service outlet, serving food and beverage to guests in their rooms. The order is placed by the guest on telephone, and is recorded on a Kitchen Order Ticket. It is then passed on to the duty captain. The duty captain in turn places the order in the kitchen or the bar, as the case may be. The room service waiter who has been assigned that order, sets the tray according to the food or beverage ordered, picks up and delivers the order when it is ready.

Carver/Trancheur

The carver is responsible for the carving trolley and the carving of joints at the table as required. The carver will plate up each portion with the appropriate accompaniment.

Floor Service Staff/Floor Waiter

The floor service staffs are often responsible for an entire floor in an establishment or, depending on the size of the establishment, a number of rooms or suites. Floor service of all meals and breakfast is offered either throughout the day or in a limited time depending on the size of the establishment. The floor service staff would normally work from a floor pantry or from a central kitchen with all food and drink reaching the appropriate floor and the required room by lift and in a heated trolley.

Lounge staff/Chef de sale

Lounge staff may deal with lounge service as a specific duty only in a first class establishment. The lounge staff is responsible for the service of morning coffee, afternoon teas, aperitifs and liqueurs before and after both lunch and dinner, and any coffee top ups required after meals. They would be responsible for setting up the lounge in the morning and maintaing its cleanliness and presentation throughout the day.

Cocktail Bar Staff

The person who works on the cocktail bar must be responsible, well versed in the skills of shaking and stirring cocktails and should have thorough knowledge of all alcoholic and non-alcholic drinks, the ingredients necessary for the making of cocktails and of the licensing laws.

Buffet Assistant/Buffet Chef/Chef de buffet

The chef de buffet is in charge of the buffet in the room, its presentation, the carving and portioning of food and its service. This staff would normally be a member of the kitchen team. The cashier is responsible for the takings of the food and beverage operation. This may include making up bills from food and drink check or, alternatively, in a cafeteria, for example, charging customers for their selection of items on a tray.

Counter Assistants

Counter assistants are found in cafeterias where they would stock the counter and sometimes serve or portion food for customers. Duties may also include some cooking of call order items.

Table Clearers

Table clearers are responsible for clearing tables and trolleys, specially designed for good stacking of crockery, glassware, cutlery, etc.

BACK-OF-THE-HOUSE TECHNOLOGY

Back-of-the-house, or *back-office,* restaurant technology consists of product management systems for purchasing, managing inventories, menu management, controlling Labour and other costs, tip reporting, food and beverage cost percentages, human resources, and financial reporting.

PURCHASING AND INVENTORY CONTROL

Product management allows managers to track product through each stage of the inventory cycle and to automatically reorder when an item falls below the par stock level. The ingredients for recipes are costed to calculate cost and selling prices. If the purchase price of an item increases, it is easy to enter this information and get the new selling price. Software solutions like Chef Tec and Chef Tec Plus include options such as importing purchases from vendors' online ordering systems and comparing vendors' pricing from purchases or bills. Additionally, the software allows restaurants to automate ordering with user-set par levels and generate customised reports detailing purchases, bids, and credits.

INVENTORY CONTROL

Back-office systems aid inventory control by quickly recording the inventory and easily allowing new stock to be added. Calculations are done rapidly and monetary tools are given for each item, plus a cumulative total. The software programmes prompt when inventory falls below the reorder point. When new menu items are added to the system, they are costed and priced according to the mark-up.

FOOD COSTING

When calculating the food (and beverage) cost percentage, a handheld device (PDA) can enter the inventory amounts into the system. Laser bar-code scanning technology is speeding up the inventory-taking process and making it more accurate. When the data are entered into the system, a variance report is generated and any significant variances are investigated. Technological improvements have made it possible to do a restaurant's food cost percentage in about one-third of the time it used to take and with more accuracy.

ChefTec and ChefTec Plus software solutions integrate programmes with recipe and menu costing, inventory control, and nutritional analysis capabilities. The recipe and menu costing programme can cost, scale, and store an unlimited number of recipes; write recipe procedures using cut and paste, customizable fonts, colours, and a culinary spellchecker; instantly analyse recipe/menu cost by portion and yield; attach photos, diagrams, videos, or company logos to recipes; print out kitchen-readable recipes; calculate costs based on highest or most recent prices paid for ingredients; save recipes in HTML, and share the data via the Internet.

MENU MANAGEMENT

There is a definite link between food costing and menu management, an example being San Diego–based Cambridge Investments, operator of 60 Arby's and five Baja Fresh units. They use MenuLink to evaluate managers' produce purchasing, test proposed recipe and pricing changes, and compare actual to expected food usage. The menu management function is used to determine what offers work best, so that coupon building may be directed towards those items. Since Menu Link use began, food costs have dropped 2 per cent and Labour costs have also dropped.

Labour Management

Labor management systems interface with both front- and back-of-the-house employee working hours, plus they handle human resources information. Labour management systems include a module to monitor applications (which can now be online and paperless), recruitment, personnel information, I-9 status, tax status, availability, vacation, and benefit information. Labour management systems also do the scheduling based on the forecasted volume of business for each meal period, and managers monitor the schedules to control costs.

The actual time worked is recorded, the data on tips are entered and later reported per IRS guidelines, the pay scale and the calculation of paychecks are made, and the check is in the mail! Windows-based Labour schedulers make it easier for restaurant operators to stay on top of their biggest controllable expense. Says John Gloe, director of special projects for constellation Concepts, of Emeryville, California, "If you don't stay on top of it, it will make a big divot in your profit-and-loss statement."

TimePro from Commeg Systems has a time, attendance, and scheduling feature. Once the manager completes the schedule, associates cannot clock in more than ten minutes early or five minutes late without a manager's override. This prevents people from coming in early and taking a socializing break out back. Obviously, schedules are geared towards expected guest counts and sales. It is better to avoid copying a schedule from week to week because either the Labour budget or the guests will suffer— since no two sales periods are identical. Forecasts are checked against actual performance, and both figures are checked against the ideal for the time period; then the numbers are tweaked for the next forecast.

It does take more up-front work, but once done it not only yields savings, but also allows managers to focus on things like pleasing guests. Savvy restaurateurs guestimate their sales for the next week and 28 days and compare the numbers with the budget, then update the numbers daily. Managers are frequently on a bonus plan, and meeting Labour costs is a big part of the programme. Managers can focus on productivity by the numbers, guests, per server, or by total sales.

FINANCIAL REPORTING

Back- and front-of-the-house systems may interface by transferring data to and from the central server. Profit (or loss) statements, budgets and variances, daily reports, and balance sheets are prepared with the aid of software programmes. The advantage of this technology is that information is provided in real time, enabling operators to make informed decisions quickly. Quicker decisions allow managers to "keep their fingers on the pulse" of the restaurant. When the back- and front-of-house systems are interfaced, it is easier for management to monitor service times, POS food costs, Labour costs, and guest counts. Again, this compilation of information helps managers make more informed decisions.

E-LEARNING

Computer-based training delivered via the Internet or proprietary Internet sites is expanding knowledge in the workplace. Darden Restaurant managers and hourly paid workers have used it to learn a new software system. About 85 per cent of Fortune 1000 companies have significant e-learning initiatives underway. Darden Restaurants, with more than 130,000 employees and 1,200 restaurants nationwide, recently introduced a PeopleSoft software system that employees use to access benefits and other information through its intranet site. "How do you train 135,000 people how to use People Soft?" asks Randy Babitt, Darden's director of operations development.

"In the old days we'd have to print up 135,000 manuals with different ones for different jobs. We'd have to send them out to all the restaurants." The National Restaurant Association Educational Foundation has several online courses, such as Serve Safe Food Safety Training and Serve Safe Manager Certification Online Course. There is also the Bar Code—Responsible Alcohol Service Programme. All front-of-the-house employees should take the Bar Code and all back-of-the-house employees should take the Serve Safe courses.

FRONT-OF-THE-HOUSE TECHNOLOGY

Front-of-the-house technology revolves around the point-of-sale (POS) system and wireless handheld devices.

POS SYSTEMS

The point-of-sale terminal is the workhorse of restaurant operations. It needs to be strong enough to withstand the rigors of daily restaurant use and versatile enough to achieve order-entry and guest-check efficiency. Restaurant operators are increasingly demanding POS terminals that work within today's conditions while leaving room for expansion or adaptation. Today it's Windows, next month or next year it may be Linux. Today most operators are robust POS units, but soon they might want to run terminals remotely via the Web. Open platform architecture, a leading trend in POS, is giving restaurant operators more flexibility when it comes to choosing operating systems, peripherals, and applications, while improved design is reducing footprint and increasing reliability.

SELECTING A POS SYSTEM

Clyde Dishman, hospitality industry vice president of NCR, suggests that because a POS system can run into thousands of dollars, any new restaurant-level system should be pre-tested in "live" environments. Additionally, because restaurants of all shapes and sizes have varying sets of technology requirements, they need to be able to combine proven hardware with multiple software modules to create flexible and customizable solutions.

NCR's Human Factors Engineering (HFE) team provides the quantitative data for evaluating current store performance levels and user interface designs. HFE concentrates on restaurant performance improvements that allow the restaurant operator to identify areas in which to increase revenues and improve operational efficiency and guest service. HFE has demonstrated the ability to assist the restaurateur in many facets of the business, whether in technology or in purely operational areas, such as work-flow design or ergonomic assessments. The two focus areas of HFE are store performance and user-interface design.

The store performance group measures key store-level metrics to assess productivity at the point of sale, as well as ergonomics and technology, and then compares that to other best-in-class restaurant practices. The resulting quantitative data are used to conduct cost/benefit analysis of recommended solutions. The second focus area relates to the usability of the system. When a restaurant's employees are not productive and customer-service levels are not up to snuff, such problems can often be traced to the design of the POS interface, ranging from complicated screen layouts to inappropriately sized buttons and the poor use of colours for different menu items.

HFE quantifies productivity levels of an existing system by surveying the needs of front-line restaurant employees to ensure that any recommended solution is easy to use. For example, HFE developed a series of more than 200 guidelines for touch-screen POS applications, which outline the best practices for designing software that improves productivity, reduces training times, and facilitates usability. Aloha has a popular POS full-range restaurant product that includes Aloha Table Service, which offers user-friendly ways of entering orders, managing guest checks, running promotions, and processing payments. Event Scheduler that lets managers programme events that are automatically activated at a specific time. Special messages can be entered to appear on the screen, keeping staff informed. Managers can also access real-time sales results and reporting features like product mix reports, employee check-in stats, and server sales.

Aloha's virtual order processing communicates between the kitchen and waitstaff. For example, with the menu availability feature, staff are able to count down selected items or specials as they're ordered so servers never order out-of-stock items. Some of the features of Table Service include intuitive touch-screen interfaces, built-in redundancy, user-customizable screens and screen flow, menu management, integrated customised table floor plan, its Microsoft Windows based performance measurement for servers, open architecture, off-the-shelf nonproprietary hardware, enterprise capabilities, extensive kitchen chit printing options, and simple check or item splitting and combining functionality.

Optional packages for Aloha's Table Service also include Aloha credit card, which authorizes, processes, and settles credit card transactions. The Aloha Customer Management includes a database to offer loyalty programmes and track vital customer information. The Aloha Kitchen Display System gives the flexibility to route orders to video monitors in the kitchen. This package can increase productivity because it notifies each station in the kitchen of orders, instead of having someone standing at the pass shouting orders to each station.

ASI has the popular Restaurant Manager POS, with easy-touse training. This, coupled with the seamless integration between Restaurant Manager and the Write-On Handheld POS system, means that servers simply jot down guests' orders and send them to the kitchen with a tap of their stylus. The Write-On Handheld also gives servers easy access to wine lists, daily specials, and recipes.

Handhelds can provide benefits to restaurants such as faster table turns, because servers no longer need to record each order twice. Another benefit is reduced errors—servers are reminded to ask for details like cooking temperature or salad dressing. The handheld system prompts servers to enter orders into the system starting with seat number one, and then moving around the table. It makes it easy to track specific items to the corresponding guest, which is especially helpful when a food expediter is needed on a busy night. This function also makes it less complicated to provide split checks— even after the order has been totaled. Yet another feature of handhelds is up-sells; because the entire menu is in the palm of their hand, servers can promote or up-sell items more easily.

If an item is 86'd, it is displayed in real time so servers will know immediately and can offer an alternative. Restaurant Manager comes with a full complement of peripheral devices that include bar code scanners, cash draws, coin dispensers, caller ID devices, customer displays, Debitek card readers, fingerprint readers, kitchen display units, liquor control devices, magnetic strip readers, order confirmation displays, printers, weighing scales and video tracking monitors.

There are several suppliers of POS. IBM offers Linux servers and Sure POS 700 series for restaurants. The Sure POS 700 open platform applications for both Microsoft Windows and IBM 4690 OS allow for customization of applications, peripherals, and displays; it also drives USB technology for plug-and-play setup and automatic configuration.

The Sure POS 700 incorporates an onboard 10/100 ether net local-area network (LAN) to handle both Internet and intranet applications. Sharp has the UP-5900 system, which is also an open platform terminal and one that is combined with Maitre'D Restaurant Management software, which can drive a variety of software modules and interfaces. NCR offers the 7454 POS Workstation with open PC-based architecture that is certified for MS DOS and Windows for flexibility and even offers full-screen, full-motion video.

Hardware solutions from NCR and its partners include the fully integrated NCR Real POS 70. It combines the reliability of the Microsoft platform and the industry leading technology of Intel with the innovation of Authen Tec. The Intel Pentium IV-based terminal sports an integrated touch screen, magnetic stripe reader, and customer display. It also features a newly designed motherboard that is based on Intel's standards-based specification. The motherboard, hard disc, and power supply are placed on user-friendly "sleds" allowing for tool-free access and servicing. That means a terminal that needs servicing can be up and running in seconds. NCR will also certify, support, and offer preloaded operating system images on the NCR Real POS 70 for Microsoft Windows 200, XP Pro, NT, and DOS. NCR's Compris runs on the NCR 7454 hospitality point of sale system.

The Compris solution includes a flexible POS application, a back-office component for managing restaurant operations, and corporate tools for remote database maintenance and consolidated reporting. The Windows-based Compris WinPOS is easy to use and has an Advanced Manager's workstation that includes Navigation—which allows inventory, operators to configure their interface with daily tasks and user-defined tabs like cash management or—view, print and balance all POS data at the back office.

The Compris Win POS also handles food cost control invoices, receipts, transfers, credits, and waste reports. Reporting includes both theoretical and actual usage and variance tracking. Labour includes controlling Labour costs, tracking time and wages, generating timecards, and avoiding employees' clocking in too early or clocking out too late. It provides a full complement of reports: daily, weekly, and period Labour costs, employee punches, hours worked, and server totals. This data can be extracted from and imported into a payroll system.

Schedule builder generates simple-to-use schedules for each shift, highlights conflicts, and tracks variances. Micros has the Eclipse PC Workstation that combines a small footprint and seams designed to channel liquids off the unit. The Eclipse also supports a number of operating systems including MSDOS 6.22 and Microsoft Windows, as well as all Micros point-of-sale applications.

POS systems have come down in price and offer the independent restaurateur the convenience of providing information for financials that obviates the need for cash registers and spreadsheets, which are time-consuming and often have to be reformatted and reentered into the accounting journals by bookkeepers or accountants. Today, POS systems have credit-card integration and interface with payroll and financial systems. The information is consolidated and an automated profit-and-loss statement is produced. Some operators choose a POS for its power beyond the point of sale. These multimedia workstations feature a large hard drive and can run customer promotions or employee training programmes when not in use as POS terminals. For some smaller restaurants, there is the old standby electronic cash register (ECR), which is now offering some of the flexibility of POS. For example, the ECR can be used as a stand-alone unit for a small restaurant.

Wireless POS has been around for a few years, but it is getting better and smaller. So, how is wireless POS being used in the restaurant business? One example is the general managers at Red Robin, who use their wireless POS as a tool to notify them when team members go on overtime, to violations of underage working rules, of birthdays and anniversaries, and of the need to void or comp a guest check. Some restaurateurs are concerned about the quality of guest contact during the order-taking process and how that might be negatively impacted by a server doing a POS transaction while standing at the table.

Several restaurant-industry technology trends are becoming more prominent. The main one is increased integration of front- and back-office systems. New technology is constantly being introduced. There is new satellite or cable entertainment; age verification units to confirm a customer's age or ferret out fake IDs; and handheld PDAs that function as pagers, data-entry pads, and inventory control devices.

The cost of installing a POS system will depend on the number of stations required. A 125-seat casual dining restaurant could use two or three stations in the dining area, one in the bar, and printers in the kitchen, plus a managers' station. The total cost would be in the $18,000 to $20,000 range. If you are opening a restaurant and do not have that kind of money, you can start with a simple cash register and work up to a more sophisticated system as business grows.

Guest Services and Web Sites

Restaurant technology has evolved to the point where a restaurant can store and recall guests' preferences for tables, menu items, wines, and servers. Tables may be booked over the Internet at any time by leaving a credit card as a form of deposit to secure the table, especially in the large cities at convention times. Hosts can use programmes to allocate tables, allowing a certain time, say one and a half hours, before that table is booked again. Guest checks can be split for payment by several people, if need be. Guest bills even come with suggested tip amounts calculated.

Another form of guest services is offered by some coffeehouses, which provide high-speed Internet access for guests. Starbucks just may be the next place for your meeting. At least when it gets boring you'll be able to check your e-mail. Other restaurants are using wireless paging to help reduce wait time for guests and loss of pagers for restaurants. When guests give their names to the hostess, they are asked for their cell phone number.

This is entered into the "Trinity" system. When the table is ready, a prerecorded message informs the guests that their table is ready. Wireless surveys allow guests to give feedback before they leave the restaurant, and tabletop pagers let guests page their server when they need something. Restaurant Web sites need an appealing, user-friendly design and functionality, including accessibility and interactivity.

When Joe Public is trying to access your site, can it be done without fault? Other features that are helpful are menus, photos of the restaurant, how to get there, parking information, frequently asked questions, and secure transaction capability. Among the higher-scoring restaurant Web sites are Red Robin, TGI Friday's, Outback Steakhouse, and Hard Rock Café.

Café Ba-Ba-Reeba, Chicago's first tapas restaurant, selected Nextology as its software programme because it could take care of a dream list of items. The restaurant has a number of special "reservation required" events such as cooking classes, wine tastings, and shows, so keeping those up to date was very important. It also needed the ability to list specials, menu changes, and other information of interest of its clientele. It now has a site that enables it to take reservations and receive payment for events online. It can also edit, change, and update information on the fly. Michael Cunningham, general manager, says that Café Ba-Ba-Reeba could not go with a generic Web site design due to the restaurant's reputation and image. Now his staff is on the phone less and bookings are up.

5

Hospitality Service

The concept of Hospitality Services, also known as "accommodation sharing", "hospitality exchange", and "home stay networks", refers to centrally organized social networks of individuals who trade accommodation without monetary exchange. While this concept could also include house swapping or even time share plans, it has come to be associated mostly with travellers and tourists staying with one another free of charge. Since the 1990s, these services have increasingly moved away from using printed catalogs and phone trees to connect users towards Internet websites. These have grown exponentially since 2000 and today it is estimated that well over 100,000 people are registered users of these networks. These vary in operational structure, place different emphasis on graphical vs. textual formatting, and cater disproportionately to specific geographic regions.

HOTEL

A hotel is an establishment that provides paid lodging, usually on a short-term basis. Hotels often provide a number of additional guest services such as a restaurant, a swimming pool or childcare. Some hotels have conference services and meeting rooms and encourage groups to hold conventions and meetings at their location. Hotels differ from motels in that most motels have drive-up, exterior entrances to the rooms, while hotels tend to have interior entrances to the rooms, which may increase guests' safety and present a more upmarket image. In Australia, a hotel may also be an establishment that serves alcoholic drinks, and usually meals in a casual setting but which does not necessarily provide accommodation. This type of establishment would more usually be called a pub or bar in other countries. In general use in Australia the terms '"hotel" and *pub* are usually taken to be synonymous. In India, the word may also refer to a restaurant since the best restaurants were always situated next to a good hotel.

The word *hotel* derives from the French *hôtel,* which referred to a French version of a townhouse, not a place offering accommodation (in contemporary usage, *hôtel* has the meaning of "hotel", and *hôtel particulier* is used for the old meaning). The French spelling (with the circumflex) was once also used in English, but is now rare. The circumflex replaces the 's' once preceding the 't' in the earlier *hostel* spelling, which over time received a new, but closely related meaning.

Basic accommodation of a room with only a bed, a cupboard, a small table and a washstand has largely been replaced by rooms with en-suite bathrooms and climate control. Other features found may be a telephone, an alarm clock, a TV, and broadband Internet connectivity. Food and drink may be supplied by a mini-bar (which often includes a small refrigerator) containing snacks and drinks (to be paid for on departure), and tea and coffee making facilities (cups, spoons, an electric kettle and sachets containing instant coffee, tea bags, sugar, and creamer or milk). In the United Kingdom a hotel is required by law to serve food and drinks to all comers within certain stated hours; to avoid this requirement it is not uncommon to come across "private hotels" which are not subject to this requirement. However, in Japan the capsule hotel supplies minimal facilities and room space.

CLASSIFICATION

The cost and quality of hotels are usually indicative of the range and type of services available. Due to the enormous increase in tourism worldwide during the last decades of the 20th century, standards, especially those of smaller establishments, have improved considerably. For the sake of greater comparability, rating systems have been introduced, with the one to five stars classification being most common.

Boutique Hotels

"Boutique Hotel" is a term originating in North America to describe intimate, usually luxurious or quirky hotel environments. Boutique hotels differentiate themselves from larger chain or branded hotels by providing an exceptional and personalized level of accommodation, services and facilities. Boutique hotels are furnished in a themed, stylish and/or aspirational manner. Although usually considerably smaller than a mainstream hotel (ranging from 3 to 100 guest rooms) boutique hotels are generally fitted with telephone and wi-fi Internet connections, honesty bars and often cable/pay TV. Guest services are attended to by 24 hour hotel staff.

Many boutique hotels have on site dining facilities, and the majority offer bars and lounges which may also be open to the general public. Of the total travel market a small percentage are discerning travellers, who place a high importance on privacy, luxury and service delivery. As this market is typically corporate travellers, the market segment is non-seasonal, high-yielding and repeat, and therefore one which boutique hotel operators target as their primary source of income.

Famous Hotels

Some hotels have gained their renown through tradition, by hosting significant events or persons, such as Schloss Cecilienhof in Potsdam, Germany, which derives its fame from the so-called Potsdam Conference of the World War II allies Winston Churchill, Harry Truman and Joseph Stalin in 1945. Other establishments have given name to a particular meal or beverage, as is the case with the Waldorf Astoria in New York City, USA, known for its *Waldorf Salad* or the Raffles Hotel in Singapore, where the drink *Singapore Sling* was invented. Another example is the Hotel Sacher in Vienna Austria, home of the *Sachertorte.*

There are also hotels which became much more popular through films like the Grand Hotel Europe in Saint Petersburg, Russia when James Bond stayed there in the Blockbuster, Goldeneye. Cannes hotels such as the Carlton or the Martinez become the center of the world during Cannes Film Festival (France). A number of hotels have entered the public consciousness through popular culture, such as the Ritz Hotel in London, UK ('Putting on The Ritz') and Hotel Chelsea in New York City, subject of a number of songs and also the scene of the alleged stabbing of Nancy Spungen by her boyfriend Sid Vicious. Hotels that enter folklore like these two are also often frequented by celebrities, as is the case both with the Ritz and the Chelsea.

Other famous hotels include the Beverly Hills Hotel, the Hotel Bel-Air and the Chateau Marmont, in California, Watergate complex in Washington DC, the Hotel Astoria in Saint Petersburg, Russia, the Hotel George V and Hôtel Ritz in Paris, Palazzo Versace hotel on the Gold Coast, Queensland, Australia, Hotel Hermitage and Hotel de Paris in Monaco (in the French Riviera) and Hotel Leningradskaya in Moscow.

UNUSUAL HOTELS

Many hotels can be considered destinations in themselves, by dent of unusual features of the lodging and/or its immediate environment:

Treehouse Hotels

Some hotels, such as the Costa Rica Tree House in the Gandoca-Manzanillo Wildlife Refuge, Costa Rica, or Treetops Hotel in Aberdare National Park, Kenya, are built with living trees as structural elements, making them treehouses. The Ariau Towers near Manaus, Brazil is in the middle of the Amazon, on the Rio Negro. Bill Gates even invested and had a suite built there with satellite internet/phone. Another hotel with treehouse units is Bayram's Tree Houses in Olympos, Turkey.

Cave Hotels

Desert Cave Hotel in Coober Pedy, South Australia and the Cuevas Pedro Antonio de Alarcón (named after the author) in Guadix, Spain, as well as several hotels in Cappadocia, Turkey, are notable for being built into natural cave formations, some with rooms underground.

Capsule Hotels

Capsule hotels are a type of economical hotels that are quite common in Japan.

Ice Hotels

Ice hotels, such as the Ice Hotel in Jukkasjärvi, Sweden, melt every spring and are rebuilt out of ice and snow each winter.

Snow Hotels

The Mammut Snow Hotel in Finland is located within the walls of the Kemi snow castle, which is the biggest in the world. It includes The Mammut Snow Hotel, The Castle Courtyard, The Snow Restaurant and a chapel for weddings, etc. Its furnishings and its decorations, such as sculptures, are made of snow and ice. There is snow accommodation also in Lainio Snow Hotel in Lapland (near Ylläs), Finland.

Garden Hotels

Garden hotels, famous for their gardens before they became hotels, includes Gravetye Manor, the home of William Robinson and Cliveden, designed by Charles Barry with a rose garden by Geoffrey Jellicoe.

Underwater Hotels

As of 2005, the only hotel with an underwater room that can be reached without Scuba diving is Utter Inn in Lake Mälaren, Sweden. It only has one room, however, and Jules' Undersea Lodge in Key Largo, Florida, which requires scuba diving, is not much bigger.

Hydropolis is an ambitious project to build a luxury hotel in Dubai, UAE, with 220 suites, all on the bottom of the Persian Gulf, 20 meters (66 feet) below the surface. Its architecture will feature two domes that break the surface and an underwater train tunnel, all made of transparent materials such as glass and acrylic.

Other Unusual Hotels

The Library Hotel in New York City is unique in that its

ten floors are arranged according to the Dewey Decimal System. The Rogers Centre, formerly SkyDome, in Toronto, Canada is the only stadium to have a hotel connected to it, with 70 rooms overlooking the field. The Burj al-Arab hotel in Dubai, United Arab Emirates, built on an artificial island, is structured in the shape of a sail of a boat.

WORLD-RECORD SETTING HOTELS

- *Tallest:* The tallest hotel in the world is the Burj al-Arab in Dubai, United Arab Emirates at 321 meters (1,053 feet). However, this title may be taken by the less illustrious Ryugyong Hotel in Pyongyang at 330 meters (1,083 feet), pending its (perhaps unlikely) completion; it has been under construction since 1987 and was abandoned in 1992.
- *Largest:* The current largest hotel in the world is First World Hotel in Genting Highlands, Malaysia. It has a total of 6,118 rooms, and is part of the Genting Highlands Resort and Casino. The First World Plaza which is adjoined to the two hotel towers boasts 500,000 square feet of indoor theme park, shopping centres, casino gaming areas, and eateries. Previously, the largest hotel in the world was the MGM Grand Las Vegas in Las Vegas, Nevada, USA with 5,044 rooms in the main building and a total of 6,276 rooms.
- *Oldest:* According to the Guinness Book of World Records, the oldest hotel still in operation is the Hoshi Ryokan, in Awazu, Japan. It opened in 717 CE, and features hot springs.

HOTEL OCCUPATIONS

The owner, chairman, or CEO of a hotel or hotel group is known as a *hotelier*. The American billionaire Howard Hughes lived much of his life in hotels. He moved with his entourage from hotel to hotel and from Beverly Hills to Boston before deciding to move to Las Vegas and become a casino baron. Less than a month after his November 27, 1966 arrival, Hughes made a public offer to buy the Desert Inn. The hotel's 8th floor became the nerve center of his empire and the 9th floor penthouse became Hughes's personal residence. Hughes moved to the Bahamas, Vancouver, London and several other locations — always taking up residence in the top floor penthouse of the hotel. Between 1966 and 1968, he also purchased several other hotel-casinos from the Mafia: Castaways, New Frontier, The Landmark Hotel and Casino, Sands and Silver Slipper.

Coco Chanel made the Hôtel Ritz in Paris her home for more than thirty years, until the day of her death, at 87, in a suite now named "Coco Chanel Suite". King Peter II of Yugoslavia spent much of the Second World War at Claridge's, a hotel in London. His son, Aleksandar was born in the hotel.

Prince Felix Yusupov lived in the Hotel Vendôme in Paris. Alois Brunner, Austrian Nazi war criminal, is believed to have lived in the Meridian Hotel in Damascus, Syria, under the name Georg Fischer.

Sultan Said Bin Taimur of Muscat lived at Dorchester Hotel in London after he was deposed by Qaboos of Oman in 1970, He died in the hotel in 1972. Eleftherios Venizelos, Greek statesman and diplomat, lived in the Hôtel Ritz Paris while he was in exile in France from 1935-1936.

HISTORY OF HOSPITALITY SERVICE

In 1949, Bob Luitweiler founded the first hospitality service called Servas Open Doors as a cross national, non-profit, volunteer run organization advocating interracial and international peace. The next earliest began in 1965 when John Wilcock set up the Traveller's Directory, originally as a listing of his mutual friends willing to host each other when traveling. This later became the Hospitality Exchange in 1988 when Joy Lily rescued the organization from imminent demise. Hospitality Club is the direct successor Hospex, the first Internet-based service, operating out of Poland since 1992. It is currently the largest hospitality exchange network, growing rapidly. CouchSurfing is a newer but also rapidly growing hospitality exchange organization founded in 2004. Just as all the individual services have their own individual creation stories and organizational histories (often including demise and resurrection), many also have specific niche markets that they cater to including students, activists, religious pilgrims, and even occupational groups like police officers. However, the trend in recent years points to a greater consolidation of users in networks without a specific group, value, or lifestyle affiliation.

How They Work

In essence, these systems employ reciprocity – users gain access to other users' information only by posting their own. Required fields normally include name and contact information, though newer services encourage users to include more detailed personal material, including likes and dislikes, hopes and dreams, and even photographs. Of course, more information included tends to improve the chances that someone will find them trustworthy enough to host or stay with while traveling.

It is very much akin to online dating services. A comfortable room, good food, and a helpful staff can make being away from home an enjoyable experience for both vacationing families and business travellers. While most lodging managers work in traditional hotels and motels, some work in other lodging establishments, such as camps, inns, boardinghouses, dude ranches, and recreational resorts. In full-service hotels, lodging managers help their guests have a pleasant stay by providing many of the comforts of home, including cable television, fitness equipment, and voice mail, as well as specialized services such as health spas. For business travellers, lodging managers often schedule available meeting rooms and electronic equipment, including slide projectors and fax machines.

Lodging managers are responsible for keeping their establishments efficient and profitable. In a small establishment with a limited staff, the manager may oversee all aspects of operations. However, large hotels may employ hundreds of workers, and the general manager usually is aided by a number of assistant managers assigned to the various departments of the operation. In hotels of every size, managerial duties vary significantly by job title.

General managers have overall responsibility for the operation of the hotel. Within guidelines established by the owners of the hotel or executives of the hotel chain, the general manager sets room rates, allocates funds to departments, approves expenditures, and ensures expected standards for guest service, decor, housekeeping, food quality, and banquet operations. Managers who work for chains also may organize and staff a newly built hotel, refurbish an older hotel, or reorganize a hotel or motel that is not operating successfully. In order to fill entry-level service and clerical jobs in hotels, some managers attend career fairs.

Resident or hotel managers are responsible for the day-to-day operations of the property. In larger properties, more than one of these managers may assist the general manager, frequently dividing responsibilities between the food and beverage operations and the rooms or lodging services. At least one manager, either the general manager or a hotel manager, is on call 24 hours a day to resolve problems or emergencies.

Assistant managers help run the day-to-day operations of the hotel. In large hotels, they may be responsible for activities such as personnel, accounting, office administration, marketing and sales, purchasing, security, maintenance, and pool, spa, or recreational facilities. In smaller hotels, these duties may be combined into one position. Assistant managers may adjust charges on a hotel guest's bill when a manager is unavailable.

An Executive Committee made up of a hotel's senior managers advises the general manager, assists in setting hotel policy, coordinates services that cross departmental boundaries, and collaborates on efforts to ensure consistent and efficient guest services throughout the hotel. The Committee may be comprised of the department heads for housekeeping, front office, food and beverage, security, sales and public relations, meetings and conventions, engineering and building maintenance, and human resources. Executive committee members bring a different perspective of guest service to the total management objective reflecting the unique expertise and training of their positions. Executive housekeepers ensure that guest rooms, meeting and banquet rooms, and public areas are clean, orderly, and well maintained. They also train, schedule, and supervise the work of housekeepers, inspect rooms, and order cleaning supplies.

Front office managers coordinate reservations and room assignments, as well as train and direct the hotel's front desk staff. They ensure that guests are treated courteously, complaints and problems are resolved, and requests for special services are carried out. Front office managers may adjust charges posted on a customer's bill.

Convention services managers coordinate the activities of various departments in larger hotels to accommodate meetings, conventions, and special events. They meet with representatives of groups or organizations to plan the number of rooms to reserve, the desired configuration of the meeting space, and banquet services. During the meeting or event, they resolve unexpected problems and monitor activities to ensure that hotel operations conform to the expectations of the group.

Food and beverage managers oversee all food service operations maintained by the hotel. They coordinate menus with the Executive Chef for the hotel's restaurants, lounges, and room service operations. They supervise the ordering of food and supplies, direct service and maintenance contracts within the kitchens and dining areas, and manage food service budgets. Catering managers arrange for food service in a hotel's meeting and convention rooms. They coordinate menus and costs for banquets, parties, and events with meeting and convention planners or individual clients. They coordinate staffing needs and arrange schedules with kitchen personnel to ensure appropriate food service.

Sales or marketing directors and public relations directors oversee the advertising and promotion of hotel operations and functions, including lodging and dining specials and special events, such as holiday or seasonal specials. They direct the efforts of their staff to purchase advertising and market their property to organizations or groups seeking a venue for conferences, conventions, business meetings, trade shows, and special events. They also coordinate media relations and answer questions from the press. Human resources directors manage the personnel functions of a hotel, ensuring that all accounting, payroll, and employee relations matters are handled in compliance with hotel policy and applicable laws. They also oversee hiring practices and standards and ensure that training and promotion programmes reflect appropriate employee development guidelines. Finance (or revenue) directors monitor room sales and reservations. In addition to overseeing accounting and cash-flow matters at the hotel, they also project occupancy levels, decide which rooms to discount and when to offer rate specials.

Computers are used extensively by lodging managers and their assistants to keep track of guests' bills, reservations, room assignments, meetings, and special events. In addition, computers are used to order food, beverages, and supplies, as well as to prepare reports for hotel owners and top-level managers. Managers work with computer specialists to ensure that the hotel's computer system functions properly. Should the hotel's computer system fail, managers must continue to meet the needs of hotel guests and staff.

THE NATURE OF SERVICES

Along with the growth in services, an appreciation for the ways in which services are different from products has developed. The traditional ways of marketing tangible products are not equally effective in services marketing. In many industries, marketing involves tangible manufactured products, such as automobiles, washing machines, and clothing, whereas service industries focus on intangible products such as travel and foodservice. However, before we can explore how services get successfully marketed, we need to examine the ways services differ from products.

Nine key differences:

No ownership by customers

A customer does not take ownership when purchasing a service. There is no transfer of assets.

Service Products

The value of owning a high performance car or the latest computer lies in the physical characteristics of the product and to some extent the brand image it conveys. The value of purchasing services lies in the nature of the performance. For example, if you decide to celebrate a birthday or anniversary by dining at an expensive restaurant, the value lies in the way in which the service actors perform. When servers come to the table and present all the entrees simultaneously, the choreographed presentation appears in the same manner as a choreographed play or performance.

Involvement of Customers in the Production

Because consumers tend to be present when receiving service within a hospitality operation, they remain involved in the service production. In many instances, they are directly involved through the element of self-service. Examples of this can be seen in fast-food restaurants as well as in hotels that provide automated check-in and checkout by means of either a machine or a video connection through the television. Airlines have greatly expanded self-service within their operations as a means of reducing labour costs. In any case, the customer's level of satisfaction depends on the nature of the interaction with the service provider, the nature of the physical facilities in which the service gets provided, and the nature of the interaction with other guests present in the facility at the time the service is provided.

People as Part of the Product

People or firms that purchase services come in contact with other consumers as well as the service employees. For example, a hotel guest waits in line at the front desk or the concierge desk with other guests. In addition, the guests share facilities such as the pool, the restaurant, and the fitness center. Therefore, service firms must also manage consumer interactions to the best of their abilities to ensure customer satisfaction. For example, a hotel's sales office would not want to book group business with a nondrinking religious group at the same time as a reunion of military veterans. The two groups are significantly different in behaviour, and the expectation is that they would not mix well within the facilities at the same time. Similarly, restaurants separate smokers and nonsmokers, and they should try to separate other patrons that show some potential for conflict.

Variability in Operational Inputs and Outputs

In a manufacturing setting, the operational production can be controlled very carefully. For example, staff carefully manage inventory and precisely calculate production times. Services, however, are delivered in real time, with many variables not being fully under the control of managers. For example, if a guest has been promised an early check-in but all of the guests from the preceding night are late in checking out, it becomes more difficult for the hotel to honour the arriving guest's request.

A service setting remains a more difficult site in which to control quality and offer a consistent service experience. Service firms try to minimize the amount of variability between service encounters, but much of the final product stays situational. There are many uncontrollable aspects of the delivery process, such as weather, the number of consumers present, the attitudes of the consumers, and the attitudes of the employees. Therefore, it becomes impossible to consistently control the quality for services in the same manner as the quality of manufactured products.

Consumers to Evaluate

Consumers can receive considerable information regarding the purchase of products; however, they often do not obtain it for services. Prior to buying a product, a consumer can research the product attributes and performance and use this information when making a purchase decision, especially an important one.

No Inventories for Services

Due to the intangible nature of services, they cannot be

inventoried for future use. Therefore, a lost sale can never be recaptured. When a seat remains empty on a flight, a hotel room stays vacant, or a table stays unoccupied in a restaurant, the potential revenue for these services at that point in time becomes lost forever.

In other words, services are perishable, much like produce in a supermarket or items in a bakery. It remains critical for hospitality and tourism firms to manage supply and demand in an attempt to minimize unused capacity. For example, restaurants offer early-bird specials and airlines offer deeply discounted fares in an attempt to shift demand from peak periods to nonpeak periods, thereby increasing revenue and profits.

Importance of Time

Hospitality services are generally produced and consumed simultaneously, unlike tangible products, which are manufactured, inventoried, and then sold at a later date. Customers must be present to receive the service. There are real limits to the amount of time that customers are willing to wait to receive service. Service firms study the phenomenon of service queues, or the maximum amount of time a customer will wait for a service before it has a significant (negative) impact on his or her perception of service quality. Airline companies offer curbside check-in for the most time-conscious passengers, and restaurants have devised practices such as providing guests with pagers and expanding the bar area in order to reduce the negative effect that results from waiting for service.

Different Distribution Channels

The distribution channel for services is usually more direct than the traditional channel (i.e., manufacturer-wholesaler retailer- consumer) used by many product firms. The simultaneous production and consumption normally associated with service delivery limits the use of intermediaries. The service firm usually comprises both the manufacturer and the retailer, with no need for a wholesaler to inventory its products. Consumers are present to consume the meals prepared in a restaurant, to take advantage of the amenities in a hotel, and to travel between cities by plane.

BENEFITS

Monetary Savings

Staying in private homes means that travellers can save lots of money on accommodation that they would usually be spending on hotels or hostels. Used over a long period of time (2 to 4 weeks), this strategy can cut overall travel budgets in half, or even more combined with hitchhiking. These savings can then be passed on towards more generously patronizing local establishments or simply staying abroad for longer periods of time.

Local Economic Sustainability

Many tourist vacations today are sold in package form, often including flights, hotels, rental cars, sightseeing tours, and coupons for chain restaurants and bars. While this makes purchasing more convenient, it also puts more money in the hands of large multinational corporations exploiting the synergy strategy of marketing their products in the context of their subsidiary companies operating in other markets.

Many years ago, this might have been termed *collusion*; today, however, it is the norm. This comes at the expense of locally owned independent businesses. Accommodation sharing helps to break apart this monopoly and hopefully redirects some of the tourist revenue back to the local or national economy.

Ecological Sustainability

While this is especially important in more rural travel venues where hotels are often built in very picturesque, though fragile environments, every night stayed at a local's home means that much less demand for such hotel rooms. Also, if accommodation sharing does in fact increase the length of average stays, it may reduce the amount of trips to and from different locations and back home again, thus reducing the overall fuel expenditures in the process.

Local Contact

Ostensibly, one of the primary reasons we travel is to experience what life is like for people living in other countries. Making interpersonal connections and fostering understanding of different cultures may in the long run also be important to international relations. However, even in our increasingly globalized world supposedly rife with diversity, in many popular travel destinations we find tourists milling around "tourist enclaves" where the companies they patronize back home have set up shop to cater to their desires while they are abroad.

Sociologist George Ritzer has referred to this phenomenon as the "McDonaldisation of society" and the more recently, the "globalization of nothing". The location of hotels near these centers only fosters more convenient envelopment of the tourist dollar. During hospitality exchanges, hosts want to show off their local knowledge and exciting "off the map" venues. Not only may travellers get a distinctly different experience, but they will also get a feel for the everyday lives of local residents.

Reciprocity

These systems foster richer and more convenient travel experiences not so much on the premise of altruism, but on the basis of social exchange theory. Implicit in the agreement to host travellers is the ability to ask to be hosted by them in the future. If one enjoys having interesting guests in their home, this works out well for both parties. It works comparatively better if you are visited by travellers from a locale you find particularly attractive.

Thus, hosting someone from New York City in Gainesville, FL seems to be an unbelievable opportunity. Moreover, if you are a Westerner visiting someone in a developing nation, your stay might be the only way that this individual or family could afford a trip to a rich nation. This may mean more than just a relaxing vacation for such disadvantaged parties.

Authenticity and Adventure

Tourism has always searched for these two qualities, but much like Midas and his golden touch, the reach of tourism has to a large extent destroyed the opportunity to encounter them in most places.

Unluckily, the experience has been thoroughly commodified by everyone who wanted to secure their opportunity to make a buck in the process. Accommodation sharing offers a way out of this bind and a viable alternative to having one's desires manipulated by corporate conglomerates who never had the best interests of the place or the people foremost in their minds.

DRAWBACKS

Lack of Guarantee

There is no contractual agreement between users in these systems. Reservations are made, but if they are for some reason broken, there is no higher authority to which one could plead for a refund or other compensation. The only repercussion will be the poor rating you give that user and your only consolation will be that your warning will deter others from visiting or hosting them. For those who feel insecure unless their travel arrangements are written in stone before departure, this system will not be comforting.

Potential Interpersonal

There is a chance that guest and host will not get along. Perhaps there will be scheduling or ideological conflicts. Maybe you will find that hosts or visitors have misrepresented themselves. Perhaps the experience will not live up to your expectations.

Intense interpersonal communications in advance and a flexibility once you have arrived is your best bet. These experiences require additional planning and courtesy towards the demands of your host. Thus, your living conditions, length of stay, and overall experience will be circumscribed by the living conditions you enter into.

Demographic Segregation

The average user is a young white person who speaks English and lives in a developed nation. While there are many users who do not fit this description, the more different they are, the less likely they will be involved.

This is especially true for persons living in the developing world who likely do not have easy access to the fundamental prerequisite for using these services: computers and the Internet. Thus, the sample population found in searches of these databases are really much less diverse than a geographical representation of worldwide users might suggest.

SECURITY

There is a distinct possibility that someone will abuse the system and that innocent users (especially women) will get hurt. All services include disclaimers that require users to waive their rights to hold anyone but themselves responsible for any harm that may come to them in using the system. They advise that the best Defence mechanism is to only involve oneself with users that have extensive personal information and interpersonal networks within the system that have been verified by others. It does seem entirely plausible that someone clever and patient enough might be able to invent an entire group of complex user identities and build histories convincing enough to fool even more cautious patrons.

Still, the difference between these systems and the other social networking platforms popular nowadays on the web (such as MySpace, Tribe, Orkut, LiveJournal and Ebay) is that any agreement reached through the accommodation sharing medium is contingent on actually meeting other people face-to-face. Other web scams are easier because interpersonal interactions rely so much on putative identities that are never actually verified in the real world. However, this does not diminish the greater risk to physical well being that this kind of traveling by definition must entertain. The best advice is to meet unknown persons in public spaces first, and try to meet some of their acquaintances in person before agreeing to a hospitality exchange.

FOOD AND BEVERAGE DEPARTMENT

Because of the diversity of services provided, the food and beverage department is typically split into subunits. The executive chef, a person of considerable importance and authority in any full-service hotel, runs the food production, or kitchen, department. A variety of culinary specialists who are responsible for different aspects of food preparation report to the executive chef.

The actual serving of food in a large hotel's restaurants is usually the responsibility of a separate department, headed by the assistant food and beverage director. The food service department is composed of the individual restaurant and outlet managers, maitre d's, waiters, waitresses, and bus help.

Because of their special duties and concerns, many large hotels have a separate subunit that is responsible only for room service. Because of the high value and profit margins associated with the sale of alcoholic beverages, some hotels have a separate department that assumes responsibility for all outlets where alcoholic beverages are sold. The person responsible for this department is the beverage manager.

Most full-service hotels also do a considerable convention and catering business. The typical convention uses small function rooms for meetings and larger rooms for general sessions, trade shows, exhibits, and banquets. As a hotel or lodging business increases the use of its facilities for conventions and meetings, it may form a separate convention services department. The convention services department and its personnel are introduced to the client, a meeting planner, or an association executive by the marketing and sales department. The convention services department then handles all of the client's meeting and catering requirements.

Individually catered events include parties, wedding receptions, business meetings, and other functions held by groups. To provide for the unique needs of these types of customers, hotels often organize separate catering and convention departments. Depending on the size of the hotel, the job of cleaning the food and beverage outlets themselves as well as of washing pots and pans, dishes, glasses, and utensils is often delegated to a subunit known as the stewarding department. It is only through continuous cooperation and coordination that a hotel's food service function can be carried out effectively. A guest who is dining in a hotel restaurant requires the joint efforts of the kitchen, food service, beverage, and stewarding departments. A convention banquet cannot be held without the efforts of the convention and catering department along with the food production, beverage, and stewarding departments.

The sequence of events and cooperation required among the food and beverage staff is even more important than in the rooms department, thus increasing the importance of communication between managers and employees alike. Another challenge faced by management is the diversity of the employees in the food and beverage department; the dishwasher in the stewarding department is at a dramatically different level than the sous chef in the kitchen.

Coordination is not as important an issue in the marketing and sales department, which is generally much smaller than the food and beverage department. The primary responsibility of the sales managers who make up the marketing and sales department is sales, or the selling of the hotel facilities and services to individuals and groups. Sales managers sell rooms, food, and beverages to potential clients through advertising, attendance at association and conference meetings, and direct contacts.

The marketing and sales department is also removed from most of the day-to-day operational problems faced by other departments. The division of work among the sales managers is based on the type of customers a hotel is attempting to attract. Individual sales managers often specialize in corporate accounts, conventions, or tour and travel markets. Sales managers' accounts are sometimes subdivided along geographical lines into regional or national accounts. The sales staff of the largest full-service hotels usually does not exceed a dozen or so. These sales managers work more or less independently in their particular market segments. The human resources department serves no customers, books no business, and prepares no meals, yet it plays a vital role in a hotel's efficient operation. The three functions of the human resources department are employee recruitment, benefits administration, and training. The director of human resources is also expected to be an expert on federal and state labour laws and to advise managers in other departments on these topics. The human resources department's major challenge is in its interactions with other hotel departments.

Although the human resources department recruits, interviews, and screens prospective employees, the final hiring decision rests within the department in which the potential employee will be working. The same is true of promotion and disciplinary decisions; the human resources department's input is, in most cases, limited to advice and interpretation of legal questions. The human resources department's effectiveness depends on its manager's ability to form effective working relationships with managers of other departments. In many hotels, the accounting department combines staff functions and line functions, or those functions directly responsible for servicing guests. The accounting department's traditional role is recording financial transactions, preparing and interpreting financial statements.

6

The Industry of Food

AN OVERVIEW

The food industry is on a high as Indians continue to have a feast. Fuelled by what can be termed as a perfect ingredient for any industry - large disposable incomes - the food sector has been witnessing a marked change in consumption patterns, especially in terms of food.

CHANGE IN CONSUMPTION PATTERNS

Increasing incomes are always accompanied by a change in the food basket, says an ICRA report, which analyses food expenditure patterns over the last three decades in India. The report observes that the proportionate expenditure on cereals, pulses, edible oil, sugar, salt and spices declines as households climb the expenditure classes in urban India while the opposite happens in the case of milk and milk products, meat, egg and fish, fruits and beverages.

For instance, the proportionate expenditure on staples (cereals, grams, pulses) declined from 45 per cent to 44 per cent in rural India while the figure settled at 32 per cent of the total expenditure on food in urban India. A large part of this shift in consumption is driven by the processed food market, which accounts for 32 per cent of the total food market. It accounts for US$ 29.4 billion, in a total estimated market of US$ 91.66 billion.

The food processing industry is one of the largest industries in India — it is ranked fifth in terms of production, consumption, export and expected growth. The Confederation of Indian Industry (CII) has estimated that the food processing sector has the potential of attracting US$ 33 billion of investment in 10 years and generate employment of 9 million person-days.

Policy Initiatives

The Government has formulated and implemented several schemes to provide financial assistance for setting up and modernising of food processing units, creation of infrastructure, support for research and development and human resource development in addition to other promotional measures to encourage the growth of the processed food sector.

- The Centre has permitted under the Income Tax Act a deduction of 100 per cent of profit for five years and 25 per cent of profit in the next five years in case of new agro processing industries set up to package and preserve fruits and vegetables.
- Excise Duty of 16 per cent on dairy machinery has been fully waived off and excise duty on meat, poultry and fish products has been reduced from 16 per cent to 8 per cent.
- Most of the processed food items have been exempted from the purview of licensing under the Industries (Development and regulation) Act, 1951, except items reserved for small-scale sector and alcoholic beverages.
- Food processing industries were included in the list of priority sector for bank lending in 1999.
- Automatic approval for foreign equity up to 100 per cent is available for most of the processed food items except alcohol, beer and those reserved for small-scale sector subject to certain conditions.

Foreign Direct Investment

- Foreign direct investment (FDI) in the country's food sector is poised to hit the US$ 3-billion mark. In the last one year alone, FDI approvals in food processing have doubled.

- The cumulative FDI inflow in food processing reached US$ 2,804 million in March '06. In '05-06, the sector received approvals worth US$ 41 million. This figure is almost double the US$ 22 million approved in '04-05.

Ready-to-eat food

The popularity of ready-to-eat packs and the bottomlines of eateries have a story to tell. Eating out no longer marks a special occasion. Not only does the traditional eat-at-home type prefer to eat out, he is very demanding too. He wants value for his money in terms of quality and variety. No wonder, multi-cuisine restaurants are mushrooming even in small towns. Italian, Mexican, Lebanese, Japanese, Cajun – the list is growing.

Corroborating this trend, Euromonitor International, a market research company, says the amount of money Indians spend on meals outside the home has more than doubled in the past decade, to about US$ 5 billion a year and is expected to double again in about half that time. The industry is estimated to grow at 9-12 per cent, on the basis of an estimated GDP growth rate of 6-8 per cent, during the tenth five-year plan period. Value addition of food products is expected to increase from the current 8 per cent to 35 per cent by the end of 2025. Fruit and vegetable processing, which is currently around 2 per cent of total production will increase to 10 per cent by 2010 and to 25 per cent by 2025.

The popularity of food and agro products is not surprising when the sector is now offering a growth of more than 150 per cent in sales. With such promise in the sector, a number of foreign companies have joined the fray. While US brands such as McDonald's, Pizza Hut and Kentucky Fried Chicken have become household names, more are on their way. The new wave in the food industry is not only about foreign companies arriving here attracted by the prospective size of the market. It is also about the migration of the Made in India tag on food products travelling abroad. Indian food brands and fast moving consumer goods (FMCGs) are now increasingly finding prime shelf-space in the retail chains of the US and

Europe. These include Cobra Beer, Bikanervala Foods, MTR Foods' ready-to-eat food stuff, ITC's Kitchen of India and Satnam Overseas' Basmati rice.

FOOD SCIENCE

Food science is a discipline concerned with all technical aspects of food, beginning with harvesting or slaughtering, and ending with its cooking and consumption. It is considered one of the agricultural sciences, and is usually considered distinct from the field of nutrition.

Examples of the activities of food scientists include the development of new food products, design of processes to produce these foods, choice of packaging materials, shelf-life studies, sensory evaluation of the product with trained expert panels or potential consumers, as well as microbiological and chemical testing.

Food scientists at universities may study more fundamental phenomena that are directly linked to the production of particular food product and its properties. In the U.S., food science is typically studied at land-grant universities. Food science is a highly interdisciplinary applied science. It incorporates concepts from many different fields including microbiology, chemical engineering, biochemistry, and many others.

FOOD PRESERVATION

Food preservation is the process of treating and handling food in such a way as to stop or greatly slow down spoilage to prevent foodborne illness while maintaining nutritional value, texture and flavour.

Preservation Processes

Preservation usually involves preventing the growth of bacteria, fungi and other micro-organisms, as well as retarding the oxidation of fats which cause rancidity. It also includes processes to inhibit natural aging and discolouration that can occur during food preparation such as the polyphenoloxidase reaction in apples which causes browning when apples are cut.

Some preservation methods require the food to be sealed after treatment to prevent re-contamination with microbes; others, such as drying, allow food to be stored without any special containment for long periods.

- Preservation processes include:
- Heating to kill or denature organisms (e.g. boiling)
- Oxidation (e.g use of sulphur dioxide)
- Toxic inhibition (e.g. smoking, use of carbon dioxide, vinegar, alcohol etc)
- Dehydration (drying)
- Osmotic Inhibition (e.g use of Syrups)
- Low temperature inactivation (e.g. freezing)

Many Combinations of these Methods

- *Chelation:* Common methods of applying these processes include drying, freeze drying, freezing, vacuum-packing, canning, preserving in syrup, sugar crystalisation, food irradiation, adding preservatives or inert gases such as carbon dioxide. Other methods that not only help to preserve food, but also add flavour, include pickling, salting, smoking, preserving in syrup or alcohol, sugar crystalisation and curing.
- *Drying:* One of the oldest methods of food preservation is by drying, which reduces water activity sufficient to delay or prevent bacterial growth. Most types of meat can be dried and this is especially valuable in the case of pig meat since this is difficult to keep without preservation. Many fruits can also be dried and the process is often applied to apples, pears, bananas, mangos, papaya, coconut etc. Currants, sultanas and raisins are all forms of dried Grapes. Drying is also the normal means of preservation for cereal grains such as wheat, maize, oats, barley, rice, millet and rye.
- *Freezing:* Probably as old as drying, many Arctic communities would preserve food in holes or larders dug into the ice. There is a tradition in Scandinavia of preserving fish and especially herrings in this way.

- Freezing is also one of the most commonly used processes commercially and domestically for preserving a very wide range of food stuffs including prepared food stuffs which would not have required freezing in their unprepared state. For example, potato waffles are stored in the freezer, but potatoes themselves require only a cool dark place to ensure many months' storage. Cold stores provide large volume, long-term storage for strategic food stocks held in case of national emergency in many countries.
- *Vacuum Packing:* Vacuum-packing stores food in a vacuum environment, usually in an air-tight bag or bottle. The vacuum environment strips bacteria of oxygen needed for survival, hence preventing the food from spoiling. Vacuum-packing is commonly used for storing nuts.
- *Curing:* Curing draws moisture from the meat through a process of osmosis. Meat is cured with salt or sugar, or a combination of the two. Nitrates and nitrites are also often used to cure meat.
- *Sugar:* Sugar is used to preserve fruits, either in syrup with fruit such as apples, pears, peaches, apricots, plums or in crystalised form where the preserved material is cooked in sugar to the point of crystralisation and the resultant product is then stored dry. This method is used for the skins of citrus fruit (candied peel), angelica and ginger. A modification of this process produces glacé fruit such as glacé cherries where the fruit is preserved in sugar but is then extracted from the syrup and sold, the preservation being maintained by the sugar content of the fruit and the superficial coating of syrup. The use of sugar is often combined with alcohol for preservation of luxury products such as fruit in brandy or other spirits. These should not be confused with fruit flavoured spirits such as Cherry Brandy or Sloe gin

PICKLING

Pickling is a method of preserving food by placing it or

companies such as Nestlé, Heinz, and others emerged to provide shops with good-quality tinned food for sale to ordinary working class city-dwellers.

Demand for tinned food skyrocketed during the First World War, as military commanders searched for cheap, high-calorie food which could be transported safely, would survive trench conditions, and which would not spoil in between the factory and the front lines. Complete meals in a tin appeared in 1916, but throughout the war soldiers generally subsisted on very low-quality tinned foodstuffs, such as the British "Bully Beef" (cheap corned beef) and Pork and Beans produced by the MacConnaughy Corporation.

Shortages of tinned food in the British Army in 1917 led to the government issuing soldiers with cigarettes and even amphetamines to suppress their appetites. After the war, companies that had supplied tinned food to national militaries improved the quality of their goods for sale on the civilian market. Canned foods were soon commonplace, and today tin-coated steel is the material most commonly used. Some food firms are currently dabbling with self-heating cans. Laminate vacuum pouches are also now used for canning, such as those found in an MRE.

JELLYING

Food may be preserved by cooking in a material that solidifies to form a gel. Such materials include gelatine, agar, maize flour and arrowroot flour. Some foods naturally form a protein gel when cooked such as eels and elvers, and sipunculid worms which are a delicacy in the town of Xiamen in Fujian province of China. Jellied eels are a delicacy in the East End of London where they are eaten with mashed potatoes. Potted meats in aspic, (the gel made from arrowroot flour) were a common way of serving meat off-cuts in the UK until the 1950s

Irradiation

A 1950s issue of Popular Mechanics details the impending arrival of "food irradiation". But the implications of irradiation are not fully understood, and the use of the technology is limited. Irradiation of potatoes, strawberries, and meat is common in many countries where refrigerated facilities and trucks are not. In 2002, the FDA permitted irradiation of meat and poultry to reduce the spread of E. coli and salmonella.

In the US and most of Europe, irradiation of spices is common, as the only alternative (treatment with gas) is potentially carcinogenic. The process is called "cold pasteurization" because it is feared that the label "irradiation" would hurt sales. Foods may also carry labels saying "Picowaved For Your Protection" as food processors may not want to openly label their foods as being irradiated.

MODIFIED ATMOSPHERE

Modified atmosphere is a way to preserve food operating on the atmosphere around it. Salad crops which are notoriously difficult to preserve are now being packaged in sealed bags with an atmosphere modified to reduce the oxygen concentration and increase the carbon dioxide concentration. There is concern that although salad vegetables retain their appearance and texture in such conditions, this method of preservation may not retain nutrients, especially vitamins.

Grains may be preserved using carbon dioxide. A block of dry ice is placed in the bottom and the can is filled with grain. The can is then "burped" of excess gas. The carbon dioxide from the sublimation of the dry ice prevents insects, mold, and oxidation from damaging the grain. Grain stored in this way can remain edible for five years.

CLAMPS

Many root vegetables are very resistant to spoilage and require no other preservation other than storage in cool dark conditions, usually in field clamps. Some foods, such as many traditional cheeses, will keep for a long time without use of any special procedures. The preservation occurs because of the presence in very high numbers of beneficial bacteria or fungi which use their own biological defences to prevent other organisms gaining a foot-hold.

FOOD PARKS

In a bid to boost the food sector, the Government is working on agrizones and the concept of mega food parks. Twenty such mega parks will come up across the country in various cities to attract Foreign Direct Investment (FDI) in the food processing sector.

The Government has released a total assistance of US$ 23 million to implement the Food Parks Scheme. It has so far approved 50 food parks for assistance across the country. The Centre also plans US$ 22 billion subsidy for mega food processing parks.

FOOD PRESERVATION TECHNIQUE

Preserving food to extend its shelf-life, whilst ensuring its safety and quality, is a central preoccupation of the food industry. As a result, there has been a steady stream of new 'minimal' preservation techniques. At the same time, the development of the hurdle concept has led to renewed interest in the use of more traditional preservation methods and the ways they can be combined with newer technologies. With its distinguished editors and international team of contributors, Food preservation techniques provides an authoritative review of these developments and the ways they can be combined to preserve particular foods.

- *Part 1:* begins by looking at the emergence of a new generation of natural preservatives in response to consumer concerns about synthetic additives. There are chapters on natural antimicrobials, bacteriocins, natural antimicrobials, antimicrobial enzymes and edible coatings, together with a discussion of how natural antimicrobial systems can be combined with other technologies.
- *Part 2:* considers current research on the application of traditional preservation techniques. There are chapters on the control of pH and water activity to prevent microbial growth, and developments in heat treatment and freezing. These are complemented by discussion of how these techniques can be combined

with each other and newer technologies to extend shelf-life without compromising safety or quality.

- *Part 3:* covers these newer technologies. It includes chapters on the use of biotechnology, developments in membrane filtration, high intensity light, ultrasound, modified atmosphere packaging, pulsed electric fields and high hydrostatic pressure.
- *Part 4:* considers the challenges in combining these techniques in a way that preserves sensory quality without compromising product safety. There are chapters on key issues such as modelling spoilage and the effectiveness of preservation techniques, the increasingly important problem of microbial resistance to the use of milder preservation methods, and setting safety criteria to account for such problems.

Food preservation techniques will be a standard reference in helping food processors extend shelf-life whilst maximising food safety and quality.

FOOD AND LIVESTOCK TREACHEBILITY

Recent devastating outbreaks such as foot and mouth disease, mad cow disease and avian flu plus contamination recalls and bioterrorism are driving strict new legislation on food traceability. In addition, consumers are also demanding more information about the food they consume (as do the police and customs).

This report analyses the need for RFID, DNA and other technologies to enable food traceability. Ten year forecasts, case studies and technology evaluations provide a complete analysis on the topic in this 250 page market intelligence report researched globally by our experts.

Traceability has become a buzzword in the food industry. Consumer demands for higher-quality foods and more variety have never been greater. Spurred on by recent food scares around the world, such as mad cow disease and bioterrorism fears, governments are forcing the adoption of food traceability systems. Everyone from producer to retailer will be affected by food traceability. This state-of-the-art review deals with the key topics of traceability - technology, law, forecasts and case studies. A must read for anyone involved in the food industry.

Although tens of millions of RFID tags have been applied to livestock and food and millions of biometric procedures have been carried out, there is no analysis of the global situation and the lessons of success and failure. The potential for RFID tagging of livestock is billions yearly and the potential for radio tagging of food is in trillions a year, but what are the forecasts for such tagging at animal, pallet/case and item level for the next ten years? Which countries are in the lead and where will the next wave of technologies, laws and mandates be applied? These and other vital questions are answered for the first time in this major new report.

This industry is on the move in a major way. It includes market pull, with McDonald's the world's largest outlet for cooked meat recently mandating full traceability from suppliers and Wal-Mart, the world's largest retailer, mandating RFID on all incoming pallets and cases. This is a prelude to tagging everything. It has legal push with the new European Union legislation in 2005 demanding "one up one down" traceability and the US Homeland Security legislation demanding unprecedented levels of traceability. China and Japan are also in the lead, and they have their own concerns. For example, Japan is convicting criminals that pass off inferior foreign fish as coming from Japanese waters.

Billion dollar businesses will be created as a consequence - much the same as happened with barcodes years ago. We believe that by 2015 900 billion food items could be RFID tagged, and 824 million livestock will have more sophisticated, more expensive tags on or in them. However, new technologies, now being developed, will be needed for the food items. The livestock figure could easily be doubled if chickens are tagged, something of vital interest to the Government of Thailand, which ships 400 million chicken carcasses yearly and could have its whole industry wiped out by the new, virulent avian flu. The safety of poultry meat and eggs continues to be a major concern for consumers. As a result, there has been a wealth of research on identifying and controlling hazards at all stages in the supply chain. "Food Safety Control in the Poultry Industry" summarises this research and its implications for all those involved in supplying and marketing poultry products. With its distinguished editor and international team of contributors, "Food Safety Control in the Poultry Industry" will be a standard reference for both academics and food companies.

RUSIAN FOOD PRODUCTION

Russia's food production is forecast to grow across the board over the next couple of years thanks to better buying power and import regulations, according to a government report. The Russian Ministry of Economic Development predicted domestic food production will have more than doubled by 2008, compared with levels in 2004.

Russia's food industry is already the country's biggest sector outside of heavy industry, including energy and steel. Some of the fastest development is expected in the dairy industry, thanks to the government's predicted rise in raw milk stocks and both domestic and foreign investment in cheese. Cheese market growth, currently around eight per cent per year, is forecast to slow to around five per cent by 2008. Imports should remain strong in the premium segment for the time being, the government said.

Meat and animal fat production are other areas forecast for good growth. The government expects there to be double-digit rises in meat production annually up to 2008, while manufacture of fish products, including fish preservatives, is expected to double. Sceptics argue that Russia has been playing with protectionism via import bans. It has banned various food products, including most recently fresh fish from Norway and dairy and meat from Ukraine, on food safety grounds.

The Russian government has said it wants average meat consumption to reach 70kg per person in Russia, and is actively promoting domestic producers to help achieve this. Current consumption is around 50-55kg. One of Russia's biggest meat import firms, Euroservice, will begin building ten new meat processing factories for Russian meat this year to help satisfy consumers' growing demand for meat, and especially sausage. The short-term results of Russia's import bans may be price increases on the market, however.

The United States Department of Agriculture's Foreign Agricultural Service said between January and October 2005 Russia imported €165m worth of fresh salmon from Norway. Russian fish processors, it claimed, now feared chilled salmon would quickly disappear from the shelves, causing a potential increase in frozen fish prices of 20-30 per cent.

UK FOOD REGULATOR

Food fraud can result in processors receiving illegally sourced meat that may be of low quality or even unfit for human consumption, posing a health risk for consumers and a business problem for manufacturers. Such trade cuts into the sales of legitimate food producers by placing cheaper products on the market. Adulterated butter, buffalo meat declared as beef, tigernuts imported as flower bulbs are some of the products that have been stopped at the EU's borders.

A task force on the issue was set up by the Food Standards Agency (FSA) board in April 2006 to initially concentrate on red and white meat fraud, but it will consider other food sector problems later in the process of making recommendations for action. The group of experts were also asked to propose sufficient legal deterrents to make it less attractive for individuals and companies to engage in food fraud.

The food fraud task force (FFTF) was launched in the wake of the FSA investigation into Euro Freeze, a Northern Ireland cold store operation that allegedly was involved in the illicit repackaging, re-labelling and distribution of meat throughout the EU. In August this year, a UK court condemned the meat from Euro Freeze as having illegal health labeling and ordered the destruction of 254 pallets.

In the first of three planned reports to the board, to be presented at the meeting on 7 December, the task force said it has not discovered to date any issues that need early action and at this time it has no recommendations.

- "At this stage in their deliberations, the Food Fraud Task Force are of the opinion that the current measures for tackling food fraud are largely adequate but may be augmented by recommendations taking into account the findings contained within this paper," the report stated.

And as the Euro-Freeze case is still before the courts, the task force has not had the full details for detailed consideration.

- " However it is hoped that before the final report of the FFTF is made in October 2007, the details will be accessible and any lessons learned from this event can be considered and commented on," the unit's first report stated as released ahead of the board meeting.

However members have identified some areas for further consideration by the board, including the problem of the possible re-use of health markings.

The FFTF says its recognises that the movement of meat and poultry no longer intended for human consumption may occur in the same premises as those used for foods. Such a situation may occur when products materials become outdated.

- "In order to prevent any possible confusion and the possibility of food moving back to human food areas, it is suggested that once moved into animal by-product areas, all food containers should have their identification marks defaced or destroyed in order to prevent any re-use of the material or containers for human food," the report stated.

In an update for an FSA board meeting on 12 October, the task force recommended that current legislation and traceability procedures need to be reviewed. The task force has also said it would consider the current controls in place to deal with food fraud and their, suitability to control and deter food fraud. The review includes a review of health marking requirements. The task force will also review inspection and audit arrangements for meat plants particularly cold stores.

It will also consider whether inspections should be made more frequent so as to assess food fraud risk. It will also review of the roles and effectiveness of the Illegal Meat Task Force, the food fraud data base and the FSA's local authorities. Laws relating to the prosecution and penalties will also be reviewed to see whether they act as a sufficient deterrent to food fraud. The members of the task force include those representing regulators, government agencies, the British Retail Consortium, the British Poultry Council, the Food and Drink Federation, consumer group Which?, and the Dungannon Meats Group.

EU laws on traceability that entered into force on 1 January 2005. The laws harmonises the bloc's requirements on the traceability of food products, the withdrawal of dangerous products from the market, operator responsibilities and requirements applicable to imports and exports. The new mandatory traceability requirement applies to all food, animal feed, food-producing animals and all types of food chain operators from the farming sector to processing, transport, storage, distribution and retail to the consumer.

All information on the name, address of producer, nature of products and date of transaction must be systematically registered within each operator's traceability system. The law requires the information to be kept for a period of five years and on request, it must immediately be made available to regulators. EU customs seized around 75 million counterfeit articles in 2005. Growth in seizures of fakes dangerous to health and safety also continued. For the first time, the number counterfeit foodstuff, drinks and alcohol products seized at the borders surpassed the five million market.

FOOD IN AMERICA

It was not the last time cannibalism would be resorted to in America. Later Virginians wanted to grow a profitable crop; they tried sugar but the climate was too cold. They settled on tobacco. Soon tobacco was bringing in so much money that people planted it on any available land—they ripped up their gardens, even grew it between graves. But who would hoe and harvest these thousands of acres of tobacco? The Native Americans who didn't die of Old World diseases refused to do it. African slaves were too expensive, although some arrived in 1619. England had the perfect Labour force: a surplus of poor, desperate young men in their late teens and early twenties. They signed an indenture— a contract—giving them a free trip to America and free room and board in exchange for four to six years of work.

Then they were supposed to get their freedom, tools, corn, and land of their own—something they had zero chance of getting in England. The person who hired the indentured servant and paid for his trip received free Labour and fifty acres of land. It was a sweetheart deal all around. Most of these young men didn't live four years after they got to America. They died from dysentery, typhoid, malaria. The ones who did live found that there was only one woman for every six men. And soon the best land was in huge plantations owned by a few wealthy men who also had all the political power.

In 1676, when former indentured servants couldn't get land, women, or the vote, they went on a rampage. Bacon's Rebellion ended with Jamestown burned and more than 20 former indentured servants hanged. Planters wanted a Labour force they could control, not these Englishmen who used violence to get their rights. In 1698, when England ended the Royal African Company's monopoly on the slave trade, anyone with a ship could get into the slave trade. With competition, the price of slaves dropped. Now it was affordable to own Africans and profitable to sell them.

THE CAROLINAS AND RICE

At about the same time, the English established a colony south of Virginia—Carolina, named after King Charles II. Many of the settlers were from Barbados. They intended to grow food for the Caribbean sugar plantations and to export more expensive items, but after failing at wine, olive oil, and silk, they decided on rice as their staple crop. Rice requires skilled Labour; Africans had this skill. They were also immune to malaria, and weren't Christian, so according to the Christian world at that time, they could be enslaved for the rest of their lives. The settlers also imported the Barbados slave code, with punishments that escalated from whipping to facial mutilation and sometimes death, which the code said was the slave's fault for forcing his master to discipline him. Charleston, South Carolina, became the primary port through which slaves entered the United States. By 1710, black slaves outnumbered white settlers in the coastal regions of the area that became South Carolina.

In spite of the conditions under which the slaves were brought to America, some of their African cuisine and culture survived. This influenced how cooking developed in the American South, since they were the cooks. Along with their knowledge of rice cultivation, cooking, and storage, they brought yams, okra, watermelon, and their love of fried food. They also brought back foodstuffs that had been taken from the New World to Africa, like the chile pepper and the peanut, and their word for it—*goober.*

They brought the banjo and the drum and the music that would become jazz. New England:" Almost Beyond Believing" In 1620, Pilgrims—Protestants who wanted to be allowed to worship without being persecuted—landed at Plymouth, Massachusetts. Before they went ashore, the men on the ship entered into an agreement. The Mayflower Compact was the first constitution in America. Only one paragraph long, it sets forth an important principle: that all would be equal and work together as a community. The Pilgrims, and the Puritans who settled the Massachusetts Bay Colony in Boston ten years later, had their work cut out for them.

These were people used to living in towns. They didn't know how to hunt or fish or farm. But they didn't like many of the strange plants and animals in North America anyway—those huge quahog clams, the slimy steamers. And the codfish and lobsters were bigger than they were, sometimes six feet long. They wouldn't eat them at first, even after the Indians showed them how. But with the help of the native tribes, the Pilgrims survived their first year and had a celebration. Thanksgiving Foods "The turkey is certainly one of the most delightful presents which the New World has made to the Old." Most of the foods Americans eat at Thanks giving dinner now are native to the Americas: turkey, cranberry sauce, mashed potatoes, sweet potatoes, corn-bread stuffing, pumpkin pie. In French the word for turkey is *dinde,* short for *poulet d'inde,* which means "chicken from India," because the French, like other Europeans, thought the turkey was from the Indies. Geese, ducks, and other wild fowl were abundant only during certain seasons in the New World, but turkeys don't migrate, so they were available all year. And they had an instinct that helped humans: when one turkey was shot, the others froze in place. It was easy to kill a dozen turkeys in a morning. Nobody ever called anybody a turkey and meant it as a compliment.

Cranberries and blueberries, both members of the heather family and both native to New England, were more than food in sauce and pies. Mashed and mixed with sour milk, they were used as paint. That is why the colours most often associated with colonial American buildings are muted cranberry and milky purple-gray. Although pumpkin was widely used in the colonies, recipes for pumpkin pie didn't appear in print until the first American cookbook, written by Amelia Simmons in 1796. She called it "pompkin" and gave two different versions. Both had pumpkin, ginger, and eggs, but one used cream and sugar, the other milk and molasses. One used the Old World spices mace and nutmeg, the other New World allspice.

THE CODFISH

The staple "crop" in the Massachusetts Bay Colony was the codfish, *Gadus morhua.* What sugar was to the Caribbean and tobacco was to the FOOD FABLE c SQUANTO AND FISH FERTILIZERC Contrary to what American myth has long held, it is quite unlikely that alewives or other fish were uses as fertilizer in Indian fields, notwithstanding the legendary role of the Pilgrims' friend Squanto in teaching colonists this practice. Squanto probably learned the technique while being held captive in Europe, and if any Indians used it in New England, they did so in an extremely limited area. Having no easy way to transport large amounts of fish from river to field, and preferring quite sensibly to avoid such back-breaking work, Indians simply abandoned their fields when the soil lost its fertility. Fertilizing fields with fish, as the English eventually did, seemed to Indians a wholly unnecessary labour.

CHESAPEAKE, COD WAS TO MASSACHUSETTS

There were millions off the coast, north to Newfoundland and Labrador. Once it was salted and dried, cod was stiff as a board and could be stacked and shipped like lumber. It was also almost 80 per cent protein. In this form it made its way to Europe: *bacalà* in Italy, *bacalao* in Spain, *bacalhau* in Portugal. According to historian Mark Kurlansky, by the middle of the 16th century, "60 per cent of all fish eaten in Europe was cod." It was the perfect food for Lent. The best grade was sent to Spain; the worst fed the slaves in the West Indies. It could also be bartered for slaves in Africa. Shipbuilders got rich because of cod, too. The cod was so important to the economy of Massachusetts that a large carved wooden cod hangs in the statehouse in Boston. Fifty-one Pilgrim men, women, and children hosted ninety men of the Wampanoag tribe and their chief, Massasoit. It was in the fall, to celebrate the good harvest of corn (wheat and barley weren't as successful).

The celebration lasted three days. There were "wild fowl" and five deer. The idea of a national day of thanks was raised in the late 1700s with the first president, George Washington, who proposed November 26 as the date. Nothing came of it until the 1850s, when magazine journalist Sarah Josepha Hale rallied the women of America to pressure the president for a national holiday. In 1863, the third year of the Civil War, President Lincoln declared that the last Thursday in November should be a day of giving thanks. It was the same year that Lincoln issued the Emancipation Proclamation freeing the slaves, and made his speech at the battlefield in Gettysburg, Pennsylvania, in which he said these famous words: "that government of the people, by the people, for the people, shall not perish from the earth."

In 1939, President Franklin D. Roosevelt wanted to extend the Christmas shopping season to give the economy a boost and help it recover from the depression. He moved Thanksgiving one week earlier. Congress objected. The president and Congress did a tug-of-war over the date until 1941, when it was settled: Thanksgiving is the fourth Thursday in November. In 1970, Wampanoag leader Wampsutta (Anglo name: Frank James) was invited to speak at the Thanksgiving celebration at Plymouth, Massachusetts. When word got out that his speech was about the oppression of Native Americans, the invitation was revoked. He gave his speech anyway, in front of the statue of Massasoit, overlooking the replica of the *Mayflower*. That was the first Native American National Day of Mourning for the culture, the religion, and the lives and lands of their ancestors. Maple Syrup: Tapping the Sap of the Sugar Tree "Maple Moon" was what Native Americans called the time in the spring when the sap started to flow in the sugar maple tree, *Acer saccharum*.

Just as the grapevine was a symbol of resurrection for the ancient Greeks, so the maple was for Native Americans. Flowing sap meant the end of winter and the rebirth of nature. The Iroquois performed a religious ritual, a maple dance, to pray for warm weather and plenty of sap. According to legend, an Iroquois chief pulled his tomahawk out of a tree where he had thrown it the night before and went off to hunt. In the meantime, the weather turned warm and sap oozed into a container left by accident at the base of the tree.

On her way to get water for cooking, his wife saw the container of liquid and used that instead; everyone agreed it was much better than water.8 Seventeenth-century European writers give Native Americans full credit for knowing how to make maple syrup and sugar, but in the 18th century, Europeans started to claim that they taught the Indians. As historians Helen and Scott Nearing have pointed out, language is on the side of the tribes. All their words for maple syrup translate as "drawn from wood," "sap flows fast," "our own tree," while they called white sugar "French snow"—a clear indication of its origin.

Maple sugar was a primary food in Native American cooking; among some tribes it was the only condiment. It replaced salt, which they did not like, and it was used to season dried cornmeal porridge, mixed with bear fat as a sauce for roasted venison, sprinkled on boiled fish, and eaten with berries or all by itself, a pound a day. It was reconstituted into a sweet drink that was used in ceremonies, along with tobacco smoked in the peace pipe. Women boiled the sap from maple, walnut, hickory, box elder, butternut, birch, and sycamore trees down to sugar crystals, which was difficult because before Europeans came, they had no metal pots.

Their vessels were made of birch bark or gourds which held between one and two gallons and could not be placed directly over fire. Instead, they dropped heated stones into the liquid until it boiled, which involved continuously taking out cool stones and replacing them with hot ones. These small amounts of liquid were then poured into hundred-gallon moose-skin vats.

It is not surprising that the Indians began to trade for metal pots and utensils as soon as the Europeans introduced them. Another way to process the syrup was to let it freeze at night, then scrape the ice off the top. This required several nights until just syrup was left. Maple sugar that was to be used for gifts was poured into molds that one European described as shaped like "bear's paws, flowers, stars, small animals, and other figures, just like our gingerbread-bakers at fairs." The American Culinary Tradition: Pocket Soup and Johnnycake American cooking developed along two parallel lines. In the South, where slave Labour did the kitchen work, cooking could take more time.

Labour-intensive cooking, such as barbecue, could be done by slaves. Barbecue needed a great deal of preparation. Either beef or pork had to be properly butchered and marinated. Then the fire had to reach just the right temperature, and the meat had to be added. The fire had to be carefully watched and the temperature maintained. This required a great deal of Labour. However, pit cooking developed differently in New England, in the form of the clambake. There, a fire was allowed to burn down in a pit; then clams, lobsters, and corn were buried under wet seaweed and left to steam for several hours. No Labour was necessary to prepare the food before or after it was placed in the pit, except to dig it out. American cooking in the North arose from the middle-class necessity of doing a great deal of work as quickly as possible. They invented shortcuts and new ways to preserve foods. Two examples are pocket soup and johnnycake. Travel was not easy in the colonies. Roads were poor or nonexistent, and there was no guarantee that travellers would be able to find food when they needed it. Sailors, too, appreciated a bit of home. Pocket soup, also known as portable soup, was the solution.

This was an early bouillon cube—soup cooked down until it was a condensed gelatinous mass, then cut into small cubes and dried for ten days. Dropped into a cup of water, it reconstituted into soup. Johnnycake or journey cake was a cornmeal cake that would keep without becoming moldy or disintegrating. Another example of New England fast food was hasty pudding, made famous in the song "Yankee Doodle" (and in the name of a Harvard University club).

This was cornmeal—called Indian or "Injun" meal—or rye meal cooked on top of the stove, not baked, so it was ready in half an hour. This is a long time by today's microwave standards, but the baking times for regular cornmeal pudding recipes in *American Cookery* range from one and a half hours to two and a half hours. Sara Josepha Hale's recipes for cornmeal pudding require three to four hours of cooking, even those that are boiled. What makes hasty pudding hasty is that the meal is soaked first and added a bit at a time, and the pudding is boiled and stirred constantly. In this cooking technique, it resembles polenta. Cobbler, Slump, Grunt, Dumpling, Crumble, and Crisp Just as regional cooking developed according to the kind of produce and Labour available in each area, different areas had different names for the same food.

For example, in most of the country, a cobbler is chopped, sweetened fruit with a sweet biscuit dough baked on top. The exception is New England, where it is called a slump, with the further exception of Cape Cod, where it is called a grunt.

Other combinations of fruit and dough are a dumpling, pieces of fruit or a whole fruit, like an apple, wrapped in a pastry square and baked. A crumble is a mixture of flour, butter, sugar, and seasonings like cinnamon and nutmeg crumbled over chopped fruit and then baked.

A crumble is different from a crisp because a crisp has more butter, which makes the topping crisper. The topping on a crisp sometimes includes oats. Brown Betty, Sally Lunn, and Anadama Women, perhaps cooks, have left their names on various foods but not much other information.Brown Betty is a thrifty New England BUONA FORCHETTA'S ANA DAMA BREAD 1 large or 2 small loaves 2 cups water 11D 2 teaspoons salt 1D 2 cup stone-ground yellow cornmeal 3 tablespoons melted unsalted butter or olive oil 1D 4 cup honey or dark molasses 2 tablespoons active dry yeast 1D 2 cup lukewarm water (85º to 95ºF) 5 to 6 cups unbleached bread flour In a large pot, bring the water and salt to a boil over medium-high heat.

With a wire whisk, slowly stir the cornmeal into the water, making sure it does not lump. When it has thickened, remove it from the heat and stir in oil or butter and honey or molasses. Transfer to a large mixing bowl and let cool completely. Dissolve the yeast in the lukewarm water. Stir into the cornmeal mixture. Stir in the flour, a cup or so at a time, mixing well as you go to incorporate it. This will form a firm dough that should not be too dry. When the dough pulls away from the sides of the bowl, stir well a few more times, rub oil on your hands, and transfer the dough to a clean oiled bowl.

Same-day method: Cover the bowl with plastic wrap and let the dough rise in a warm place until doubled in volume, about 1 hour. Proceed with the shaping instructions. *Overnight method:* Cover the bowl and refrigerate overnight. The dough will rise in the refrigerator and acquire flavour from the slower yeast action. Remove the dough 3 hours before shaping and let stand, covered, in a warm place. Proceed with shaping instructions. *To shape into loaves:* Preheat the oven to 500ºF. Oil one seasoned nonstick, ovenproof 9-inch skillet or two 5-inch skillets. Shape the dough into 1 large or 2 small round loaves.

Place the loaf or loaves in the oiled pan or pans and let rise for about 40 minutes or until doubled. Brush the tops of the loaves with olive oil, if desired.

TO BAKE LOAVES

Place the bread in the oven and reduce the oven temperature to 400ºF. Bake for about 40 minutes or until nicely browned and loaf sounds hollow when tapped with your finger. Remove the loaf from a pan and cool on a wire rack. dessert that layers leftover bread with fruit, usually apples, and is baked. It isn't a bread pudding because it lacks eggs to make the custard binder. Sally Lunn is a very light, yeast-risen egg bread. Anadama is supposedly named after Anna, who kept cooking only one thing— a cornmeal and molasses bread—until her husband finally burst out, "Anna, damn her!" Suzanne Dunaway's Buona Forchetta Bakery in southern California makes an updated version of this bread.

BEER A GOOD FAMILY DRINK

As food historian John Hull Brown points out in *Early American Beverages*, men, women, and children in colonial America drank alcoholic beverages. Beer, familiar from England, was the earliest drink in the colonies. Women were the brewers; they made beer from nearly anything that grew. They made vegetable beers from corn, tomatoes, potatoes, turnips, pumpkins, and Jerusalem artichokes. They made tree beers from the bark of birch, spruce, and sassafras, and from maple sap. Fruit-based beers were brewed from persimmons, lemons, and raisins.

There were herb beers using wintergreen, and spice beers made of ginger, allspice, and cinnamon. Even flowers became beer: rose beer. There was molasses beer. They made their ale two barrels at a time, from 8 or 9 bushels of malt, 12 pounds of hops, 5 quarts of yeast, and 72 gallons of water. And, of course, just as in ancient Egypt, once they had beer they had leavening for bread, either from the beer itself or from the "leavins"—the dregs. They also distilled "spirituous waters" and cordials using spices from the Middle East like coriander, cardamom, and anise seed, and the stones of apricots, peaches, and cherries. Wine was made from ginger, currants, and cherries, but sweet wines, sack, and Madeira were imported. Later, the Scots-Irish brewed whiskey from corn, barley, or oats. Colonial Americans drank hard cider distilled from apples, peachy made from peaches, and perry made from pears. The colonists liked to dress up their alcoholic beverages with cream, sugar, eggs, mace, and nutmeg—like eggnog. "Kill-Devil" Rum, Stonewall, Bogus, and Flip Rum, distilled in New England after 1670, was cheap and available.

It was called by a variety of names—rhum, rumbullion, rumbooze— and used in a variety of mixtures: stonewall, which was cider and rum; bogus, which was unsweetened beer and rum; blackstrap, made with molasses and rum; and flip, a popular drink that appears at least as far back as 1690 in New England. Here's one way to make it. Punch, with its five ingredients of tea, arrack, sugar, lemons, and water, arrived from India via the British East India Company. New Englanders added a sixth ingredient, and rum punch was born. Life was good to New Englanders; they could expect to live ten years longer than if they had stayed in old England. But since they attributed their longer life to drinking alcohol, it became difficult to enforce laws restricting its intake.

Life was longer, but food preparation was still difficult and time consuming. Before the modern stove with a cooktop and an oven was invented in the mid-19th century, most cooking was done with the quadriceps, because it involved long hours of squatting to stir foods in front of the open hearth. A stool or rocking chair could be pulled up next to the fire, but it still involved long hours next to open flames, as the picture on the following page shows. On wealthy southern plantations, meats were hung in a separate smokehouse, as the picture on the following page shows.

THE GOLDEN AGE OF THE NETHERLANDS

Between England's colonies in New England and the Chesapeake was the Dutch colony of New Netherland. The Dutch knew that they would have to entice people from other countries to settle New Netherland, because the Dutch people, prosperous and free to practice the religion of their choice, had no reason to leave their own country. The Dutch settlers who did go to New Netherland found oak trees that grew seventy feet high and made logs that burned hot and bright for hours. As in the Netherlands, bread was a staple in New Nether- land, but it was baked at home.

The Netherlands was urbanized, so commercial bakers made bread, but parts of the colony were very sparsely populated, so it was necessary for people to have their own brick ovens built into the wall next to the fireplace. American ingredients like corn and pumpkin found their way into standard Dutch recipes like pancakes. Bread was more than food in the Dutch colony; it was a trade item so much sought after by the Native Americans— especially white breads and sweet cakes—that by 1649 there were laws against making bread to trade with the Indians.

New Netherland was just a small part of a vast Dutch empire. The Dutch replaced the Italians—the Medicis of Florence and the Venetians—as the international bankers, and the world banking center moved to the Netherlands. The Dutch dominated or controlled the world shipping trade in spices, sugar, coffee, slaves, precious gems, and grain. The Dutch fleet of 10,000 ships also delivered oil, wine, and salt from Portugal, Spain, and France to northern Europe, and gold and silver from New World mines to Old World vaults. One of the reasons the Netherlands rose to power was that it was unique—a unified, religiously tolerant republic.

During the 16th century, while the European monarchies fought with the Church and within their own countries over religion (and in some places killed a greater percentage of the population than the Black Death had), the Netherlands was open for business. Many of the Jews who had been driven out of Spain by the Inquisition went north to the hospitable Protestant Netherlands and contributed their knowledge of banking and business to an already flourishing economy. The stock exchange, called the *bourse* (French for "purse"), was created in Amsterdam in the middle of the 16th century. In

1609, the Bank of Amsterdam opened. It had an international money exchange, it used the system of writing checks invented by the Arabs in the Middle Ages, and the Dutch government guaranteed the safety of deposits—something not available in the United States until 1933. The Dutch florin was accepted as payment all over the world, much as the American dollar is today. "God Made the World, but the Dutch Made Holland" Dutch life was tied to the sea and was a constant battle with it. The Dutch invented windmills to pump water out of the fields and reclaim land from the sea, and dikes, walls to hold back the sea. Much of Dutch food and industry centered around the sea. Twenty-five per cent of the Dutch population was connected to the herring industry, from fishing and selling to preserving by smoking, salting, and pickling.

In a time when the economy of other European countries was suffering, the Dutch were extremely prosperous, with a large middle class and a high standard of living. Dutch virtues were cleanliness and thrift. Every morning, Dutch housewives washed not only their own stoops but also the public sidewalks in front of their houses. They lived and ate well. At fish markets, the Dutch bought only live fish. They threw away dead fish, as well as mackerel and red mullet.

Even workers could afford meat, cheese, and butter, and the urban poor were provided for in poorhouses that had been recycled from monasteries or convents when the Netherlands converted to Protestant from Catholic. Sailors on warships were fed a 4,800-calorie-per-day diet of mutton, beef, pork, smoked ham, bread, beans, peas, and smoked and pickled fish, much of it herring. They were a country that grew no grain and made no wine, but they controlled trade from the breadbasket of Europe, the countries around the Baltic Sea. "French *haute cuisine* did not appear until a century later and then showed little Italian influence; and there is no evidence that Catherine's cooks had any impact on French cooking in the early 16th century."

Catherine supposedly introduced frozen ices, artichokes, parsley, and the fork to France. Wheaton says further that Catherine didn't have much power at court because she didn't have children for 14 years; because her husband was not supposed to become king, but his brother died; and because her husband's mistress set court fashions.

There was a dramatic shift in French cuisine in the middle of the 17th century. In 1651, a French chef named La Varenne published a cookbook called *Le Cuisinier françois*—The French Cook. As Anne Willan, who has named her cooking school in France after him, pointed out, *Le Cuisinier françois* "is a seminal work; it marks the end of medieval cooking and the beginning of *haute cuisine.*" More fresh fruits and vegetables appear in these recipes, because they are more readily available and because gardening had advanced considerably, especially among the upper classes. However, there were still not many foods from the New World. La Varenne used the foods that were trendy among the French nobility, like peas, lettuce, and artichokes. People *had* to have peas.

Woe to the host who served asparagus instead, although asparagus could be served disguised as peas. *Le Pastissier* is the first thorough pastry cookbook, with precise, clear instructions and definitions of weights and measures, perhaps the influence of the Scientific Revolution that was then taking place in Europe. However, Willan thinks that *Le Pastissier* was probably not written by La Varenne or was written by him and an anonymous Italian pastry chef, because Italian pastry chefs were the best in the world at that time.

Also, cooking and pastry were two separate professions. In any case, it is sophisticated—there are fifteen varieties of marzipan. It also has the first cakelike biscuit recipes.

HYGIENE IN FOOD PROCESSING

A high standard of hygiene is a prerequisite for safe food production, and the foundation on which HACCP and other safety management systems depend. Edited and written by some of the world's leading experts in the field, and drawing on the work of the prestigious European Hygienic Engineering and Design Group (EHEDG), Hygiene in food processing provides an authoritative and comprehensive review of good hygiene practice for the food industry.

- An authoritative and comprehensive review of good hygiene practice for the food industry
- Draws on the work of the prestigious European Hygienic Engineering and Design Group (EHEDG)
- Written and edited by world renowned experts in the field
  - *Part 1:* looks at the regulatory context, with chapters on the international context, regulation in the EU and the USA.
  - *Part 2:* looks at the key issue of hygienic design. After an introductory chapter on sources of contamination, there are chapters on plant design and control of airborne contamination. These are followed by a sequence of chapters on hygienic equipment design, including construction materials, piping systems, designing for cleaning in place and methods for verifying and certifying hygienic design.
  - *Part 3:* then reviews good hygiene practices, including cleaning and disinfection, personal hygiene and the management of foreign bodies and insect pests.

Drawing on a wealth of international experience and expertise, Hygiene in food processing will be a standard work for the food industry in ensuring safe food production.

CHICKENS SHOWS PATHOGEN

While critics from the US Agriculture Department (USDA) have labelled the report "junk science" for not doing a wide enough sampling, the publishing of the survey by an influential consumer organisation is a direct attack on the food safety practices at leading poultry processors.

As well, the USDA's own figures show that samples in broilers, ground chicken and ground turkey testing positive for salmonella at US slaughter and processing plants have surged since 2002, indicating that companies might soon be pushed to do more to bring down the levels. Broilers had the highest rates of salmonella, with 16.3 per cent of samples testing positive in 2005, up from 11.5 per cent in 2002, USDA figures released earlier this year showed. The highest level was reached in 1998, when salmonella was found in 20 per cent of the broilers sampled. Meanwhile the Consumer Reports survey tested 525 chickens – including samples from Perdue, Pilgrim's Pride and Tyson Foods. Campylobacter was present in 81 per cent of the chickens, salmonella in 15 per cent and both bacteria in 13 per cent. Only 17 per cent had neither pathogen. That's the lowest percentage of clean birds in all four of the organisation's tests since 1998, and far less than the 51 per cent of clean birds it found in a 2003 survey, the organisation stated.

- "Leading chicken producers have stabilized the incidence of salmonella, but spiral-shaped campylobacter has wriggled onto more chickens than ever," Consumer Reports stated. "And although the US Department of Agriculture tests chickens for salmonella against a federal standard, it has not set a standard for campylobacter."

Overall, chickens labeled as organic or raised without antibiotics and costing $3 to $5 per pound were more likely to harbor salmonella than were conventionally produced broilers that cost more like $1 per pound, the study found.

Moreover, most of the bacteria we tested from all types of contaminated chicken showed resistance to one or more antibiotics, including some fed to chickens to speed their growth and those prescribed to humans to treat infections. Among all brands, 84 per cent of the salmonella and 67 per cent of the campylobacter organisms showed resistance to one or more antibiotics.

- "The findings suggest that some people who are sickened by chicken might need to try several antibiotics before finding one that works," the organisation concluded.

No major brand fared better than others overall. Foster Farms, Pilgrim's Pride, and Tyson chickens were lower in salmonella incidence than Perdue, but they were higher in campylobacter. There was an exception to the poor showing of most premium chickens. As in its previous tests, Ranger—a no-antibiotics brand sold in the Northwest—was extremely clean. Of the 10 samples the organisation analysed, none had salmonella, while two had campylobacter.

To keep contamination in check, processors follow procedures collectively known as Hazard Analysis and Critical Control Point (HACCP) analysis as a means of reducing the risks. HACCP requires companies to spell out where contamination could be controlled during processing, then build in procedures—such as scalding carcasses—to prevent it. The report cited the example of Bell and Evans, which spent $30 million to modernize its processing plant in 2005. The sum included $9 million for a high-tech air-chill system designed in part to reduce cross-contamination.

The system whisks carcasses on two miles of track through chambers in which they're misted and chilled with air, then submerged in an antimicrobial dip. Tom Stone, the company's marketing director, says the measures helped reduce the rate of salmonella to less than 3 per cent in recent in-house tests of chickens done before packaging. But in Consumer Reports tests of 28 store-bought chickens, five of the Bell and Evans samples had salmonella and 19 had campylobacter, the organisation stated. Other government studies back up the growth trend, while reporting significantly lower levels of the pathogens compared to the Consumer Reports survey. SDA testing shows that Salmonella is found in about 12 per cent of broiler chickens in a sample of 3,242 nationwide in the third quarter of 2006. The industry association also cited a large-scale study by Dr. Norman Stern, an expert with the USDA Agricultural Research Service, which showed that 26 per cent of the chickens sampled had detectable level of Campylobacter.

Stern's study took place over 13 months, in 13 poultry complexes, and included 4,200 samples. This study was published in the Journal of Food Protection earlier this year.

- "As for the suggestion that bacteria that may be found on raw chicken are becoming more resistant to antibiotics, the fact is that Campylobacter is notoriously resistant to some antibiotics regardless of whether they are used in chicken or not," the associtation stated. "We are not aware of any actual human cases in which antibiotics have failed to work because of any usage in live chickens. The use of antibiotics in live chickens has declined sharply in recent years."

Another criticism of the Consumer Reports study came this week, with Reuters news service quoting a spokesman with the USDA as saying the Consumer Reports study was riddled with flaws such as a small sample size and uncertainty over the report's methodology. Steven Cohen, spokesman for the agency, said the report did not go back to all the stores used.

- "There is virtually nothing or any conclusion that anyone could draw from 500 samples," Reuters quotes Cohen as stating. "They're passing along junk science and calling it an investigation."

The federal Centers for Disease Control and Prevention (CDC) this month published USDA figures showing that the presence of Salmonella enterica serotype Enteritidis in broiler chicken carcass rinses collected from 2000 through 2005 increased four-fold over the period. The proportion of establishments with Salmonella Enteritidis–positive rinses increased nearly three fold during the same period.

- "We present US Department of Agriculture (USDA) Food Safety and Inspection Service (FSIS) Salmonella testing programme data collected from 2000 to 2005 that suggest a need for interventions to prevent the emergence of this Salmonella serotype in broiler chickens in the United States," the CDC stated in its study.

Campylobacter and salmonella from all food sources sicken about 3.4 million Americans and kill about 700 annually, according to the latest estimates from the CDC. The CDC said that in 2004, poultry was involved in 24 per cent of infection outbreaks in which a single product was identified, up from 20 per cent in 1998. In 2004, about 53 per cent of campylobacter samples and 18 per cent of salmonella samples were resistant to at least one antibiotic. In July 2006, Food and Water Watch, an environmental health organization, published the names of 106 chicken processing plants that failed federal salmonella standards in at least one test period between 1998 and 2005. In August 2006, the USDA reported that the rate of positive salmonella tests in broilers had jumped to 16.3 per cent in 2005, up from 11.5 per cent in 2002.

THE USE OF THIN WALLED PACKAGING FOR FOOD

In a survey of the segment, Applied Market Information (AMI) says thin-walled packaging has become an increasingly well delineated sub-segment of the rigid plastics market. In total in Europe the segment accounts for about two million tonnes of thermoplastics. The report indicates some of the trends in this plastic packaging segment, as the market responds to higher raw material costs, and changes in demand for particular types of food products. Thin walled packaging is used mainly to display goods for sale, but the format may also incorporate features for extending shelf-life and other functions. Thin walled packaging is defined to include yoghurt pots, butter and margarine containers, meat and fruit trays, blister packaging and similar containers. It excludes CD, DVD and blow moulded packaging. The largest single application of thin-walled packaging is dairy products, which account for 22 per cent of the market. The fastest growing application is in the chilled ready meals segment, in which demand is growing at about six per cent.

While some of the applications for thin-walled packaging are mature others are evolving rapidly such as meat packaging, which is in the process of shifting from being packed within store to being packed centrally. The fruit and vegetables segment accounts for eight per cent of the demand, meat, fish and poultry another eight per cent, frozen foods eight per cent, delicatessen products for seven per cent, bakery for five per cent, yellow fats for five per cent, chilled meals for four per cent and ambient products two per cent. Disposable products account for another 17 per cent of the demand and non-food products 14 per cent. In terms of composition, PET and PP are gaining market share, while polystyrene (PS) and polyvinyl chloride (PVC) are losing market share. Recently, plant-based and compostable polymers have emerged that offer brand owners exciting new opportunities to align sustainable and natural food propositions — such as organic food — with the packaging itself.

VISION FOR INDIAN POULTRY INDUSTRY

India is the fifth largest producer of eggs and ninth largest producer of poultry meat in the world, producing over 34 billion eggs and about 1,715,000 Metric ton of poultry meat in 2004. In the overall market for poultry products, India was positioned 17 in World Poultry Production. And analysts estimate that the poultry sector in India has been growing at a much faster rate, along with other industries such as BPO and Securities market. Over the past decade the poultry industry in India has contributed approximately US $229million, to the Gross National Product (GNP).

Several breakthroughs in poultry science and technology have led to the development of genetically superior breeds capable of higher production, even under adverse climatic conditions that offer opportunities for overseas entrepreneurs to expand export and import of poultry products on a large scale. The average per capita poultry meat consumption is also estimated to increase from 0.69 to 1.28 kilograms, during the 2000-2004. Overall, analysts studies that the total egg consumption is estimated to increase from 34 billion in 2000 and to 106 billion in 2020, while poultry meat consumption is predicted to increase from 687 million kilograms to 1,674 million kilograms. The market research report "Vision for Indian Poultry Industry: Current Scenario and Future Prospects" predicts a relatively strong growth for the egg and poultry meat industry, in both the urban and rural areas, in the next two decades. It has been found that egg consumption has grown at a much faster pace, than the consumption of poultry meat. With the continual rise in income, it is estimated to nearly triple by 2020. The report also examines the consumption pattern of egg and poultry meat for 2010 by taking into account urbanization and differences in consumption patterns across various income groups, both in urban and rural areas. The report deals in detail with the market structure, as well as highlights the production, consumption, import/export statistics etc., of the Indian poultry market, including broilers and processed poultry.

Report Highlights

- Assesses recent trends in Indian poultry production and consumption.
- Growth in India's poultry sector relative to other countries.
- Economic factors affecting food demand, including population, income, and urbanization.
- Consumption shares of poultry products.
- Gains in real per capita incomes and changes in poultry prices.
- Religion and regional preferences for poultry products.
- Structure and costs of production in the Indian poultry meat industry from region to region.
- Poultry production practices by geographic regions like facilities and equipment, breeding and feeding practices.
- Foreign direct investment inflow (FDI) in poultry inputs.
- Policies affecting market integration and feed trade, key to future growth.
- Performance indicators and variable costs for poultry in India, according to region.
- Marketing practices in Indian poultry industry.
- Regional variations in retail prices and margins.
- Tariff levels, regulatory barriers, and import potentials in the Indian poultry sector.
- Trends in supply and demand for key broiler feeds, corn, and soy meal.
- Key factors behind the recent growth of the Indian poultry sector.

- Impact of increase in income, integration, and corn free trade on the Indian poultry sector.

Report Features

This report assesses the supply/demand structure, and policy factors affecting the growth of the Indian poultry industry. The objectives of the report are twofold: to gain a better understanding of the prospects for the poultry industry, in one of the world's largest and fastest growing developing economies, and to take advantage of the information developed on India's diverse sector, to arrive at the implications for growth prospects in the poultry sectors, in other developing countries. To help meet these objectives, this report analyses the impacts of alternate economic, technical, and policy assumptions on poultry supply and demand prospects and the implications for the feed trade.

FOOD AND BEVERAGES

While U.S. hotels have enjoyed a strong increase in room revenue during the current recovery period, growth in hotel food and beverage sales, while improving, lacked the same kind of sizzle, according to an recent study by a leading hospitality consultant. Fortunately, tight cost controls by management have enabled food and beverage profitability to keep pace with the profit growth of other operating departments. In 2004, hotel food and beverage (F&B) revenues grew 6.7 per cent, the result of a 6.9 per cent increase in food sales and a 5.5 per cent bump in beverage sales. The 6.7 per cent growth rate is certainly very healthy, but it does fall short of the 8.6 per cent growth in rooms revenue, and 7.6 per cent increase in total hotel revenues achieved during the same time period.

Table. Mix of Food and Beverage Revenues 2004

Banquet Food	38.2%
Food Outlets/ In Room	25.0%
Other	15.5%
Beverage Outlets/ In Room	11.1%
Banquet Beverage	6.1%
Banquet Meeting Room Rental	4.1%

"While the magnitude of the increase in food and beverage revenue may have fallen short, the pace of profit growth equaled that of the other operated departments within a hotel. This can be attributed to good expense control practiced by F&B management," Woodworth concluded. In 2004, food and beverage departmental expenses grew 6.2 per cent versus and an average of 6.9 per cent for all other operated departments. The bottom- line was an 8.1 per cent growth in food and beverage profits for 2004. This equals the increase in total Operated Department Income for all hotels.

Food and beverage revenues and expenses are just some of the 200 discrete hotel revenue and expense items captured in 2005 Trends in the Hotel Industry report. The 2005 report marks the 69th annual review of U.S. hotel operations conducted by PKF. This year's sample draws upon year-end 2004 financial statements received from more than 5,000 hotels across the country. Hotel managers use the PKF Trends report to benchmark the performance of their hotel's revenues, expenses, and profits.

Revenue Gains

The growth in food and beverage revenues appears to be driven more by increased guest and customer counts, as opposed to increases in pricing. While food and beverage revenues measured on a per-available-room basis grew 6.7 per cent in 2004, food and beverage revenue measured on a per-occupied-room basis grew 2.3 per cent. "The implication from these two statistics is that the increase in F&B revenue was more attributable to the fact that there were 4.3 per cent more rooms occupied, as opposed to any substantial increase in the F&B expenditures per occupied room. Of course, another reason could be a boost in food and beverage patronage from local residents.

When looking at the sources of food and beverage business for the typical hotel in PKF's sample, revenues from banquet events account for 44.3 per cent of the total sales. This compares to 36.1 per cent of the total sales volume that comes from the restaurants, lounges, and room service. The remaining 19.6 per cent is derived from the rental of meeting and banquet rooms, as well as other miscellaneous sources. When looking at growth by the revenue source, we found sales emanating from restaurants and lounges increased 6.1 per cent in 2004, while banquet and catering related revenues grew 7.0 per cent.

Expense Controls

For hotel food and beverage departments, the "prime costs" are Labour and cost of goods sold. In 2004, the cost of food and liquor purchased for re-sale averaged 25.6 per cent of total food and beverage revenue. Salaries, wages, and employee benefits combined for another 56.1 per cent of the dollars spent in the department. Like most other departments in a hotel, labour costs are the biggest expense item. In 2004, F&B labour costs rose 6.1 per cent. This compares Favourably to the 6.3 per cent overall growth rate in Labour costs throughout the hotel. It also looks like the chefs and bartenders did a good job in the back-of-the-house limiting food and beverage cost increases to only 4.9 per cent." As a result of the tight cost controls, food and beverage department profit margins improved from 30.4 per cent in 2003 to 31.0 per cent in 2004. While food and beverage sales accounted for 26.2 per cent of total hotel revenues in 2004, F&B department profits were only 11.1 per cent of total Operated Department Income for the year.

Free Food

Since the proliferation of limited-service and all-suite hotels, a growing percentage of travellers have grown accustomed to complimentary breakfast and/or cocktail receptions. These expectations have become so prevalent that an increasing number of full-service, resort, and convention hotels are now offering complimentary food and beverages as part of special packages, preferred guest programmes, or corporate rate contracts. The amount of money U.S. hotels spent on complimentary food and beverage increased 13.1 per cent from 2003 to 2004. For the industry segments that have traditionally offered complimentary breakfast, growing competition and evolving social patterns have resulted in an increase in both the quantity and healthiness of the food offered. "When measured on a dollar per-occupied-room basis, limited-service and all-suite hotels increased their spending on complimentary food and beverage by 5.0 per cent. Clearly, these segments are making an effort to upgrade the quality and quantity of the food and beverages they offer to their guests. Stale doughnuts just don't cut it anymore," Woodworth said. Food and beverage serving and related workers are the front line of customer service in restaurants, coffee shops, and other food service establishments. These workers greet customers, escort them to seats and hand them menus, take food and drink orders, and serve food and beverages. They also answer questions, explain menu items and specials, and keep tables and dining areas clean and set for new diners. Most work as part of a team, helping coworkers to improve workflow and customer service.

Waiters and waitresses, the largest group of these workers, take customers' orders, serve food and beverages, prepare itemized checks, and sometimes accept payment. Their specific duties vary considerably, depending on the establishment. In coffee shops serving routine, straightforward fare, such as salads, soups, and sandwiches, servers are expected to provide fast, efficient, and courteous service. In fine dining restaurants, where more complicated meals are prepared and often served over several courses, waiters and waitresses provide more formal service emphasizing personal, attentive treatment and a more leisurely pace. They may recommend certain dishes and identify ingredients or explain how various items on the menu are prepared. Some prepare salads, desserts, or other menu items tableside. Additionally, they may check the identification of patrons to ensure they meet the minimum age requirement for the purchase of alcohol and tobacco products. Waiters and waitresses sometimes perform the duties of other food and beverage service workers. These tasks may include escorting guests to tables, serving customers seated at counters, clearing and setting up tables, or operating a cash register. However, full-service restaurants frequently hire other staff, such as hosts and hostesses, cashiers, or dining room attendants, to perform these duties. *Bartenders* fill drink orders either taken directly from patrons at the bar or through waiters and waitresses who place drink orders for dining room customers. Bartenders check identification of customers seated at the bar, to ensure they meet the minimum age requirement for the purchase of alcohol and tobacco products. They prepare mixed drinks, serve bottled or drought beer, and pour wine or other beverages. Bartenders must know a wide range of drink recipes and be able to mix drinks accurately, quickly, and without waste. Besides mixing and serving drinks, bartenders stock and prepare garnishes for drinks; maintain an adequate supply of ice, glasses, and other bar supplies; and keep the bar area clean for customers.

They also may collect payment, operate the cash register, wash glassware and utensils, and serve food to customers seated at the bar. Bartenders usually are responsible for ordering and maintaining an inventory of liquor, mixes, and other bar supplies. The majority of bartenders directly serve and interact with patrons. Bartenders should be friendly and enjoy talking with customers. Bartenders at service bars, on the other hand, have less contact with customers. They work in small bars often located off the kitchen in restaurants, hotels, and clubs where only waiters and waitresses place drink orders. Some establishments, especially larger, higher volume ones, use equipment that automatically measures, pours and mixes drinks at the push of a button.

Bartenders who use this equipment, however, still must work quickly to handle a large volume of drink orders and be familiar with the ingredients for special drink requests. Much of a bartender's work still must be done by hand to fill each individual order. *Hosts and hostesses* welcome guests and maintain reservation or waiting lists. They may direct patrons to coatrooms, restrooms, or to a place to wait until their table is ready. Hosts and hostesses assign guests to tables suitable for the size of their group, escort patrons to their seats, and provide menus. They also schedule dining reservations, arrange parties, and organize any special services that are required. In some restaurants, they act as cashiers. *Dining room and cafeteria attendants and bartender helpers* assist waiters, waitresses, and bartenders by cleaning tables, removing dirty dishes, and keeping serving areas stocked with supplies. Sometimes called backwaiters or runners, they bring meals out of the kitchen and assist waiters and waitresses by distributing dishes to individual diners. They also replenish the supply of clean linens, dishes, silverware, and glasses in the dining room and keep the bar stocked with glasses, liquor, ice, and drink garnishes. Dining room attendants set tables with clean tablecloths, napkins, silverware, glasses, and dishes and serve ice water, rolls, and butter.

At the conclusion of meals, they remove dirty dishes and soiled linens from tables. Cafeteria attendants stock serving tables with food, trays, dishes, and silverware and may carry trays to dining tables for patrons. *Bartender helpers* keep bar equipment clean and wash glasses. *Dishwashers* clean dishes, cutlery, and kitchen utensils and equipment. *Counter attendants* take orders and serve food in cafeterias, coffee shops, and carryout eateries. In cafeterias, they serve food displayed on steam tables, carve meat, dish out vegetables, ladle sauces and soups, and fill beverage glasses. In lunchrooms and coffee shops, counter attendants take orders from customers seated at the counter, transmit orders to the kitchen, and pick up and serve food. They also fill cups with coffee, soda, and other beverages and prepare fountain specialties, such as milkshakes and ice cream sundaes. Counter attendants also take carryout orders from diners and wrap or place items in containers. They clean counters, write itemized checks, and sometimes accept payment. Some counter attendants may prepare short-order items, such as sandwiches and salads. Some food and beverage serving workers take orders from customers at counters or drive-through windows at fast-food restaurants. They assemble orders, hand them to customers, and accept payment. Many of these are *combined food preparation and serving workers* who also cook and package food, make coffee, and fill beverage cups using drink-dispensing machines.

7

Catering Industry

INTRODUCTION

Hospitality is probably the most diverse but specialized industry in the world. It is certainly one of the largest, employing millions of people in a bewildering array of jobs around the globe. Sectors range from the glamourous five-star resort to the less fashionable, but arguably more specialised, institutional areas such as hospitals, industrial outfits, schools and colleges. Yet of these many different sectors, catering has to be the most challenging. Whatever the size of the catering operation, the variety of opportunities available is endless. "The sky is the limit with catering".

CATERING INDUSTRY

The food service industry encompasses those places, institutions and companies that provide meals eaten away from home. This industry includes restaurants, schools and hospital cafeterias, catering operations, and many other formats, including 'on-premises' and 'off-premises' caterings. Catering is a multifaceted segment of the food service industry. There is a niche for all types of catering businesses within the segment of catering.

The food service industry is divided into three general classifications: commercial segment, noncommercial segment, and military segment. Catering management may be defined as the task of planning, organizing, controlling a n d executing. Each activity influences the preparation and delivery of food, beverage, and related services at a competitive, yet profitable price. These activities work together to meet and exceed the customer's perception of value for his money.

CATERING SEGMENTS

Catering management is executed in many diverse ways within each of the four segments. The first, commercial segment, traditionally considered the profit generating operation, includes the independent caterer, the restaurant caterer, and the home-based caterer. The food service catering industry is segmented. The non-commercial segment, or the 'not-forprofit' operations, consists of the following types of catering activities: business / industry accounts, school, college and university catering, health care facilities, recreational food service catering, social organizations and transportation food service catering. The military segment encompasses all catering activities involved in association with the armed forces and / or diplomatic events.

TYPES OF CATERING

There are two main types of catering on-premises and offpremises catering that may be a concern to a large and small caterer. On-premise catering for any function - banquet, reception, or event - that is held on the physical premises of the establishment or facility that is organizing / sponsoring the function. On-premise catering differs from off-premise catering, whereby the function takes place in a remote location, such as a client's home, a park, an art gallery, or even a parking lot, and the staff, food, and decor must be transported to that location. Off-premise catering often involves producing food at a central kitchen, with delivery to and service provided at the client's location. Part or all of the production of food may be executed or finished at the location of the event.

Catering can also be classified as social catering and corporate catering. Social catering includes such events as weddings, bar and mitzwahs, high school reunions, birthday parties, and charity events. Business catering includes such events as association conventions and meetings, civic meetings, corporate sales or stockholder meetings, recognition banquets, product launches, educational training sessions, seller-buyer meets, service awards banquets, and entertaining in hospitality suites.

ON-PREMISE CATERING

All of the required functions and services that the caterers execute are done exclusively at their own facility. For instance, a caterer within a hotel or banquet hall will prepare and cater all of the requirements without taking any service or food outside the facility. Many restaurants have specialized rooms on-premise to cater to the private-party niche. A restaurant may have a layout strategically designed with three separate dining rooms attached to a centralized commercial food production kitchen. These separate dining rooms are available at the same time to support the restaurant's operation and for reservation and overflow seating. In addition, any of the three dining rooms may be contracted out for private-event celebrations and may require their own specialized service and menu options. Other examples of on-premise catering include hospital catering, school, University/ college catering.

OFF-PREMISE CATERING

Off-premise catering is serving food at a location away from the caterer's food production facility. One example of a food production facility is a freestanding commissary, which is a kitchen facility used exclusively for the preparation of foods to be served at other locations. Other examples of production facilities include, but are not limited to, hotel, restaurant, and club kitchens. In most cases there is no existing kitchen facility at the location where the food is served. Caterers provide single-event foodservice, but not all caterers are created equal. They generally fall into one of three categories:

Party Food Caterers

Party food caterers supply only the food for an event. They drop off cold foods and leave any last-minute preparation, plus service and cleanup, to others.

Hot Buffet Caterers

Hot buffet caterers provide hot foods that are delivered from their commissaries in insulated containers. They sometimes provide serving personnel at an additional charge.

Full-Service Caterers

Full-service caterers not only provide food, but frequently cook it to order on-site. They also provide service personnel at the event, plus all the necessary food-related equipment-china, glassware, flatware, cutleries, tables and chairs, tents, and so forth. They can arrange for other services, like décor and music, as well. In short, a full-service caterer can plan and execute an entire event, not just the food for it.

TYPES OF CATERING ESTABLISHMENTS

Various catering establishments are categorised by the nature of the demands they meet. The following are some of the catering establishements.

RESTAURANT

A restaurant is an establishment that serves the customers with prepared food and beverages to order, to be consumed on the premises. The term covers a multiplicity of venues and a diversity of styles of cuisine. Restaurants are sometimes also a feature of a larger complex, typically a hotel, where the dining amenities are provided for the convenience of the residents and for the hotel to maximize their potential revenue. Such restaurants are often open to non-residents also.

TRANSPORT CATERING

The provision of food and beverages to passengers, before, during and after a journey on trains, aircraft and ships and in buses or private vehicles is termed as transport catering. These services may also be utilised by the general public, who are in the vicinity of a transport catering unit. The major forms of modern day transport catering are airline-catering, railways catering, ship catering and surface catering in coaches or buses which operate on long distance routes.

Airline Catering

Catering to airline passengers on board the air craft, as well as at restaurants situated at airport terminals is termed as airline catering. Modern airports have a variety of food and beverage outlets to cater to the increasing number of air passengers. Catering to passengers en route i s normally contracted out to a flight catering unit of a reputed hotel or to a catering contractor or to the catering unit operated by the airline itself as an independent entity.

Railway Catering

Catering to railway passengers both during the journey as well as during halts at different railway stations is called railway catering. Travelling by train for long distances can be very tiring; hence a constant supply of a variety of refreshment choices helps to make the journey less tedious. On-board meal services are also provided on long distance trains.

Ship Catering

Ship catering is catering to cargo crew and passenger ship passengers. Ships have kitchens and restaurants on board. The quality of service and facilities offered depends on the class of the ship and the price the passengers are willing to pay. There are cruises to suit every pocket. They range from room service and cocktail bars to speciality dining restaurants.

Surface Catering

Catering to passengers traveling by surface transport such as buses and private vehicles is called surface catering. These eating establishments are normally located around a bus terminus or on highways. They may be either government run restaurants, or privately owned establishments. Of late there has been a growing popularity of Punjabi style eateries called dhabas on the highways.

OUTDOOR CATERING

This catering includes the provision of food and drink away from home base and suppliers. The venue is left to the peoples' choice. Hotels, restaurants and catering contractors meet this growing demand. The type of food and set up depends entirely on the price agreed upon. Outdoor catering includes catering for functions such as marriages, parties and conventions.

RETAIL STORE CATERING

Some retail stores, apart from carrying on their primary activity of retailing their own wares, provide catering as an additional facility. This type of catering evolved when large departmental stores wished to provide food and beverages to their customers as a part of their retailing concept. It is inconvenient and time consuming for customers to take a break from shopping, to have some refreshments at a different location. Thus arouse the need for some sort of a dining facility in the retail store itself. This style of catering is becoming more popular and varied nowadays.

CLUB CATERING

Club catering refers to the provision of food and beverages to a restricted member clientele. Some examples of clubs for people with similar interests are turf clubs, golf clubs, cricket clubs etc. The service and food in these clubs tend to be of a fairly good standard and are economically priced. Night clubs are usually situated in large cities that have an affluent urban population. They offer entertainment with good food and expensive drinks.

WELFARE CATERING

The provision of food and beverages to people to fulfil a social obligation, determined by a recognised authority, is known as welfare catering. This grew out of the welfare state concept, prevalent in western countries. It includes catering in hospitals, schools, colleges, the armed forces and prisons.

INDUSTRIAL CATERING

The provision of food and beverages to 'people at work,' in industries and factories at highly subsidised rates is called industrial catering. It is based on the assumption that better fed employees at concessional rates are happy and more productive. Catering for a large workforce may be undertaken by the management itself, or may be contracted out to professional caterers. Depending on the choice of the menu suggested by the management, catering contractors undertake to feed the workforce for a fixed period of time at a predetermined price.

LEISURE-LINKED CATERING

This type of catering refers to the provision of food and beverages to people engaged in 'rest and recreation' activities. This includes sale of food and beverages through different stalls and kiosks at exhibitions, theme parks, galleries and theatres. The increase in the availability of leisure time and a large disposable income for leisure activities has made it a very profitable form of catering.

RELATIONSHIP BETWEEN CATERING INDUSTRY AND ALL OTHER INDUSTRIES

Food is the sustainer of life regardless of whether they belong to animal kingdom or plant kingdom. All living beings consume food as they come in nature. Subsequently they may convert the raw natural food into usable form on their own. This transformation never involves the art and science of coking, which is a speciality of human beings alone. Importance of food for the human beings is amply, accurately and appropriately stated in the following age old sayings: "hungry man is an angry man" and "even the army marches on stomach" where stomach implies food Employment of largest number of people in the world in general terms and in commercial terms is in food preparation and servicing. Roughly half the world population is actively engaged in the art and science of food production and then alone comes reproduction. Food production, simply stated, is the transformation of raw food material into palatable, appetizing and easily palatable tasty food. Unlike all other living organisms, man has to "buy" food by paying money. Where does the money come from? It comes only from industries. Any industry in the world has the primary objective of making money. Money so generated by the industrial activity is shared between the employer and the employee, however disproportionate it may be. Money so shared is used to take care of the three important objectives: food, clothing and residence. Whatever left after meeting these primary objectives may go towards acquiring wealth. Food is the very basis of existence or survival.

To buy food, man needs money. The money comes or must come from industries, all of which have the primary objective of making money and share with those who help generate it. Since the raw food needs to be transformed into palatable food fit for consumption which is achieved, as already stated, through general cooking or commercial cooking. Therefore, there is no industry in the world which is not directly or indirectly, one way or the other, related to the food industry. Commercial food industry or the catering industry is the only industry that provides food, at a price, away from home. Various types of catering services available would include general or speciality services such as transport catering, welfare catering, industrial catering, etc.

CATERING AND CUSTOMER

CATERING TO DIVERGENT

It sounds rather crass, but when they die, in the next 10-15 years, all of their money-some $10 trillion dollars-is going to another group of people, most of whom don't like banks. They would rather go to Fidelity, play the market, not having lived through a downturn. One of the challenges as we go forward is how the banking industry is going to transform itself, move from the current group who provides the bulk of our earnings, to a second group who will assume society's wealth, and who does not realty like us. Who likes banks? Those 55 years and older plus those who have lower incomes and less education, according to a 1997 ABA survey-valued customers, but not a group we can solely survive on. Also customer satisfaction is slipping somewhat for banks. You need to know when you should allocate resources from the group giving you the bulk of your earnings now, to the group that does not like you. You will also get a boost from the federal government's change to electronic benefits transfer on January 1, 1999. Most states will have an EBT environment by the end of 1998. The people who now get a Social Security check will have to become accustomed to an electronic transaction, and that's in your favour.

A lot of the back-office work, you can change through electronic transactions. EBT will provide a large infusion of the infrastructure required for electronic commerce, by increasing the number of point-of-sale terminals. The ABA asked the Federal Reserve and the Treasury to review the regulations surrounding transaction accounts, because the existing regulations are all in the realm of paper-based accounts. We would really like to get rid of the periodic statement under Regulation E because a purely electronic account will not have any outstanding items so you don't realty need a statement. Banks will have to do some new things, though-electronic benefits transactions on automated teller machines, and maybe statements on demand. What can you do today on the Internet? You can do consumer education; you can have interactive advertising; you can distribute forms and applications; you can provide account information. You can do some internal transactions, some bill payment and, perhaps, some electronic commerce for the more daring. Electronic commerce, a broader term than electronic banking, better describes what ultimately we might want to do. What customers want today is not necessarily what they are going to want next year. You have to continually reassess.

Reliability on Tomorrow's Systems

Today, most of you keep your real stuff on a mainframe, a rather secure system. On the Internet, how are you going to let people like me hack around in your computer? You are going to be doing the same kinds of things on the Internet that you do today to render service and security to your customers.

You will have a lot of the same, concerns. Yo1 could have a saboteur on the inside. You could have a huge virus or software that fails. The new one is the hackers, but then you've got people who forge checks, too; they just attack in a different way. Whatever system you have must be reliable, sound, and secure.

What kinds of things will give you these qualities? Well, you have technical standards; you have best practices, and the regulators providing guidance to the industry. You are going to a much more efficient system and you should have greater margins as you implement it, but meanwhile, many larger institutions have proprietary systems that work very well. Probably nobody here has had a customer question, in the past 50 years, whether her check is going to clear. You are coming off of that kind of reliability.

Bankers have systems that, perhaps, can be expanded to an Internet environment. Determining who has the best products to help you is part of creating a plan. You want, perhaps, to start small, with, say, electronic bill payment, see how secure it is, how your customers accept it, and then go forward. You may lose money, but you are going to do it because your customers want it. There are threats to banks' dominance of the payments system, one of the biggest of which is the post office. You may say that will never happen because it is not an insured depository, but I would submit, for example, that the largest financial institution in Japan is the post office. Financial modernization, after 30 years, seems finally to be coming.

Companies with unlimited capital, such as, say, General Electric Corp., will be able to compete very effectively, not for the little old ladies' $50,000 CDs but for their kids' money. That's why ABA is very concerned. With direct deposit, a customer need never walk into a branch. A customer in Alaska can directly deposit funds into a bank in Alabama and write checks or use his debit card all day long in Alaska. All across the country, community bankers are saying to themselves "Aha! Maybe I have an opportunity here." This stuff is coming. How are you going to respond? You are concerned about how your customers perceive you. Are you stodgy-as one of ABA's new industry ads shows -or are you out there on roller-blades? Now, you have to be concerned about customer perception beyond the community where you do business.

The Growth of Service Activities

Service sector economics now constitutes a major branch of economic studies although it is a field which no more than a decade ago was variously referred to as the 'poor relation' and the 'Cinderella of academics and politicians alike'. The explanation of the interest recently evinced in the economics of the service sector is to be found in the extent to which service industries have expanded relative to other economic activities. Whilst the tendency for the tertiary sector to grow in comparison to primary and secondary activities has been identified and commented on for many decades special factors, such as the potential for services to generate new jobs, have helped thrust the sector to the forefront of economic analysis in the last few years.

The relative growth of services in the British economy since 1971, quantified on the basis of official statistics, could well stand as on outline of events in most developed economies during this period. Between 1971 and 1986 the output of the service sector increased by 2.5 per cent a year, or more than twice the rate, 1.1 per cent, achieved by other economic activities. Within the sector commercial services-distribution, catering, financial, business, recreational and personal services-expanded faster than other services, 3.1 per cent compared with 1.7 per cent a year, whilst specific commercial services grew very rapidly indeed-banking and business services by as much as 5.1 per cent per annum.

As a result, by 1985, service activities in Britain accounted for three-fifths of GDP and commercial services themselves were responsible for a third of total output. The importance of service activities is no less when judged by labour force size. On the basis of both numbers of employees, and by numbers of employees plus the self-employed, by 1985 services accounted for 66 per cent of Britain's labour force compared with 53 per cent in 1971. Commercial services alone provided jobs for 37 per cent of all employees in 1985.

The Need for New Measures

At a time when the bases, compilation, accuracy and usefulness of a range of official economic statistics have come under close scrutiny, the measurement of service outputs has not escaped attention. Recently there has been some shift away from a simple acknowledgement that service output measures may be subject to a degree of unreliability towards an apprehension that any errors they contain might lead to a downward bias in the measure of service output, and therefore, GDP growth rates. It has in fact been suggested that output increases in services may have been underestimated in recent years by as much as 2-1/2 per cent a year implying that annual growth of GDP itself should have been substantially higher.

For both conceptual and practical reasons the outputs of many service activities are notoriously difficult to quantify both absolutely and in terms of change over time. Yet because of their size and growth it is especially important that a reasonable degree of accuracy must attach to service output measures which should reflect current best practice given the data and resources available. If this is not the case then, because of the weight of service activities in the total economy, the accuracy of the registred change in GDP and national productivity, the relative contribution to growth of service and non-service activities, the pattern of structural change within the service sector and the policies to which these various phenomena have given rise, must all be called in question.

This assembles some of the principal results which have emerged from a study of alternative output measures for British service industries. The study reviews the methods currently used by the CSO to measure real output changes in specified services and seeks to devise, develop and implement new measures for these activities. For this purpose an empirical approach has been adopted. Whilst basic conceptual considerations are taken fully into account in that the alternative measures which are compiled can be integrated into the national accounting framework, it is felt that the theoretical complexities associated with service output measurement have received due attention elsewhere whilst very little has been done at the practical level. When compiling new service output measures the two principal uses for which they are employed must be borne in mind.

The original raison d'etre for measuring service sector output is for use, in conjunction with output indicators for industrial activities, to yield a measure of real growth in total GDP. This is the primary role for which the CSO devises and compiles output measures for service sector activities. Increasingly, however, as the weight of services in the economy has grown service output indicators are now used extensively, in conjunction with labour force and other relevant economic series, for the analysis of long-term developments in individual service industries.

Their employment in the latter context accentuates the requirement that they fulfill minimum reliability criteria: it is possible that offsetting errors in individual service industry output measures may modulate their impact on the reliability of overall GDP measurement but this does not apply when attention is focused on the analysis of developments in a specific service industry.

The results obtained in the present exercise suggest that official measures of GDP growth may well have been marginally understated as a result of the methods used to track service output changes. Even more significantly, perhaps, the alternative measures which have been compiled portray patterns of development for some individual commercial service industries which are very different from those yielded by official output measures.

When considering alternative output measures attention has been directed first at the strengths and weaknesses of official practice as a prelude to an attempt to improve the rationale and reliability of the resulting output indicators. However in some cases it is necessary to regard the new measure simply as an alternative to the official index: an alternative with a different, rather than superior, base and/or derived from quite separate data sources. Another feature of the search for alternative indicators is that it has been conducted with an eye to the improved reliability of service output measurement in the future. To some extent this means that data series which are available only for recent years have been drawn upon.

Nevertheless a major objective of the study has been to assess the extent to which the official picture of past service sector developments is changed if alternative output measures are used. The alternative measures have therefore been carried backwards in some cases to 1971, in others to 1973 and for a large number to 1978, using 1985 as the base year.

There are three reasons for the latter choice. First data limitations mean that all series cannot be uniformly taken back to a common early date so that a recent year must be adopted as the base. Secondly at the time when the research was initiated 1985 was the latest year for which data-whether values, 'quantities' or 'weights'-were generally available. Thirdly, the CSO was then in the process of re-basing its output indicators using 1985 GDP weights.

The new output measures draw much more extensively on unofficial data sources than do those compiled by the CSO. Broadly such sources can be divided into two types: those which yield data series covering an industry-wide set of activities; and those which contain data relating to individual service industry organisations and firms. Typically the assistance of the latter was enlisted to provide weights with which industry-wide quantity series for different kinds of output can be combined to produce a single output measure for the service sector in question.

It is to the credit of the CSO that there has been a continuous attempt to modify service output measures in the light of methodological developments and the emergence of alternative data sources. Whilst this has had the desired result of improving the reliability of service output measurement inevitably it also introduces inconsistencies and breaks in the time series where-either on practical or other grounds-the new methods have not been carried back to earlier years. A feature of the new measures postulated below is that every effort has been made to ensure temporal consistency in the series which they yield. It has not proved possible to devote to 'quality' aspects of service output the attention they properly merit. In part this reflects the fact that the incorporation of quality changes in output measures may be even more difficult in services than in goods-producing industries where frequently its assessment is equally neglected.

This in turn is due to the consideration that the quality of a given service varies greatly and in many cases is highly subjective. Nevertheless the results do have implications for this aspect of service output measurement, especially in the case of the catering trades. Were quality aspects taken into account more fully, further consideration would need to be given to the relative merits of measures based on deflated value series and service output units.

Coverage of the Measures

The search for alternative output measures has been restricted to the commercial service industries, essentially distribution, catering, financial, business and personal services, for which suggests that output has risen especially rapidly. Within this group of commercial services the CSO distinguishes for output measurement purposes as many as 37 service industries, output changes in which are currently assessed by a total of 114 indicators. These services accounted for some 30 per cent of total GDP in 1985 and about a third of people employed in Great Britain.

Given the vast range of service activities which must be covered by official output measures it is natural that the CSO makes use of readily available, relevant, series to yield the required indicators, series which themselves are normally official in the sense that they are compiled by other government departments. Since the quest for new measures has entailed a search for and detailed examination of, alternative data, involving the identification, location and perusal of non-official sources and also the co-operation of individual firms and organisations it proved necessary to regard the full range of commercial service activities as no more than a frame from which individual service industries could be selected for intensive analysis. When choosing industries from this list for which alternative measures of output change are identified and implemented, several criteria have been applied. A principal consideration has been to direct efforts to services where, on the face of it, current practice appears to be weak.

At one end of the scale this principle tends to divert attention away from activities such as retailing, where the measures are generally regarded as being relatively sound, towards such services as advertising where the official output indicator is based on an employment series.

Secondly some priority was given to activities for which at first blush-sometimes deceptive-alternative measures appeared feasible. Thirdly an attempt has been made to cover the larger service industries such as banking and insurance, and ceteris paribus, attention was focused on service activities which, a priori, are thought to be rapidly expanding, a criterion which points to the inclusion of, especially, financial and business services.

Since a systematic attempt has been made to base alternative output measures on numbers of service units produced, such service industries as estate agents, stockbroking and legal services where official output measurement is already founded on numbers of service units-of property transfers, transactions, and court proceedings-have not been considered as candidates for alternative measures.

The service industries for which new measures were ultimately compiled fall neatly into three groups. First, there are ten selected financial and business services: banking, building societies, finance leasing, hire-purchase, insurance, accountants, architects, advertising, computer services and construction plant hire. Secondly eight recreational services have been covered: broadcasting, theatres, libraries, museums, professional sports, participatory sports, local authority leisure centres and betting and gaming. Thirdly, the five catering trades-restaurants, public houses, clubs, catering contractors and hotels-have also been included.

Alternative Output Measures

Continuous CSO action to modify and improve service output measures means that they have developed from year to year in an essentially ad hoc manner with considerable diversity in their conceptual underpinning. Output measures for the commercial service sector rely heavily on deflated value and employment indicators and whilst output measurement for some service activities is based on counting numbers of service units, such practice applies to only a fraction of the output of the commercial service sector. In fact it has emerged that the use of this type of measure can be extended to a considerable number of commercial services and an attempt has therefore been made to generalise and implement this approach, especially in the case of the financial and recreational services.

This method can be summarised as the compilation of [sigma]poqo where q represents the industry's output quantities of the industry's output prices and 0 and 1 refer to the years compared. This is 'the traditional [measure] used for multi-product industries wherein an index of production is constructed from a weighted sum of various outputs produced by the industry'. Such a deflated value approach to output measurement will yield the required result-as measured by the traditional direct method based on weighted quantities-only if the deflator, the price index, relates specifically to the products or services in question. This condition is not fulfilled in the case of many service output measures where for practical reasons some form of general price index is used.

It is partly to remedy this weakness in service output measurement that, wherever possible, alternative measures have been based in this exercise on the traditional direct methodology using numbers of service output units. A fundamental requirement for the use of this 'traditional' or 'direct' approach is that, for purposes of practical measurement, the outputs of the industry or service in question should be relatively homogeneous. No economic activity yields a single, identical, product or se~vice so that in practice it is sufficient if the bulk of an industry's activity is represented by a limited range of output types. It is their supposed inability to fulfill this criterion which has discouraged the application of the traditional, direct, measurement methodology to service activities. Generally it has been assumed that there exists, virtually, an infinite variety and range of outputs in the case of most, especially financial, services: that no two life insurances, mortgages, bank accounts, and the output activities associated with them, are the same.

It is argued that this view is based largely on a misconception, associated with what, for want of a better term, we shall call the 'digit illusion', and that in fact many service industries-including betting and gaming-fulfil the basic criterion for the application of the traditional, direct measurement methodology in that the bulk of their output is accounted for by a limited range of essentially homogeneous activities. For the impression of enormous diversity in the output of most financial services derives from the fact that the values associated with a specific activity-the sums assured by a life company, sizes of mortgages provided by a building society, the amounts loaned under hire-purchase agreements by a finance house, the values of cheques cleared by a commercial bank, the car insurance premiums charged by an insurer etc-do have an infinitely large range.

It has been assumed in the search for new output measures that such differences can be essentially ignored. In the case of mortgages, for example, the output associated with writing 500,000 pounds sterling in a deed is, with some relatively minor qualifications, little different from that associated with inscribing 50,000 pounds sterling or even 5,000 pounds sterling; differences in the numbers of digiis required in this and other financial instruments-cheques, insurance policies, hire-purchase agreements, betting slips-have relatively little bearing on the amount of output involved. In brief for a given type of financial activity it is normally legitimate, when measuring output, to ignore the 'digit illusion'. This has the effect of rendering homogeneous a wide range of financial activities, making them amenable, in principle, to the traditional direct, measurement methodology. It means, by way of illustration, that output changes for the life insurance industry can be based on changes in numbers of policies. It must be stressed however that a distinction must be drawn, and numbers counted, for each major type of service/activity provided by the service industry in question where value added per service unit varies significantly between activity types.

This means, for instance, in the case of the life insurance industry, that numbers of policies must be counted separately for ordinary life insurance, industrial life, annuities and personal pensions. It also means that attention needs to be drawn to a feature of this approach which is peculiar to financial service industries: the distinction between stocks and flows. Clearly, the resources devoted to, and therefore the amount of output associated with, the annual 'maintenance' of pre-existing mortgage will be substantially less than required when initiating a new mortgage. In principle, and where practical, it is as important therefore to draw a distinction when measuring output between numbers of existing mortgages issued in a given year and the numbers of existing mortgages as it is to count separately the numbers of, say, different kinds of policy issued by life insurance companies. Indeed the same distinction needs to be drawn in the case of life insurance-between new policies and policies in force-and in principle at any rate in many other financial service industries: between new and existing contracts for hire-purchase and finance leases for instance.

The practicability of extending the traditional measurement methodology to commercial services thus hinges, in the case of each activity, on the availability of two kinds of data: industry-wide series of numbers of each type of principal product, the series q; and appropriate weights with which these various product series can be combined to yield an aggregate output measure for the service industry in question. To a degree inadequacies in the measurement of service output changes simply reflect the relative lack of interest with which they were regarded in the past and a consequent failure to devote sufficient resources to the collection of basic output data. Also, it is to some extent, due to the 'insubstantiality' of most services, the fact that they 'pass away' in the moment of production, that a systematic effort has not been made to base their output measurement to a much larger extent on numbers of service units produced. In fact regardless of whether or not a service has any kind of physical embodiment, in the vast majority of cases there exists a physical record or token that a particular service has been performed.

The outputs of all kinds of commercial service industries are very well 'documented'-by the ticket required for entrance to Wimbledon, the bill for a meal, the contract which records the finance leasing of a fleet of aircraft-in a form which in principle allows the numbers of each type of service to be recorded. In this sense, and at this level, the output of service activities is registered at least as well as the products of industrial pursuits. The nig universal existence, at the 'grass roots' level, of this detailed record of service sector outputs, to an ever increasing extent in computerised form, augurs well for the future extension and development of the kind of direct output measurement advocated here. This comprehensive data base has not yet been properly exploited to yield aggregate series of the numbers of each type of service produced on an industry-wide basis.

However research and enquiry have revealed that representative bodies of various kinds at the industry level-especially trade associations-have come to regard the compilation of aggregate numbers of each kind of service produced, using these data bases, as one of their primary tasks, and such sources have been widely drawn upon. That they may not be based on series for numbers of service units which are fully comprehensive for the industry in question should not be regarded as a major weakness of the alternative output measures. Usually only the major 'products' are counted and in this respect the circumstances are no different from those which exist when the method is applied to industrial activities. For both industrial and service activities so measured the implicit assumption is the same: that real changes in the non-covered outputs parallel the aggregate change measured for the covered operations. Unfortunately, with few exceptions, service industry organisations, do not collect, process or publish, the kind of data which are needed to obtain the 'weights' required for aggregating these various output series into a single measure for the industry in question. In these circumstances it has proved necessary to have recourse inter alia to the goodwill of individual firms in order to derive suitable weights which must be accepted as typical for the service industry in which they operate.

Wherever possible alternative measures have been derived from an application of the traditional, direct methodology based on numbers of service output units. However even when allowance is made for the 'digit illusion' some service industries-such as architecture and accountancy-remain in that class where output units are, in essence, infinitely variable in nature. In these cases an attempt has nevertheless been made to upgrade the output measure, usually by identifying and compiling a more appropriate price deflator. This presents the results of the search for new output measures for the selected commercial activities. Initially the new output series are presented separately for the three major service complexes-financial and business services, recreational services and the catering trades-which have been covered and compared with the official measures. The part concludes with a consideration of the implications of the results for future developments in the measurement of service output.

Financial and Business Services

In 1985 the ten financial and business services for which new output measures have been compiled contributed, in total, about 35 pound sterling billion to GDP and employed approximately a million people. In the case of banking, the largest of the services in this sector, it proved possible to base the new measure wholly on numbers of service units-numbers of accounts, clearings, cash and credit card transactions. This contrasts with official practice in which indicators derived from deflated series for deposits and loans, as well as employment, carry the bulk of the weight. In life insurance, also, numbers of policies of various types, distinguishing between new policies and policies in force, replace the official series comprising deflated consumer expenditure. Similarly the new building society measure is founded wholly on numbers of service units-shareholders, existing borrowers and new loans-instead of, as is the case with the official measure, a combination of deflated liabilities, employment and numbers of advances.

For general insurance, a measure reflecting broadly the stock of insurable assets has been substituted for the official indicator based on deflated premiums. In the case of two services, architects and advertising, a deflated value series places officla measures based on employment. The primary feature of the new measures used for accountants, computer services and hire-purchase, is the use of deflators which have been specially constructed to reflect more closely than those officially employed developments in the activities in question. The official practice for both construction plant hire and finance leasing has been to base indicators on output developments in user industries.

Instead of this approach the new measures are derived from gross output in the case of construction plant hire and the value of assets newly leased and of the stock of leased assets in the case of finance leasing, each deflated by price indices specifically compiled for the activities in question. The new measures for the covered financial and business services are set alongside the official indicators. The basic date series from which these were derived are such that not all of them cover the full span of years, 1971 to 1986, so that it is convenient to combine them into three groups: five industries-building societies, hire-purchase, insurance, advertising and construction plant hire-for which growth rates are available for the whole period 1971-86; six industries where the information is shown for 1973-86; and all ten covered financial services, architects, finance leasing and computer services-for which alternative and official growth rates can be compared for the period 1978-86. In the case of the first group, for which measures extend over the full period 1971-86, whilst there are some very significant differences between alternative and official growth rates-for building societies the former is appreciably higher than the latter whilst the opposite is true for hire-purchase-the arithmetic average growth rate for all five services, at 4.1 per cent per annum, is identical for both alternative and official measures.

The same generalisation applies to the group of six industries over the period 1973-86: for hire-purchase, advertising, construction plant hire and banking the two measures yield quite different results but these contrasts offset each other so that the average alternative growth rate is identical with the average official growth rate. Results for the group of ten industries, relating to the period 1978-86, paint a very similar picture; of individual industry diversity but overall similarity. In this case only for building societies, insurance, advertising and accountants do alternative and official methods yield rates of output change that are at all akin. Yet, overall, the average alternative growth rate, 7.4 per cent per annum, is not much greater than the 7.0 per cent registered officially.

The official measure for finance leasing is constructed to minimise distortion in GDP measurement whilst the alternative measure has been compiled in such a way as to enhance the reliability of the industry's growth indicator per se. If this service industry is left out of account, the average alternative growth rate, at 6.6 per cent, is below the average official rate, 7.6 per cent. This set of results contains a further point of interest. Whilst, as pointed out, there are substantial differences in the case of most industries between the alternative and official measures, the inter-industry growth patterns are remarkably similar whether gauged by alternative or official indicators: again leaving out finance leasing the correlation coefficient for the remaining nine pairs of, alternative and official, growth rates is +0.95. Although comparisons of unweighted average growth rates can be quite instructive more attention should be focused on differences between alternative and official measures revealed by weighted aggregate indices of the kind. These output indices, derived from the alternative and official measures for individual industries and relating to the same groups of industries and periods specified have been obtained from an aggregation procedure which is based on 1985 contributions to GDP.

The results contained are summarised in the form of average annual rates of growth that also contains growth rates obtained from weights derived from 1980 industry contributions to GDP and 1985 industry employment levels, to test the sensitivity of the results to alternative weighting systems. In the case of the five industries for which there is full coverage over the period 1971 to 1986 the alternative growth rate is 4.4 per cent and the official one 4.8 per cent on the basis of 1985 GDP weights. A discrepancy of no more than a tenth between the two versions is also suggested by 1980 GDP weights. This group of five industries accounted for only 20 per cent of the contribution to GDP and an estimated 27 per cent of employment of all financial and business services in 1985. In contrast the group of six was responsible for 56 per cent of output and an estimated 42 per cent of employment and the group of ten for as much as 74 per cent of output and 56 per cent of employment.

Greater significance should therefore be attached to the results obtained for these latter two groups. All three weighting systems show that for the group of six industries, over the years 1973 to 1986, the official measure understated growth by about a fifth when compared with the aggregate alternative measure; much the same picture emerges for the group of ten industries during the period 1978 to 1986 where, on the basis of both 1985 and 1980 GDP weights, the official measure, compared with the alternative, underestimates growth by about a fifth. When considering this disparity two industries merit special attention: banking which is by some way the largest of the ten industries; and finance leasing on account of the fundamental difference in the methods underlying the alternative and official measures. In fact if banking-with alternative and official growth rates of respectively 8.2 and 6.5 per cent per annum for the period 1978 to 1986-is left out of account the picture hardly changes at all: the alternative aggregate growth rate for the remaining nine industries over the period 1978 to 1986 emerges as 8.0 per cent per annum compared with an official growth rate of 6.0 per cent. This is in sharp contrast to the effect of excluding finance leasing. In this case the alternative growth measure for the nine remaining industries falls to 7.5 per cent whilst the official measure rises to 7.2 per cent so that most of the differential disappears.

Recreational Services

In 1985, recreational services, SIC class 97, contributed almost 6 billion pounds sterling to GDP and provided employment for 430,000 people. Apart from cinemas, for which the official output indicator is based on numbers of attendances, the measures used by the CSO rely for the most part on deflated series of turnover or consumers' expenditure on the service in question. In the case of local authority libraries, however, employment-based indicators are used. In the search for alternative measures it has proved possible, for these services, to base the new indicators largely on numbers of service units. Thus the output index for 'group' 974, broadcasting and theatres, reflects changes in numbers of radio and television hours transmitted and of attendances at theatres etc, whilst that for libraries and museums has been founded on numbers of books issued and numbers of visitors.

The new measures for sport, 'group' 979, an activity that accounts for almost half of the output of recreational services, has been derived from a variety of indicators which reflect, inter alia, changes in numbers of attendances at paying spectator sports, sports hours transmitted by television and radio, membership of participatory sports clubs and measures which trace changes in numbers of betting slips and football coupons. Only in the case of local authority leisure facilities was recourse made to conventional deflated value series. The output series set out for cinemas and for authors and artists are those used officially: that for cinemas being already based on numbers of service units whilst no alternative measure could be readily identified for 'group' 976. For comparison with the overall official measure for recreational services the five component output measures have been combined into a single output index using weights based on 1985 contributions to GDP.

The official measure suggests that the output of this service industry complex grew, between 1973 and 1988, at an average annual rate of 2.9 per cent; the alternative points to a significantly slower rate of increase of 2.0 per cent. One factor which may go some way towards explaining this discrepancy is that whilst in principle the alternative measure includes local authority libraries and leisure facilities throughout the period, the official indicator embraces these activities only since their transfer to class 97 of the 1980 SIC. Yet it can be seen that even in recent years the official measure has registered a significantly higher rate of growth for this industry than that shown by the alternative measure.

THE CATERING TRADES

In 1985 the catering trades' contribution to GDP totalled 7-1/2 pounds sterling billion and the industry employed more than a million people. Output measures for these trades are summarised, in terms of average annual growth rates. In the early years of the period covered the official indicator was based on turnover data supplied by a voluntary panel of catering organisations deflated by price indices specific to each of the catering trades.

From the beginning of the 1980s the official measure has been derived from changes in the margins of the individual catering trades as recorded in the DTI's annual catering trades' enquiry, again deflated by specific price indices. Although in principle it should be possible to measure output in the catering trades on the basis of numbers of service units-hotel bed occupancy, numbers of bar transactions etc-attempts to use this approach proved, for practical reasons, to be fruitless. Therefore to test the sensitivity of the official measure alternative output series were constructed using the price indices officially compiled but applying them throughout to turnover data yielded by the catering trades inquiries, interpolating results for early years where no such inquiries were conducted.

It is clear that these alternative measures alter the picture quite significantly for some trades. Whilst for restaurants, clubs and catering contractors changes in output are not greatly different whether measured on the official or alternative bases, sharply contrasting developments emerge for public houses and the hotel trade: the substantial growth recorded for public houses by the official measure virtually disappears with the alternative, whilst the opposite occurs in the case of hotels. These quite significant modifications to the subsectoral picture, in effect, cancel out: on both official and alternative methods catering output increased over this period by about 1 per cent a year.

The reliability of catering output changes cannot, however, be allowed to rest there. For when these changes are compared with labour force developments there would seem to have been substantial long-term declines in labour productivity: taking the official output measure in conjunction with changes in the number of employees in catering, labour productivity appears to have fallen by as much as 1.7 per cent a year between 1971 and 1986. To help determine whether these results reflect real developments in this service industry or whether they arose from statistical series which are sufficiently unreliable as to produce a misleading picture of events, alternative, more sophisticated, full-time equivalent labour force series have been constructed.

Since both part-time working and self-employment are important features of the catering trades' labour force, allowance for developments in both these aspects has been made in the FTE series shown. Whilst the introduction of FTE labour force series improves the productivity picture there nevertheless remains an apparently substantial fall in catering productivity: an annual average decline of 1.7 per cent a year using numbers of employees is modified to a deterioration of 1.2 per cent on an FTE basis. Of the individual trades only catering contractors emerge with enhanced FTE productivity, displaying an improvement of 1.7 per cent a year. The other four trades register deteriorations: restaurants by 2.1 per cent a year, public houses 0.1 per cent, clubs 3.6 per cent and hotels 1.2 per cent.

It is theoretically feasible, on the basis of most formulations of the production function, that in certain circumstances output in any economic activity might increase over the long term at a rate below that registered for labour inputs. This could arise in particular if there were a fall in capital intensity but such a development does not appear to have been a feature of catering during this period. A measure compiled for the industry suggests that between 1971 and 1986 the stock of equipment grew at an annual average rate of 3.6 per cent a year which, in conjunction with an annual rise of 2.3 per cent in the FTE labour force, points to a 1.4 per cent annual increase in capital intensity. In these circumstances it is difficult to accept that either the official or alternative output measures presented adequately reflect output growth in the catering trades.

A probable explanation of this deficiency is that the measures fail to take sufficient account of developments, in some general sense, in the quality of catering output, be it a reflection of changes in the range of services offered, the milieu in which they are provided, the nature of the food and drink supplied or the standards of customer service. It is relevant that following comparatively little change in its size during the 1950s and 1960s the catering industry's labour force has grown substantially over the last two decades, especially during the early 1970s. These developments have generally been explained by contrasts in the nature of the labour market between, on the one hand, the earlier decades and on the other the 1970s and 1980s. The earlier prevalence of full employment meant that because catering work was notoriously unattractive and ill-paid the industry was able to adjust its labour force towards its basic manning requirements. This kind of effect was reinforced by the impact of the selective employment tax which led to a significant fall in catering employment when it was implemented during the later years of the 1960s and a rapid increase in the early years of the 1970s after its abandonment. This thesis is also supported by case studies of the impact on the industry of technological innovations. A recent survey of organisations operating in the catering trades revealed that rather than causing redundancies 'the time saved by new technology and improved productivity was being used wherever possible to enhance customer service'.

A stagnant productivity performance in catering is equally difficult to reconcile with the rapid growth of both take-away food facilities and self-catering accommodation. In the event it has been decided to use labour inputs, to be precise the FTE measure shown, as a surrogate output measure for this industry. It is felt that whilst far from ideal it provides a less unsatisfactory output measure, over the period in question. On this basis an annual average growth rate of 2.3 per cent emerges for catering output, hardly an unreasonable achievement for what is largely a leisure industry during a period when GDP increased, on average, by 1.7 per cent a year. Furthermore when applied to the individual catering trades this labour force based method yields results, for changes in real output over these years, which are intuitively much more plausible than those derived from either the official or alternative methods. It suggests that between 1971 and 1986 output in all five trades increased substantially: in restaurants by 2.4 per cent a year, in public houses by 2.5 per cent, in clubs by 3.1 per cent, in catering contractors by 2.8 per cent and in hotels by 1.6 per cent.

Measure for all Covered Services

The alternative output measures compiled for financial services, recreational services and the catering trades are combined and compared with their official counterparts. Group 1, for which the series relate to the full period 1971-86, comprises five financial services and the catering trades. Group

2 covering the period 1973-86 includes in addition banking and recreational services. Whilst group 3, for which the output indicators are available for the period 1978-86, embraces all the service industries for which alternative measures have been compiled. These aggregate output indices, both official and alternative, are derived from those presented in the relevant tables using as weights the 1985 contribution of each activity to GDP. The results are summarised in the form of average annual rates of change. To check the sensitivity of these final results alternative and official measures of growth are also compared using as weights the services' 1985 employment levels and 1980 contributions to GDP.

The picture which emerges is one in which the alternative measure consistently points towards a higher growth rate than that indicated by its corresponding official index. Moreover the size of the differential varies comparatively little regardless of the group, period or weighting system to which attention is directed. If most attention is attached-in view of the size of their coverage-to the results for groups 2 and 3, it appears that compared with the alternative methods the official indicators have understated growth by between 13 and 18 per cent. Given that in most cases the alternative measurement methods differ radically from those officially employed it is perhaps remarkable that, overall, the discrepancy should be no greater than this.

To what extent, as it stands, would the official measure of GDP growth be changed if the alternative measure is substituted for the official indicator? The answer is: very little. Basing this adjustment on the alternative/official differential revealed for group 2 the annual average GDP growth rate for 1973-86 is unchanged at 1.3 per cent per annum, and using the group 3 results the annual growth rate for 1978-86 rises from 1.6 per cent to 1.7 per cent. If the disparity between official and alternative growth rates depicted held for the commercial services excluded from this exercise then the official GDP growth rate of 1.3 per cent registered for the period 1973-86 is boosted to 1.5 per cent per annum and the GDP growth rate of 1.6 per cent for the years 1978-86 is raised to 1.9 per cent a year. There are good reasons for supposing that these upward revisions to the GDP growth rate will understate rather than overstate the actual shortfall. In the first place output measures which lean towards numbers of service units will to some extent be biased downwards compared with those derived from deflated sales or turnover values because the data sources in question tend to cover any new services in the latter but not the former. Secondly whilst official output measures which rely on employment series usually incorporate some productivity improvement, this has not been applied to the FTE based measure compiled for catering so that it may well underestimate actual output growth in this activity.

Thirdly salary indices which have been used as surrogate price deflators in the case of accountancy and computer services will tend to overestimate actual output price increases-and therefore bias downwards the resulting output measure-since no allowance is made for the impact on unit labour costs of any productivity improvements in these services. While the implications for GDP measurement of the substitution of alternative aggregate service output indicators may not be unduly significant it is clear that they are more substantial for the commercial service sector as a whole. They are even more significant for individual service complexes. Although the new measure for financial and business services differs relatively little from the official measure, especially if account is taken of the contrasting conceptual treatment of finance leasing in the respective approaches, the alternative obtained for recreational services points to a significantly lower growth rate and that compiled for catering is about twice the official growth rate. Contrasts between alternative and official measures are even more pronounced for individual service industries.

Service Output Measurement

Substitution of the new output measures for those officially compiled would have made little difference to GDP growth rates in recent years. In effect discrepancies which emerged between alternative and official output measures for individual service industries have tended to offset each other. There is no guarantee that this condition would hold in the future and for this reason alone the search for alternative, improved, measures of service output change should be pursued. In contrast significantly large differences between alternative and official output measures have emerged for particular services and these have very important implications for the analysis of economic developments in individual service industries.

The validity of the economic analyses to which these activities are now widely subjected depends crucially on the accuracy of the output and productivity measures that are employed to map their development over time. For this reason, especially, new and improved service output measures are required. The research which lies behind the results is that new service output measures can be further developed both extensively and intensively. Whilst the service industries examined were chosen as systematically as possible on the basis of specific criteria, only limitations imposed by time and resources prevented other service activities being subjected to a similar kind of scrutiny. Moreover in many of those service industries which have been surveyed scope for further measurement improvements remain. In this connection attention needs to be drawn to the results obtained for building societies and the catering trades. In the case of the former serious doubts attach to the alternative measure which, although it yields a growth rate higher than the official one, nevertheless implies, as it stands, a long-term fall in labour productivity in this service industry.

Also it is clear that the search for improved catering output measures needs to be continued: the labour force indicator adopted for the purpose of this exercise must be regarded as no more than a stop-gap strategem though on the basis of existing statistical sources there is at present little immediate prospect of new measures being based on numbers of service output units. None the less the data deficiencies are essentially practical, not conceptual, in nature and with appropriate statistical arrangements could no doubt be remedied eventually: already there is some experience of collecting data relating to hotel room utilisation which some time in the future might form the basis of a service unit-based measure. Generally there seems to exist a large reservoir of data relating to both output indicators and weights, collected by a variety of service industry organisations, which lies outside the purview of official sources. It is difficult to avoid the impression that the current exercise has barely scratched the surface of this fund of material and that, in particular, much is available at the firm level which has yet to be systematically collated in a way that it can be used to measure developments for whole industries.

Certainly it is clear that within the firms in question most service outputs are documented in detail, increasingly in computerised records, so that alternative measures based on numbers of output units should become progressively more practicable. There appear to be two basic options for tapping into this kind of data base. One would comprise an official periodic survey of each of the main service industries in which, as in the case of some industrial censuses, questionnaires would seek information about numbers and values of those output units which are best measured for each service. The inquiries into the distributive, catering and service trades periodically conducted by the Business Statistics Office might be developed in this direction. The alternative is to adopt the approach followed, in the main, in this exercise and base new output measures on the information which is collected by trade associations and other industry organisations. This option is less attractive than the systematic collection of the requisite data, on a comprehensive and consistent basis, by means of an official census.

IMPORTANCE AND USAGE OF DRESS CODES

A survey was conducted to investigate the nature and use of employee dress codes of organizations that market professional services. The study sample consisted of personnel administrators employed in selected service organizations that are members of the American Society of Personnel

Administrators; the total sample included 1000 administrators. The analysis of responses revealed that dress is important in marketing services and that compliance to a dress code is a criterion for employee performance evaluation. While most administrators agreed that dress is a significant factor in their companies' success, few organizations had formal written dress codes; dress codes are most often communicated orally. Traditions in the professions, the expectations of customers, Chief Executive Officers of the organizations, and past experiences were the factors that dominate the development of dress codes.

On the question of dress code requirements for male vs. female employees, the study revealed that more service organizations specify dress for males than for females. For traditional business attire, comparing the dress codes of the different service organizations revealed several significant relationships. In recent years much emphasis has been placed on the importance of dress and appearance for professional success. Often organizations make an effort to manage dress and appearance so as to communicate to the client/customer in the most effective manner. Such controls have traditionally been manifested in policies called "dress codes." The responsibility for the administration of dress codes has conventionally been treated as a personal function. "Proper" business dress has long been a part of the norms of professional services practitioners such as bankers, accountants, stock brokers and management consultants.

However, it is interesting to note that in the marketing literature there is little attention devoted to dress as it relates to the marketing of professional services. This is particularly interesting when one considers the growth of professional service industries as a part of the U.S. economy and the broadscale increases in attention focused on services marketing by practitioners and academicians. The marketing literature does, however, address the issue of personal appearance as it relates to the personal sales interview. It is well documented from a behavioural standpoint that dress has a significant impact upon perception and image formation as a part of the interpersonal communication process. Peak discovered that when personality traits are correlated with clothing styles, persons who wear conservative clothing are perceived as being more intelligent, mature, generous, sincere, trustful, understanding and dependable than those wearing more "daring" styles. Premeaux and Mondy, dress establishes a level of respect and authority.

This is often necessary to get the work done. In a study on occupation and grooming it was found that less positive characteristics are attributed to those who were groomed "poorly" than to those well groomed. There is an essential difference between the professional salesperson and the professional service practitioner which underlies the justification of this study. Sales personnel are designated as the "front-line" customer contact persons for an organization which markets goods. Management, as well as salespersons themselves, are not only aware of the role of personal appearance and dress in interpersonal communication, but have employed the resources necessary to incorporate dress codes into promotion and marketing strategies. On the other hand, it is argued that professional service practitioners see themselves as "doers" rather than, sellers".

Therefore, it is felt by some that these employees do not focus the necessary attention on those behavioural factors important in selling or marketing as would designated marketing personnel. As Denny states: One of the fundamental misconceptions many accountants have about marketing is that...someone else can bring in the new clients and then they can take over and do the work. Unfortunately they are wrong...It takes an accountant to sell accounting services. The literature dealing with services marketing ends support to the premise that the dress behaviour of employees could be a salient attribute of the buyer when involved in the purchase process of a professional service.

Two commonly cited characteristics of services, intangibility and inseparability, give credence to this postulate. Because services are intangible in nature, perceptual and communication problems exist during the exchange process which make the true quality of the service difficult to evaluate and distinguish. Pricing and valuation problems result, leading the buyer to feel uncertainty. With complex technical services such as legal, financial or consulting research, the problem is magnified because of the lack of knowledge of the buyer. It can be argued that because the buyer cannot see the true quality of the service for evaluation that he might use surrogate criteria such as the behaviour of the practitioner, the physical appearance of the facility or other tangible cues. Dress behaviour, then, can become a tangible evaluative criteria for the buyer, regardless of the relationship dress has to the skills of the practitioner or quality of the service performed. Another theoretical argument offered which distinguishes services from goods is that of inseparability. Often production and consumption of services cannot be separated temporally or spatially.

Consequently, personal contact exists between the producer and consumer, allowing the buyer to have the perceptual exposure necessary to observe behavioural and physical characteristics of the seller. The premise set forth as the rationale for this study is that through their behaviour, each practitioner in a service organization which has customer/client contact plays a role in marketing that organization's service. Since dress is an important aspect of that behaviour which plays a role in the communication process during this interaction, dress behaviour can be a salient factor in the exchange process. If this premise is accepted, and dress is perceived to be important in marketing of professional services, then the question of management or control of employee dress arises. One would assume that organizations would make an effort to manage appearance so as to communicate to the client/customer in the most effective manner.

The purposes of this study were to identify the nature and extent of usage of dress codes among selected service organizations and to determine the importance of dress in the marketing of professional services as reflected in the attitudes and opinions of personnel administrators and in the policies of their organizations. The study sample consisted of personnel administrators employed in selected service organizations that are members of the American Society of Personnel Administrators; the total sample included 1000 administrators. The study involved a questionnaire designed to secure information about the perceived importance of dress codes among selected service organizations. Questions concerned the importance of employee appearance for service organizations, the factors used in developing dress codes, the requirements of dress codes, the effect of dress codes on employee performance evaluations, and the dress code requirements for male and female employees.

Questionnaires were returned by 304 personnel administrators, a 30.4 per cent return. Data was analysed using frequency distributions, and cid-squares were computed to determine statistical significance. The number of respondents from various types of service industries which were used in this study: Type of Service Organization Number in Sample Management/Marketing Consultants 51 Health Care and Human Services 47 Hotel/Restaurant/Entertainment 40 Financial 39 Employment Agencies 39 Other 35 Engineering and/or Computer Services 30 Legal 13- Total 304 The personnel administrators responding to the questionnaire clearly indicated that appearance of professional employees was a significant factor when a potential client or customer evaluated their company's services.

Most of the respondents indicated that personal appearance was a "very important" factor in this evaluation process. Of the 304 responding personnel administrators, 73% indicated that a dress code, either formally or informally communicated, had been established for their service organizations. Among those respondents whose organizations employed any type of dress code, 67% noted that individual employee compliance to the code was a criterion for employee performance evaluation. Eighty-five per cent of the respondents indicated that compliance to a dress code was either absolutely necessary or very important when employers underwent performance evaluation. The employment of an established dress code varied little by type of services, ranging from 66 per cent for management consultants to 83 per cent for employment placement services. But the differences in the formalization and use of compliance varied more dramatically. While only 19 per cent of management consulting firms had established written dress codes, 60 per cent of the hotel/ restaurant/entertainment groups used written codes. The data revealed that differences in the use of written codes existed between types of services, and that these were statistically significant at the.05 level. Only 42 per cent of management consulting firms considered dress code compliance in evaluation of their employees, while 80 per cent of employment placement/personnel services considered dress compliance as a factor in performance reviews.

The respondents were asked to rank the level of importance of eleven factors when developing a dress code. The scale ranged from "very important," "fairly important," "of little importance," to "no importance," with each given numerical weights of 1, 2, 3, and 4 in corresponding order. Mean scores and the percentages responding to each level of importance are reported. Customer expectations, tradition/ convention in the profession, and the opinion of the organization's C.E.O. were the three most important factors listed by the respondents in the development of dress codes. Among those respondents whose organizations employed any type of dress code, chi-square analysis was performed to compare the classifications of the companies to the formality of the dress codes.

Though not statistically significant, the study revealed that more of the local/independent service organizations used formal written dress codes, while more of the multi-located firms utilized dress codes which were informally communicated. Over one-third of the respondents indicated that their dress codes had been established within the last 20 years. Many of the companies had made changes in their dress codes within the last 10 years. Though not statistically significant, it was found that the firms with revised dress codes were more relaxed in requiring a traditional business look. The differences in the degree of requirement for wearing a "traditional business suit" by type of business organization. Of all types of services in the sample, financial services most required business suits, and engineering/computer least. Those organizations classified as personnel services expected the wearing of suits with skirts more often than others, and again the engineering/computer services required the traditional suit with skirt to the least degree. Most of the respondents indicated that dress is important in marketing services and that compliance to a dress code is a criterion for employee performance evaluation.

While most administrators agreed that dress is a significant factor in their companies' success, few organizations had formal written dress codes; dress codes are more often communicated orally. The results of this study lend support to the premise that dress and appearance of employees could be a salient attribute of the buyer when involved in the purchase process of a professional service. Although the usage of dress codes differed among service organizations, many administrators agreed that dress and appearance are particularly important in making an initial impression and in progressing in a business career. More needs to be known about the actual impact of dress and appearance on the communication process with clients and customers in professional service organizations.

QUALITY INTO SMALL- AND MEDIUM-SIZED HOTELS

Total Quality Management can be defined as a satisfaction of social shareholders via implementing effective planning, programmes, policies, and strategies, as well as using human and other assets efficiently and continually within an organization. This approach will continue to be one of the hot topics among practitioners, academics, and professionals in the new millennium. This presents how a new TQM readiness model can be utilized for providing social shareholders' satisfaction and continuous improvement in small- and medium-sized hotel organizations. Five-star hotel staffs appear to have better organizational strengths than four-star hotel staffs in North Cyprus. Four-star hotel employees indicate substantial differences in their perceptions concerning TQM readiness elements. An extensive literature review has been conducted.

Issues examined include the following:

- Where to start?
- Is it valuable to bring such a total system?
- Should some parts be imported instead of the whole? and
- Is there any cheap way to bring TQM to small- or medium-sized organizations?

Oakland, the first decision of where to begin can be daunting, referred to as the Total Quality Paralysis problem in quality-management literature. This has been confirmed by other experts and academics who state that small- and medium-sized enterprises generally are less comfortable in bringing TQM into their organizations than large companies are due to limited managerial knowledge, skill, ability, incentives, resources, and time. Only a few studies have been developed on TQM readiness assessment criteria in small- and medium-sized firms. Scholars and others have a common understanding that the more clearly the TQM readiness factors are assessed, the healthier a transition can be achieved to the TQM process.

The TQM literature states, "Organizations, which are ready for change in climate, have more opportunity to achieve a successful implementation in a shorter period of time". A common point endorsed in the literature is that there must be a readiness survey before designing, developing, and implementing a TQM programme. This may help to determine TQM factors within an organization and to identify potential problems that may create resistance to TQM and will help to develop a database for future comparisons. Walker and Salameth have stated that only a small percentage of hotels have heard "the siren call of TQM implementations" even in the U.S. It is interesting to note that after 10 years, the literature regarding hotels is still sparse. Although some viable hotels in limited geographical areas have reported that their TQM performance resulted in profit increased, employee satisfaction, and better usage of economic resources, only a few case studies have been published. As Bloomquist and Breiter indicate, "While those case studies are important in elaboration on the theme of quality management, there remain no reliable statistical data on industry-wide performance credited to quality management."

CHALLENGE FOR HOTEL ORGANIZATIONS

Cyprus is the third-largest island in the Mediterranean. Cyprus has a great historical heritage, conserved environment beauties, and a good climate, and after the war in 1974, the island was divided into north and south parts. No study has been conducted on how TQM can be applied in small- and medium-sized hotel organizations in North Cyprus, which is a major deficiency since tourism is the leading sector. North Cyprus is certainly not the only country where tourism is the most important business sector. The World Tourism Organization statistics, tourism in the world is expected to reach a volume of $US 4 trillion after 2000. This will mean that one out of nine people in the world will be employed in tourism industry in 2010.

The aim of this analysis is to provide a better understanding of how different groups of managers, chiefs, and employees perceive their readiness towards the TQM philosophy in North Cyprus four and five-star hotels. In June 1999, a preliminary investigation was carried out through one-on-one interviews with several assistant general managers, department managers, chiefs, and other lower-level employees from the four- and five-star hotels of North Cyprus. The aim was to design a more realistic TQM readiness model, as well as to prepare a better quantitative questionnaire for the targeted hotels.

The hypotheses of this study are as follows: There is no difference between small-and medium-sized hospitality organizations' hierarchical levels concerning their TQM readiness. There is a difference between small-and medium-sized hospitality organizations' hierarchical levels concerning their TQM readiness. A new model with its first selected eight factors of TQM culture was identified. These factors are leadership, participation, teamwork, employee satisfaction, empowerment, influence, change, and training. It is important to mention that the assessment factors may not represent all the TQM readiness culture factors. In time, other related factors may be added to this group.

THE ASSUMPTIONS UNDERLYING THE MODEL

The assumptions underlying this model include the following:

- The readiness model factors are iterative; in other words, every organization may use several different preassessment factors, and the rank of these factors also may be different.
- TQM is not a completely new strategic system but rather is a process of developing the current system, opening its way to continuous improvement.
- The readiness model will decrease the total cost, time, and energy of an organization in transforming it into a new TQM culture.

The model involves two important stages. The first stage is to understand and to monitor the present organizational system, especially when dealing with the factors of TQM philosophy and its soft components such as leadership, teamwork, participation, influence, empowerment, and employee satisfaction.

The second stage is the process of examining the gap between upper, middle, and lower layers of personnel in order to prevent possible resistance from different layers at the time of transitioning to a new TQM culture, as well as preparing a database for future assessments. This database may serve as a benchmark where yearly data can be compared with the previous year, necessary precautions can be taken against weaknesses, and the organization can open its way to a continuous improvement process.

Of course, if the necessary proactive precautions can be taken successfully every year, the actual gap among the layers of staff will be narrowed in terms of employee resistance and inefficient use of time, money, and energy. As a result of successful TQM applications, the social shareholders will be more satisfied, and effects of internal challenges will be minimized for the organization. The data in this study were obtained from four- and five-star hotels. In these hotels, the general manager, usually the owner or a relative who has a very close relationship to the investors, has overall responsibility for all activities. The department managers work under the control of the general managers and report directly to them.

Department chiefs largely serve the role of supervisors, reporting to the department manager. The rationale for selecting four- and five-star hotels is because they attract the majority of tourists in North Cyprus. A total of seven out of 10 hotels were included in the study. There are two hotels that are identified as five-star hotels; the remaining five are four-star hotels.

All seven of these five- and four-star hotels were sampled, which provide an overall 100 per cent sampling ratio among five-star hotels and 87 per cent sampling ratio among four-star hotels. This stratified-sampling ratio is very high, and therefore the research is designed to be representative. Stratified sampling has been used in determining the number of employees of four- and five-star hotels. The stratified sampling technique "separates the population into relative homogenous groups".

The hotels employed approximately 550 permanent staff according to statistics gathered from the tourism ministry at the time of the research. The average return rate from the quantitative survey collected from the managers, chiefs, and employees was 73 per cent, 85 per cent, and 39 per cent respectively. Among the 500 questionnaires distributed, 267 were returned, 10 were not completely answered, and 13 were considered biased. Consequently, 23 responses were deleted from the analyses. The net return rate of 43.8 per cent was quite adequate for the set of questions. A perception survey, a self-administered questionnaire addressed to all managers, chiefs, and employees of the targeted hotels, was prepared in order to collect the necessary readiness data from a more comprehensive perspective. Respondents were asked to indicate their degree of agreement with each statement on a five-point Likert scale: 1=strongly agree, 2=agree, 3=somewhat agree /disagree, 4=disagree, and 5=strongly disagree. Furthermore, three questions were asked about the ranking of the hotel, type of ownership, and the job position. Items for each subscale were subjected to a reliability assessment. The Cronbach coefficient alpha value for the total scale was .9602, and the subscales were 9092, .8425, .8812, .7177, .6993, .7164, .6976, and .7744 for leadership, team, influence, empowerment, participation, training, change, and satisfaction. Usually, a reliability coefficient above 0.50 is considered to be a sufficiently high reliability.

A factor analysis of the TQM readiness questions in the survey was performed. In order to identify the actual factors in the survey, all questions that did not load cleanly on one factor were dropped from further analysis, which left 61 questions. The frequency and one-way analysis of variance were calculated as a second statistictical technique. Levin and Rubin, ANOVA tests are used for determining the significance of the differences among more than two sample means. The critical mean scores of the TQM readiness survey for the four- and five-star hotel mangers, chiefs, and staff. A one-way ANOVA analysis is used to explore whether there is a significant difference in the perceptions among upper-, middle-, and lower-level employees of the hotels.

In terms of highest and lowest scores, it has been observed that there is little consistency in perceptions among the three staff levels. Results for five-star hotels indicate that employees have significantly higher scores on seven items: teamwork, leadership, and influence. For those seven items, employees had the highest mean scores. Considering all 61 questions, four-star hotel employees are less positive than five-star hotel employees. They have significantly higher scores on 32 items. For those 32 items, all staff has different scores on each item. Interestingly, the managers have higher mean scores than chiefs and employees on eight items, which are mainly dealt with through satisfaction, empowerment, participation, and leadership. The chiefs gave negative scores to change, empowerment, teamwork, and participation factors through six questions. Four-star hotels had aggregate means for the 61 items indicated by managers, chiefs, and employees. Both managers and chiefs expressed a moderate level of TQM readiness, while employees exhibited a low level of TQM readiness.

However, in five-star hotels, the aggregate means for the same items were managers, chiefs and staff, where all expressed a moderate level of TQM readiness. Therefore, the null hypothesis was rejected, and the alternative hypothesis was accepted. North Cyprus is a suitable island for tourism because of its undeveloped industry, rich historical and cultural heritage, natural beauty, and relatively unspoiled environment.

The various governments that have come to power all have stated that tourism is the primary sector in achieving economic development. The aim of this research was to find out how different groups of managers, chiefs, and employees of four- and five-star hotels in North Cyprus perceive their readiness towards the TQM philosophy With this study it is possible to point out to the owners arid managers the weak and strong aspects of the TQM soft side components they are practicing, and it also provides an opportunity to remove the resistance and conflicts that arise because of perception differences about this philosophy Some researchers point out that in many cases, TQM has been applied without any readiness research and has thus resulted in failure.

As Weeks, "The perceptions of managers, chiefs, and employees are crucial because individuals act as if their beliefs or perceptions are real." Social shareholders are defined by the author as interested or chain parties who are in the same business arena and are a part of the same business life in a free market economic system such as customers, owners, employees, suppliers, government, municipality, and so forth. Two of the five-star hotels are in the same complex and therefore are considered as one hotel. Two hotels have been excluded from the research due to extraordinary reasons.

COMPETITIVE ADVANTAGE

This offers an in-depth treatment of conversion franchising, where new franchisees are added to a franchised system by recruiting existing independent entrepreneurs or competitors' franchisees. The first part of the paper examines conversion franchising as a source of competitive advantage. This discussion leads to the articulation off our propositions. The second part of the paper looks at the empirical results of our study of 72 North American franchisors. Seventy-two per cent of these firms use conversion franchising in their domestic markets, and 26 per cent use conversions in international locales.

The propositions relating to a franchisor's decision to use conversions based on increased levels of experience, economic resources, and to a lesser extent skills! knowledge, all were supported. These results lend support to the literature indicating that resources and skills serve as sources of competitive advantage. Implications for research and practice are discussed. Franchising is emerging as a preferred method of doing business throughout the global economy.

A recent study by the International Franchise Association estimated that, by early in the new millennium, nearly 50 per cent of every U.S. consumer dollar would have been spent in franchised locations. Business franchising has spread rapidly to most continents during the past decade. Given the widespread use of franchising, how can firms leverage better this method of doing business? Some firms have gained increased advantage by adding mobility to their franchised operation by bringing their products/services to the customer where and when they demand them.

But increasingly, firms are turning to conversion franchising as a way of enhancing growth and of gaining competitive advantage in multiple markets. Conversion franchising occurs when a franchisor adds new franchisees to the system by recruiting existing independent businesses or competitors' franchisees. The purpose of this paper is to examine closely this emerging phenomenon by drawing on relevant literature and by reporting the results of an exploratory study of conversion franchising. Before discussing some of the competitive advantages that can accrue from employing conversion franchising, it first is instructive to review some of the advantages of traditional franchising. Franchising's longevity and success also may be due to the fact that, organizationally, it represents a collaborative alliance. The alliance depends on the cooperation of two entrepreneurs in order to be successful. Further, these partners depend on cooperation among a network of entrepreneurs to advance common methods and goals, like the sharing of information on innovations that potentially could benefit all franchise partners.

Franchising traditionally has offered many competitive advantages over independently formed and operated businesses. The franchisor has access to capital at lower risk; cost sharing with the franchisee; rapid market penetration at a relatively lower cost than establishing one's own distribution system; economies of scale; a motivated workforce of indigenous entrepreneurs; and reduced monitoring and control costs. The franchisee gets an opportunity to enter a business at less cost with a proven product or service and brand name. Additionally, the franchisee frequently receives management assistance in the areas of business location, facilities design, operating procedures, purchasing, and marketing. These advantages have been born out by a superior survival rate for franchising over independent ventures. Next, we turn to a discussion of conversion franchising and its competitive advantages.

Conversion franchising occurs when a franchisor adds new franchisees to the system by recruiting independent businesses, chains, and/or franchisees from other franchised systems. Conversion franchising offers additional advantages to those discussed under traditional franchising. The use of conversion franchising appears to be expanding in recent years, as several industries have experienced changing environmental conditions that often have combined to favour this form of franchising. The environmental conditions fostering conversions include economic, market, competitive, and technological changes. A contracting economy can mean tight credit policies, making it difficult to raise funds for new projects. During one such period, 3.7 per cent of the domestic hotels converted to a new brand affiliation. A restricted real estate market has led many fast food franchisors to convert existing urban locations to their system rather than to devel op new sites. Saturated markets and increased competition coupled with the growing consumer demand for rejuvenated brand names have generated conversions in the real estate and hospitality industries. Independents have converted to ReMax and ERA, while Holiday Inn has converted some Ramada Inns and vice versa.

Keeping abreast of changing technology has forced firms to seek conversions with systems on the cutting edge of technology, such as Century 21 and Coldwell Banker in Real Estate or Marriott's reservation system in the lodging industry. Resource-based models of organization indicate that established know-how serves as a basis for competitive advantage. Experienced franchisors have developed such managerial capabilities. Moreover, experienced firms often operate in more competitive arenas, in turn forcing them to try innovative strategies such as conversions. Experienced franchisors have learned to share their know-how with franchisees and have established a record of strong performance, in part because they have taken the time to build brand equity and economies of scale in purchasing, advertising, and distribution, all of which are attractive to independent businesses.

Thus, we suggest the following proposition: Proposition 1: The decision to use conversion franchising is associated positively with the experience of the franchisor. Once a business has converted to a new franchise, is the conversion likely to lead to sustainable competitive advantage? Possible answers to this question are examined in the ensuing discussion. Using the framework of competitive advantage from the field of strategic management is consistent with the view expressed by Castrogiovanni and Justis that researchers need to consider findings from outside the franchising field to assess their generalizability to franchisors. Competitive advantage is concerned with developing a value-creating strategy by uniquely combining bundles of valuable firm resources and skills to yield positional advantages that result in positive outcomes. Firm resources include both tangible and intangible assets. Firm skills include organizational, technical, and market knowledge, among others. Aaker argues that a retail location superior to the competition's can act as a key asset, leading to competitive advantage. Barney suggests that a valuable location can act as an imperfectly imitable physical capital resource for the firm, while Day and Wensley see location as a tangible resource that can enable a firm to exercise its capabilities, leading to positional advantage.

An existing location may be the only space available on a crowded playing field. This is particularly true in the restaurant, retail, and hotel industries, where location is a key element. Franchisors can acquire location resources in tight real estate markets by converting independents or chains that possess strategic locations. A strong brand name may be regarded as a superior resource or as a key asset, leading to competitive advantage for today's firms. Consumers in every industry are increasingly brand conscious. At the core of the franchising concept is the bundling of a brand or a trade name with a good or service to sell to entrepreneurs in return for fees or royalties. The need to maintain brand equity motivates franchisors to grow their systems in order to develop promotion economies and, therefore, to spread promotion costs over more units.

Converting independents to a franchise system allows for rapid growth and increased name recognition. For example, in the hotel industry converting members of other chains has been shown to lead to increased occupancy rates. Thus, conversions permit firms to reposition themselves under a new brand to enhance their competitive position. Human resources are critical to the proper execution of any strategy Franchising taps into entrepreneurs who sign on as franchisees to manage individual business units. Sen provides an extended discussion of the franchisee as a source of managerial talent. While entrepreneurs may be motivated to do well, they often are inexperienced and require considerable training on the part of the franchisor. Using inexperienced franchisees poses a risk of adverse selection, that is, the franchisee misrepresents his/her abilities to the franchisor. Conversion franchising enables the franchisor to bring in experienced franchisees who already have managed a similar business in the industry, either as an independent or as a franchisee for a competitor, thereby reducing the risk of adverse selection.

Experienced managers are more likely to enhance a repositioned unit's performance than one with less industry experience. Furthermore, such an experienced franchisee requires less training support. An existing customer base is a major resource that independents and members of other chains possess that can be internalized by the franchisor upon conversion. Since converts can resume business rapidly with existing customers, royalty streams also can begin flowing quickly to the franchisor. Of course, an additional benefit is that a competitor now has been co-opted into the system instead of working against it. We suggest the following: Proposition 2: The franchisor's decision to use conversion franchising is associated with the potential resource advantages provided by conversions. It has just been argued that conversion franchising brings together key resources of the franchisor and franchisee that have a high potential for improving the competitive positioning of each alliance member. We now will examine important skills that can play a role in creating competitive advantage.

As a cooperative alliance, conversion franchising facilitates the sharing and enhancement of skills to improve the competitive position of both the convert and the franchisor in expanding markets. Skills or capabilities are those attributes that enable the firm to coordinate and to exploit its resources. At the core of the firm's capabilities are its knowledge base from which the skills originate. Thus, we now examine the role knowledge of markets, technology, and organization plays as key sources of competitive advantage provided by a firm's skills. When a franchisor enters a new market, he or she does so with a limited knowledge of local market conditions and consumer preferences. Since cultures, consumer behaviour, and marketing methods are often different in various markets, franchised systems may need to be adapted to fit local requirements better. Feltenstein argues that firms need to think globally but to act locally and that much of the variability in sales, service, costs, and margins is determined by local market knowledge. Experience in growing the business provides enhanced knowledge for franchisors in areas such as market and site selection.

Acquiring experienced converts helps leverage the advantage of such experience. Moreover, converting independents or other chain members who have been operating in the local market for some time allows the franchisor to internalize these skills into the franchise system. Newly allied members also can aid the franchisor in maneuvering around local rules and regulations that otherwise could slow down or could block a venture. Since conversions typically are of firms operating in the same type or in closely related businesses, converts bring their technical knowledge and expertise to the partnership. Two general types of technical knowledge are especially relevant in the case of conversions: industry and franchising knowledge. Knowledge relevant to the industry in terms of competitors, substitutes, methods of distribution, and general industry practices are critical to determining competitive advantage.

A convert brings new perspective on industry knowledge to the franchisor, broadening the latter's knowledge base and vice versa. Experience in a particular type of franchising is critical to a system's competitive advantage. The franchise concept is developed on what is believed to be a successful set of practices, and then knowledge bundles are replicated for franchisees. Independents who convert may obtain the immediate advantages of competing with a proven franchise concept. Converts who are previous franchisees presumably

have switched because they perceive the new franchisor to have a superior franchise concept. Such franchise-experienced converts, however, also may provide additional knowledge from their prior franchising experience to enhance the concept of their new franchisor, thereby providing advantages for the entire system. Converts' technical skills are enhanced by the franchisor through extensive training of new members through operating manuals and procedures, and through technical guidance and support. For example, PIP Printing, a leader in the quick-printing industry, offers its franchisees training workshops. The technical skills of the franchisee are enhanced further by the introduction of sophisticated computer systems. In real estate, 20 per cent of the firms in the U.S. are organized as a franchise. New franchisees in this industry gain access to nationwide databases of existing housing stock. Franchising enables a firm to harness the efforts of entrepreneurs while reducing the costs of monitoring a large multiunit organization.

Thus, organizational skills revolve around monitoring to prevent franchisees who either may under invest in their units or may shirk on product quality because these actions affect the entire franchise system. The scale or size of the system contributes to improved organizational coordination. Increased size of the firm enhances monitoring capabilities of the franchisor by reducing the lower per unit costs of monitoring. Conversions enable a franchisor to expand more quickly, thereby strengthening the organizational monitoring skills of the franchisor. Another way to control opportunism is through the payment of fees to the franchisor; this provides financial incentive not to behave opportunistically because the franchisor risks forfeiting the fee if the franchisor suspends the relationship. Monitoring capability also can be enhanced by learning how best to control the franchisee's behaviour over time.

Thus, the longer the franchisor has been offering franchises, the greater the likelihood of improved monitoring skills. Independents can gain other improved organizational efficiencies, such as increased purchasing power, joint or

pooled advertising, and other benefits of similar economies of scale, by joining a franchise system. We offer the following proposition: Proposition 3: The franchisor's decision to use conversion franchising is associated with the potential skill advantages provided by conversions. The literature on competitive advantages stresses those factors that facilitate the development of competitive advantage. However, traditional strategic management theory also notes that the acquisition of skills and resources may also be seen as threats or as challenges confronting the firm when undertaking a new strategy.

Anecdotal evidence from franchise experience suggests that certain problems may be encountered when making conversions. Some of the resource-related challenges posed by conversions include the added time it takes to implement a programme or to socialize or to retrain converts. Newly acquired entrepreneurs may be experienced but may be unwilling to work as part of a team or to readily adopt new business methods, thus diluting the advantages of a conversion. Market, technical, and organizational capabilities may be threatened because of the need to adopt new rules or methods to accommodate a new local market or to attract a convert to join. In short, the franchise concept and standard contract may be changed for opportunistic rather than strategic reasons in order to attract and retain new converts. The reality of the existence of such threats or barriers suggests the following: Proposition 4: The franchisor's decision to use conversion franchising will he associated negatively with the perceived existence of threats posed by the conversion.

The purpose of this empirical part is to provide a description of the current nature and extent of the use of conversion franchising among North American franchisors; and to provide an initial examination of the propositions relating to the factors behind the decision to use conversion franchising by franchisors. A random sample stratified by size and industry of 250 North American franchisors were selected for the study from the Franchise Annual. The top manager of each firm was sent a cover letter and a two-page questionnaire

concerning their use of conversion franchising; one follow-up mailing was sent three weeks later. Seventy-eight firms responded. Six decided not to participate because of mergers, company policy, etc.; 72 firms returned useable questionnaires for a 29 per cent response rate. This compares favourably with other surveys of franchise companies that have reported similar return rates. The profile of franchisors in our sample reveals a good distribution of firms across eight broad industry sectors. The firms are large, averaging 746 total units and having an average of 23 years experience in franchising. The majority of responding managers hold sufficiently high level positions in their organizations to be considered knowledgeable about their firm's franchise strategies. A comparison of respondent firms to a random sample of 40 non respondents in terms of industry, size, and age revealed no significant differences.

This should reduce concerns of response bias in our sample. The survey instrument consisted of 10 questions. After defining conversion franchising, the first question asked the respondents to indicate their agreement concerning 18 characteristics of conversion franchising. These characteristics represented the advantages and barriers of conversion franchising. Responses were made on a Likert-type scale ranging from 1 = not at all to 5 = highly descriptive of your experience. Other questions asked whether the firm used conversion franchising and explored the extent and reasons for doing so. The last three questions explored the use of conversions in international markets. We describe the variables used to explore the four propositions. The decision to convert was assessed by the following survey question: Has your firm used conversion franchising now or in the past? A simple yes/no response was recorded. This is the categorical dependent variable for investigating the propositions.

The remaining variables serve as the independent variables. Franchisor experience was expressed as the number of years the firm had been in business. These were combined further into two factors using principle components analysis with varimax rotation; these factors explain 50 per cent of the variance in conversion advantages. One factor represents "market/location skills" and is comprised of 4 items and has an eigenvalue of 1.58 and a reliability of = .60. The second factor represents "economic resources" and is comprised of five items and has an eigen-value of 2.87 and a reliability of varies = .73. Two items did not load on any factor. A third item was dropped from the market factor due to reliability problems. These latter three items were not included in any tests of the propositions. Other sources of competitive advantages based on skills were drawn from the Franchise Annual. Technical advantages included seven dummy variables representing eight industry sectors.

Franchising knowledge was assessed by the number of years the firm had been franchising. The organizational skills assessed were monitored through scale and financial bonding. Scale was measured by the number of franchised units possessed and financial bonding was measured using the initial franchising fee charged by the franchisor. Competitive barriers/threats were assessed strictly with subjective measures drawn from the eighteen conversion franchising characteristics described earlier.

Seven of the items represented potential barriers or threats. These were reduced to two factors using principle components analysis. The factors explain 49 per cent of the variance in conversion barriers. One factor was labeled "changes" because of the adjustments to existing procedures required by conv ersions. This factor was comprised of three items and has an eigenvalue of 1.52 and a reliability of infinity = .50. The second barrier was labeled "effort" because of the extra effort required by the franchisor to make conversions and was comprised of four items and possesses and eigenvalue of 1.89 and a reliability of infinity = .60 The nature and extent of conversion franchising is described using descriptive statistics.

The exploration of the propositions was analysed using discriminant analysis. The decision to convert represents a nominal dependent variable. The analysis derives a linear combination of independent variables that will discriminate best between the firms that use conversion franchising and the nonusers. The analysis determines whether the competitive advantages and barriers posed by conversion franchising account for a significant variance in the decision to convert. In addition, this method of analysis determines both the predictive accuracy of the independent variables and their relative importance in explaining the decision to convert. Seventy-two per cent of the firms surveyed use conversion franchising in their domestic markets. Almost half began using conversions prior to 1987; the remaining firms have started using conversions since that time. Among the firms using conversions, an average of 26 per cent of their units are conversions. In responding to an openended question as to why businesses converted to their franchise, our respondents identified eight major reasons. The most frequently cited reasons were to acquire a brand name, which represents one of the major competitive resources conversions can provide businesses.

Awareness, identity, and recognition on a national or global level were cited as the chief benefits of branding. Franchisor characteristics and operating results were tied for second as the most frequently cited reasons for conversion. Key franchisor characteristics included proprietary products and quality of operation and system. Operating performance benefits of conversions included better pricing, leading to increased sales and profitability. Support services such as technology and research and development, as well as training, each were tied for third in importance for conversions. These represent technological and organizational skills frequently mentioned as advantages of joining a good franchise system. Cost savings and other marketing benefits represented the fourth and fifth major reasons why franchisors believe that businesses convert to their system.

These reasons appear to be congruent with the expected competitive advantages of conversion franchising discussed previously. One of the difficulties in using conversions is that franchisors may have to make adjustments to their normal franchise plans in order to attract well-run businesses to convert. However, less than 25 per cent of the franchisors using conversions needed to make any changes to their normal conversion franchise plan. Most changes made to attract converts included reduced fees; added training; reduced royalties; covered remodeling costs; additional capital; longer contracts; and other. Thus, a variety of changes are made by a minority of franchisors in order to attract businesses to convert to their system. The majority of franchisors who are currently using conversions to grow plan to continue using them in the future. Thirty-one per cent plan to increase their use of conversions; 25 per cent plan to use them at the same rate as in the past. Only two per cent of the franchisors plan to decrease their use of conversions in their domestic markets. These intentions indicate that franchisors are satisfied that conversion franchising delivers distinct advantages over other forms of doing business.

The survey also briefly explored the franchisors' use of conversions in international markets. Twenty-six per cent of the respondents use conversion franchising in international markets. Half of these franchisors began using conversions internationally in 1990 or after, and currently an average 5.8 per cent of their overseas units are conversions. The country markets in which they have the largest number of conversions include Canada, Germany, France, and the U.K.. Importantly, of the franchisors using conversions internationally, 61 per cent intend to increase their future use of conversions internationally. By way of summary, the descriptive data reveal that a substantial proportion of North American franchisors are using conversion franchising. Businesses were attracted to convert because of numerous competitive advantages associated with conversion franchises. The future of conversions appears to be quite promising, especially in international markets, as the domestic market becomes more saturated.

All four propositions advanced regarding the factors associated with a franchisor's decision to use conversion franchising were examined using discriminant analysis. Since there were only two categories for the dependent variable, a single discriminant function was derived. The function, using competitive advantages and barriers to predict the decision to convert, is meaningful. The function accounts for 55 per cent of the variance in the decision to convert. The validity of the function is ascertained by how well it predicts the classification of firms between those that use conversion franchises and those who do not. The derived function correctly classified 93 per cent of the firms. This is almost a 33 per cent improvement over chance alone. A statistically significant and valid function also may be interpreted. For interpretation, we use the discriminant loadings from the structure matrix. These loadings are simple correlations between each independent variable and the discriminant function. The loadings can be interpreted similar to factor loadin gs to assess the relative contribution of each independent variable.

The analysis of the discriminant loadings and their ability to discriminate between franchisors who convert and those who do not reveals five variables that significantly explain the decision to convert. Proposition 1, the decision to convert is associated with franchisor experience. Only experienced franchisors with an established reputation and system can use conversions meaningfully. Proposition 1 is supported as "experience," has a relatively high, positive loading, and is also a significant discriminator between franchisors who use conversions and those who do not. Proposition 2, concerning the resource advantages associated with conversion franchising, is supported. "Economic resources" has a high positive loading, and its mean is also significantly different between the two groups of franchisors. Firms that use conversions perceive that they derive greater competitive resource advantages than firms who do not u se conversions. Proposition 3 concerning the association of "skill/knowledge" advantages of conversion partially is supported. Franchise skills market skills, and industry knowledge all are associated with the decision to convert.

Franchise and market skills have the two highest, positive loadings and are significant discriminators as indicated by tests of mean differences. The retail industry sector has a moderate but negative loading. The negative loading suggests that nonretail industry experience is more relevant in the decision to convert; other industry categories did not have high loadings, however. The ability of this variable to discriminate between the two groups is marginal. Organizational monitoring skills achieved through scale and bondings had relatively weaker loadings and were not significantly different among the two groups of franchisors, contrary to our proposition. Finally, competitive barriers did not add significant discriminating information to the decision to convert, contrary to Proposition 4. Neither effort nor changes had strong loadings, nor were their means significantly different between the two groups of franchisors. However, the negative sign of the loadings for effort was in the predicted direction.

Overall, our implicit model of franchisor experience and the competitive resources and skill advantages provided by conversion franchising appear to be significant predictors of the decision to use conversions. Although competitive barriers appear to exist, they do not appear to contribute significantly to the decision to convert, at least among this sample of franchisors. Although conversion franchising appears to have been used for some time, its use has accelerated recently. Over half of the firms have started using conversion franchising since 1987. While conversions appear to be more prevalent in domestic rather than international markets, a greater proportion of firms intend to increase their use of conversions in international versus domestic markets.

The descriptive data also seem to support the franchising and strategy literature regarding why firms convert to a franchise system. Resources such as brand identity, franchisor support, and training were among the most frequently cited reasons. Three of four propositions concerning the factors affecting the decision to use conversion franchising were supported in whole or in part. The most significant discriminant variables explained 69 per cent of the variance accounted for by the discriminant function. Our results confirm that firm experience, economic resources, market skills, franchising knowledge, and selected industry experience all contribute significantly in explaining why franchisors use conversion franchising as part of their growth strategy. These results support the strategy and marketing literature, indicating that resources and skills serve as sources of competitive advantage. The results also support the franchising literature regarding the various benefits of this form of business organization. Competitive barriers were related negatively to the decision to use conversions but did not have strong loadings, nor did the means of the barriers differ significantly between those firms that use conversions and those that do not.

It seems reasonable to assume that franchisors tend to focus more on the advantages rather than on the threats when considering whether or not to use conversion franchising. The results of this study should be examined in the light of its potential limitations. The sample size may be considered somewhat small, especially when analyzing the propositions due to missing data. The results are pertinent only to North American franchisors. However, North American franchisors are the most mature and therefore are the most likely to consider conversions. Our data reveal that business experience is a significant factor in the decision. Our respondent companies had similar profiles to nonrespondents, minimizing response bias. Our measures of competitive advantages and barriers were drawn mostly from the field rather than the literature; this may reduce their explanatory power.

However, both subjective and objective measures of competitive advantages were used to reduce same-source bias. Slightly more than half of the variance in the decision to convert was accounted for by the variables examined in this study. Thus, these results provide a partial but not a complete picture of the factors affecting a firm's decision to use conversion franchising. With the limitations in mind, we offer some implications for practice and research. North American franchisors considering the use of conversions should possess significant experience in their business to develop both their business concept and a strong identity for their brand. Having done so, franchisors then have something to offer to businesses seeking to join their franchise system. When investigating potential businesses to convert, franchisors must evaluate carefully the resources needed to attract technically qualified businesses with a good track record in order to gain resource advantages. Conversions may enhance the franchisor's market skills if the new franchisees are located in more distant markets and possess a prime business location. Conversions appear to be more attractive in nonretail sectors such as business and personal services and lodging. However, additional research is warranted to confirm these results. North American businesses seeking to convert to a new or different franchise system are advised to seek a franchise with a proven concept and a strong brand identity in the markets in which they want to expand. Successful business converts should have a proven track record of financial performance.

These potential converts should demonstrate that their management team is well experienced and qualified in their industry; however, they may lack some key resource or skill that the franchisor can provide. This has demonstrated the relevance of employing theories of competitive advantage to guide systematic studies of conversion franchising. Future studies should develop more robust measures of competitive advantages and threats. Larger samples from other parts of the world also should be included to determine if the factors affecting the decision to use conversion franchising are the same in other national or regional markets. A particularly fruitful avenue for future research suggested by our data is the use of conversion franchising for international expansion. While a minority of the North American firms currently are using international conversions, the majority of these firms intend to increase the use of conversions for international growth. Studies examining the factors affecting the international conversion decision also would be a valuable addition to the franchising knowledge base.

CATERING AND FOOD SERVICE

Catering is the business of providing food service at a remote site. Mobile catering is the business of selling prepared food from some sort of vehicle. It is a feature of urban culture in many countries. The food service generally encompasses those places, institutions, and companies responsible for any meal eaten away from home. This industry includes restaurants, school and hospital cafeterias, catering operations, and many other formats. The companies that supply foodservice operators are called foodservice distributors. Foodservice hard goods like ovens and refrigerators are often sold by large buying groups. Some companies manufacture products in both consumer and foodservice versions. The consumer version usually comes in individual-sized packages with elaborate label design for retail sale.

The foodservice version is packaged in a much larger industrial size and often lacks the colourful label designs of the consumer version. Foodservice sales to restaurants and institutions are estimated to be approximately $400 Billion, about equal with consumer sales of foods through grocery outlets. A food cart is a motorless trailer that can be hauled by automobile, bicycle, or hand to the point of sale, often a public sidewalk or park. Carts typically have an onboard heating or refrigeration system to keep the food ready for consumption.

Foods and beverages often served from carts include:

- Halal food such as lamb or chicken over rice, or in a gyro
- Ice cream and other frozen treats
- Coffee, bagels, donuts, Egg sandwichs and other breakfast items

Food Truck is a mobile kitchen, known colliqually in some regions as a "X" Truck, is a mobile venue that sells food. Some, including ice cream trucks, sell mostly frozen or prepackaged food; others are more like restaurants-on-wheels. Food trucks make frequent appearances at carnivals, construction sites, and other temporary venues where large numbers of people gather. Some college campuses and surrounding areas boast many food trucks with loyal followings; for example, visitors to Harvard University or MIT in Cambridge, Massachusetts or the campus of the University of Pennsylvania in Philadelphia may see some very popular trucks parked outside the main entrances to buildings at lunchtime. At Rutgers University, the Grease Trucks serve "fat sandwiches" that contain an ensemble of ingredients such as steak, cheese, chicken fingers, french fries, mozzarella sticks, jalapeño poppers, and more. In the United Kingdom, these are known as burger vans and can be found on nearly all major trunk roads at the side of the road selling their food. A 1/4lb burger can be purchased for about £2. Many people prefer to stop at one of these Burger vans when travelling due to the cheap price, rather than stop at a motorway service station where prices can be extremely high. Sometimes also called "maggot wagon," "roach coach," or "gut truck," these rolling restaurants can frequently be found at or near construction sites. An early version of the food truck was the US Army's mobile canteen and before that the old West's chuckwagon. A mobile kitchen is a modified van with a built-in grill, deep fryer, or other cooking equipment.

It offers more flexibility in the menu since the vendor can prepare food to order. A vendor can choose to park the van in one place, as with a cart, or to broaden the business's reach by driving the van to several customer locations. Examples of mobile kitchens include taco trucks on the west coast of the United States, especially Southern California, and fish and chips vans in the United Kingdom. A concession trailer has preparation equipment like a mobile kitchen, but it cannot move on its own. As such it is suited for events lasting several days, such as funfairs. In addition to being operated as private businesses, mobile catering vehicles are also used after natural disasters to feed people in areas with damaged infrastructure. The Salvation Army has several mobile kitchens that it uses for this purpose.

An event caterer serves food with waiting staff at dining tables or sets up a self-serve buffet. The food may be prepared on site, made completely at the event, or the caterer may choose to bring prepared food and put the finishing touches on once they arrive. The event caterer staff isn't responsible for preparing the food but often help set up the dining area. This service is typically provided at banquets, conventions, and weddings. Any event where all the attenders are provided with food and drinks or sometimes only hors d'oeuvres is often called a catered event. A catering company or specialist is expected to know not just food preparation, but how to make it attractive. Many events require working with the entire theme or colour scheme.

Catering companies have moved towards full-service taking charge of not only food preparation but also decorations, such as table settings or lighting. It's not that food is no longer a focal point, but rather that it is part of a broader mission. Many suggest that catering is about satisfying all the senses. A caterer and his or her staff should be friendly and coorperative because, after all, they are in the food service industry and should follow the motto "the customer is always right". Catering is typically sold on a per-person basis, where adding additional people is a flat price per person. Keeping the cost of the food and supplies below this is required to make a profit on the catering. With the correct atmosphere, professional event caterers experience can bring clients satisfaction of all the senses in a way that makes an event special and memorable. Of course, beautifully prepared food can appeal to your sense of taste, smell and sight - perhaps even touch, but the decorations and ambiance should play a significant part in the clients enjoyment as well.

Industrial catering includes providing food for airline passengers, schools, prisons and other institutional settings. It can include contract management of client foodservice facilities. Airlines often have divisions or hire third parties to provide food for passengers. Catering is covered by two different groups. "Independent caterers and companies with a catering business on the side" is a phrase that could be combined with the previous sentence.

CATERING TIPS AND TRICKS

CHOOSINGRIGHT CATERING SERVICE

Food is an integral part of any party so one must choose a catering service wisely. But how does one choose the right caterer for an event? It is important to do a lot of research, check references, and often request a sampling to make your final decision. List your catering needs In order for a caterer to provide an accurate estimate for your party or event, you must communicate your needs clearly.

Do you have a location for your party/event reserved and is there a kitchen on site? How many guests are coming to your event? Find out if the potential caterer has a minimum guest requirement. Take into consideration that some of your guests may have special dietary needs and be certain to communicate this with your caterer. A great caterer will be ready for any surprise that may surface, but at what cost to you? Discuss your budget with your caterer and what options are available. Ask yourself, do you prefer a buffet style or a silver-service sit down dinner for your guests?

Be clear about your proposed menu, do you have a theme or style at the event that will be reflected in the cuisine? Your budget may or may not determine how flexible your caterer is to meet your needs. Keep in mind; it is the type of food that often determines the bulk price of the catering job. Find out, and possibly request, if the caterer will provide a detailed contract of service and outline what the payment terms will be. Does the caterer use fresh or frozen food for recipes? Is the produce grown locally?

Is it organic? Will any of the dishes be pre-made and then frozen until the party/event? Does anything come from a can? Does the potential caterer supply decorations, linens, tables and chairs? Very often there will be a brochure catering services supply with examples of past event and table decorations. It is important to be very clear in what your event needs and what the caterer will be supplying. Is a menu board provided for the guests that describes the ingredients of the dishes being served? Will the catering company provide a wait-staff? What is their required dress code? What is the ratio of servers to guests? A rule of thumb is one server for every 10 guests. Be certain to ask your potential caterer if taxes and gratuities are included in the final bid. What happens to the leftovers? Often, upon request, a catering service will compile a food basket at no additional charge for the host or hostess of the event. Remember, it is critical that you communicate with your potential caterer exactly you want; the result, you get what you want and the caterer can provide an accurate bid for the job as well as the exceptional service your event deserves.

SERVING ALCOHOL AT YOUR EVENT

When one commits to planning an event or party, one must decide whether or not to serve alcohol to the guests. There are a few considerations to keep in mind and discuss with your caterer. Where will your event or party be taking place? It is important to confirm that your event or party site will allow alcohol on its premises. Once you have made certain that you can serve alcohol at your chosen site, ask your caterer if he or she holds a liquor license. He or she must have a valid liquor license. If he or she does not hold a liquor license, then you must contact a liquor-licensed dealer. Prepare to provide a guest estimate for your caterer to work with.

The caterer in turn will supply you with a quote for the number of bartenders that must attend bar and the quantity of ice, glasses, and mixers necessary. The amount of bartenders depends on the number of guests. Your caterer or licensed liquor dealer will be responsible for setting up the bar. You must now determine what you wish to be served from the bar as well as if you require your guests to pay for alcohol themselves. A cash bar requires the guest to pay for their drinks. Guests tend to consume less alcohol when it isn't free. This is a basic bar with all the works and at no charge to the guests. The open bar includes hard liquor for mixing drinks, wine, beer, and soft drinks. A limited bar will set boundaries on what will be served and in what moderation. An example of a limited bar is an event in which beer and wine is offered to the guests at no charge and hard liquor is offered at a pre-determined price. Whatever you decide in regards to serving alcohol at your event or party is up to you.

WEDDING CATERING

After watching the happy couple exchange vows and

begin their married life together, your guests will be hungry. Many of the guests may have scaled back on eating in order to look good for pictures or just because they were so busy during the day. When you're putting together such a large assortment of people, there are bound to be those that have certain ways or preferences of eating. You may find that there are vegetarians or those that can not eat dairy. You might have a diabetic in the crowd or some other health restriction. You should certainly try to have options for any sort of eating arrangement. In the case of those that don't eat meat, you might want to have a cheese lasagne available or other pasta dish. This is becoming widely popular to have two options anyways, so why not offer them?

Another way to cope with varied needs is to serve dinner in a buffet style. This allows each person to pick only what they want or what they can eat. A lot of wedding caterers rely on word of mouth to get their services recognized. If you can, talk to other people that have gotten married in your town to see who they recommend. Of course, you will still want to see them for yourself, but this list can be a great starting point. Another way to find good catering is to talk to the reception hall coordinators. Many times they will either require the use of a particular caterer or they have a list of those that they recommend. Of course, you will want to schedule an appointment with all of the catering candidates in order to do a taste test of their menu options. At that point, you can pick what you think your guests will enjoy. A good meal is a great way to send your thanks to your guests for coming to your wedding. This is the part that shouldn't be skimped on for any reason. Of course, that doesn't mean that you can't find moderately priced options.

Try your favourite restaurant, for example. If they're able to cater, then you may be able to get a better deal because you're buying food in bulk. Having a friend who is a cook is even better-so long as they don't mind working through the wedding. So you've tasted the offerings of the caterer and you've selected your main menu options. What about drinks? Much like selecting the menu options, you will need to factor in what kinds of drinks everyone would like to drink. The easiest way to take care of this is to offer a full service bar. In this way, guests can have mixed drinks of all varieties or they can stick to wine and beer. You want to plan this option out carefully as you may end up paying more than you would like. Check with the provider as to how many drinks each guest can have, or can expect from the supply that will be brought. In most cases, there is no limit. A word of advice: Don't ever have a cash bar. Making your guests pay for their drinks when they may also have paid for their outfits and transportation is just a lot to ask.

In terms of wine and beer, tastes and varieties are enormous-how does someone choose? The best advice is to select four to five different kinds of beer with each one having enough to fill everyone's glass. This may surprise you, but sometimes all of your guests will like the same thing and you may want to make sure that they can have it. As for wine, you may want to have at least one of each a red varietal and a white varietal. This ensures a milder and more acidic selection. A way to make sure that everyone is happy is to find blends of each of these wines. By blends, this means to find a red that includes a merlot, syrah, and pinot noir, while the white might include a chardonnay, reisling, and zinfandel. These can be tricky to find, but they are crowd pleasers. Toasts are just not toasts without a little glass of champagne. It's common sense to make sure that the new couple and their wedding party have the very finest in champagne, while the rest of the guests have another variety. In many reception halls or catering services, the champagne for the wedding party is provided. Of course, there will also be designated drivers at the wedding, so you will also want to have water, sodas, coffee, and juices available as well. When you're planned it thoroughly, everyone will be well-watered throughout the evening.

HOW TO START A CATERING BUSINESS

The catering industry in the United States is estimated to be worth $5 billion a year. Caterers are hired to perform an assorted number of jobs-everything from cooking to serving, mixing drinks, and whipping up delicious desserts. Functions range from dinner parties that serve a handful of guests to enormous events that serve thousands of guests. Normally a caterer will define their niche, meaning a caterer will choose what type of functions to specialize in as well as their job description. For example, you may offer the best fondue table for up to 100 guests, perhaps you would rather prepare meals for business catering parties that are held within banker's hours. There really are no limits in regards to catering styles. Once you have arrived to the idea stage it is great to begin a business catering plan. Be meticulous when you detail how the catering business will be operated, managed and capitalized.

The following checklist can help you organize your ideas into the beginning of a business catering plan:

- What services will your catering business offer? Will you run a full service catering business, corporate catering service, custom event catering service, or a scheduled events catering business?
- Research necessary permits and requirements your local government imposes on a catering business.
- Determine your start up costs of your catering business. Remember to include everything-permit fees, catering equipment, marketing, uniforms, catering supplies etc.
- Construct a budget, forecast and projection.
- How will you finance the start up of your catering business?
- Research liability insurance needed to protect your catering business.
- Where will you house your catering business office and how will you manage your business? Prepare to think about cancellations, payment policies, consultations, menu-planning as well as samples, contracts and the transportation of food.
- What food suppliers do you intend to work with?
- Will your catering service rent equipment for special requests?

- What will you name your catering business?
  Owning a catering service not only includes cooking but also be prepared to wear many hats such as: accountant, manager, marketer, sales representative, and bill collector. Additional questions to consider when constructing your catering business plan:
  - Is my business idea practical and is it in demand?
  - What is my competition?
  - What is my advantage over existing services?
  - Can I deliver a better quality service?
  - Can I create a demand for my business?
  - What will be my legal structure?
  - How will I compensate myself?

Your answers to these questions will help you create a focused, well-researched catering business plan that can serve as a blueprint for your new catering service. Whatever you choose to specialize in, running a catering business offers creativity, flexibility, and growing opportunities. Maybe you've got the details of the actual wedding ceremony worked out, but what about the reception? One of the major costs of the wedding reception will definitely be the food, so you'll want to make sure you'll have enough food for everyone without spending too much money. Here are some top ways to cut on your catering bill that will ensure that your guests enjoy your reception-and you save money. Most couples want to order an extra tray or two of hors d'oeuvres in case extra guests show up.

This is fine but you should still make sure that you're not order more appetizers than you actually need; use your discretion based on the guest list. For instance, if you know a number of your guests are vegetarian, you may not need to order as many appetizers with meat. Also, ordering two or three types of hors d'oeuvres will help to reduce your catering bill. If you buy more of the same dish, you can usually save money with most catering companies-different kinds of foods will increase the bill, so it's important to keep it classy but simple at the wedding-even when it comes to food. Caterers will also try to encourage you to spend more than you may need to on the actual meal as well. You may not need a five course meal if you've already purchased three types of appetizers and a salad, or three extra desserts if you already have a pretty large wedding cake.

The time of day that you hold your wedding will give you a good indication of how much food to serve; if you're having the ceremony in the afternoon or early evening, you may want to serve more food. There are some foods that are always going to be expensive, even if you only order small amounts. So, since you have to order a considerable amount of food, ordering dishes that aren't so costly will help you to keep your catering bill reasonable. Certain seafood, like shrimp, lobster and salmon will definitely make your catering bill higher, so if you have to have them, try to use them as only one of the course choices for dinner, or purchase these fo1ods as appetizers to save on costs.

Food stations are a unique way to serve a variety of foods at your wedding reception, and you can be sure that everyone will find something they like to eat. This way, you won't have to worry about people changing their minds about their meal choices once they arrive at the reception. A food station with different types of pasta is usually a hit with most guests, and can be very economical. You can also include food stations with other types of the ethnic foods, such as Mexican or Indian fare, to celebrate the cultures of the people who will be attending your wedding, or to acknowledge your backgrounds. You may also be able to cut your catering bill by not requesting an elaborate setup for your food stations and tables. Using a single colour for tablecloths, usually white, will cut down on labour costs.

Bibliography

Andrews, S.: *Food and Beverage Service,* Philadelphi: University of Pennsylvania Press, 1980.

Bernard D.: *Food and Beverage Management,* New York: Oxford University Press, 1998.

Chen, Wei: *International Hospitality Management: Concepts and Cases,* UK: Cambridge University Press, 2007.

Coskett, David: *Food and Beverage Management,* London: Harvard University Press, 1999.

Cousins, John: *Food and Beverage Management,* Philadelphia: University of Pennsylvania Press, 1999.

Gillam, Scott: *Food, Agriculture, and Natural Resources,* UK: Cambridge University Press, 2007.

Hayes, David K.: *Food and Beveruge Cost Control,* New York: Columbia University Press, 2010.

Kandampully: *Services Management,* India: Long life Publication, 2000.

Lockwood, A.: *Food and Beverage Management,* Berkeley, CA: University of California Press, 1998.

Meldrum: *Leisure Services Management,* Philadelphia: University of Pennsylvania Press, 2008.

Mukherji, Anupam: *Food and Beverage Management,* New York: Oxford University Press, 2006.

Ojugo C.: *Practical Food and Beverage Cost Control,* London: Jessica Kingsley Publication, 2009.

Rutherford, Denney G.: *Hotel Management and Operations*, UK: Cambridge University Press, 2010.

Verghese, B.: *Professional Food and Beverage Services Management*, New York: Transnational Publication, 2000.

Welsons, Julia.: *Risk Management for Meetings and Events*, Chicago: University of Chicago Press, 2007.

Wentz, Bill: *Food Service Management*, Aldershot: Dartmouth Publication, 2007.

Wood: *Strategic Questions in Food and Beverage Management*, New York: Oxford University Press, 2000.

Index